Harmon's Journal
1800-1819

DANIEL WILLIAMS HARMON ESQ^r.

Harmon's Journal
1800-1819

DANIEL WILLIAMS HARMON
A PARTNER IN THE NORTH WEST COMPANY

WITH A FOREWORD BY

Jennifer S. H. Brown
Professor of History, University of Winnipeg

VICTORIA • VANCOUVER • CALGARY

TouchWood Editions
#108–17665 66A Avenue
Surrey, BC V3S 2A7
www.touchwoodeditions.com

Library and Archives Canada Cataloguing in Publication

Harmon, Daniel Williams, 1778–1845.
    Harmon's journal 1800–1819/Daniel Williams Harmon; edited by
W. Kaye Lamb. — 1st TouchWood edition

First published as: Sixteen years in the Indian country. Toronto:
    Macmillan, 1957.
Includes index.
ISBN-13: 978-1-894898-44-7
ISBN-10: 1-894898-44-3

    1. Harmon, Daniel Williams, 1778–1845—Diaries. 2. Northwest, Canadian—Discovery and exploration. 3. Indians of North America—Northwest, Canadian—History. 4. Fur traders—Northwest, Canadian—Diaries. I. Lamb, W. Kaye (William Kaye), 1904-1999. II. Title.

FC3205.1.H37 2006   971.1'02   C2005-907755-7

Book design by Rodger Reynolds and Joanne Poon
Cover design by Erin Woodward
Front-cover photo: Carrier women in the Fort St. James area (Glenbow Archives NA-1164-3)
Printed in Canada

TouchWood Editions acknowledges the financial support for its publishing program from the Government of Canada through the Book Publishing Industry Development Program (BPIDP), Canada Council for the Arts, and the British Columbia Arts Council.

The Canada Council | Le Conseil des Arts
for the Arts | du Canada

BRITISH COLUMBIA
ARTS COUNCIL
Supported by the Province of British Columbia

This book has been produced on 100% post-consumer recycled paper, processed chlorine free and printed with vegetable-based dyes.

Contents

Contents

❖

Foreword

by

Jennifer S. H. Brown, University of Winnipeg

My interest in Daniel Williams Harmon and his life in the fur trade goes back thirty years and more. In the early 1970s, I began research on Hudson's Bay and North West company fur traders and their Native families for a doctoral dissertation at the University of Chicago. I soon discovered that at the same time, Sylvia Van Kirk was doing doctoral research on women in the fur trade at the University of London; we had independently decided that these families and their stories had been too long neglected. Our confluence of interests led to fruitful conversations, and as it happened, our books on these topics found publication in the same year, 1980.[1]

Twenty-five years later, it appears that our work helped to initiate a whole new field of study. Fur-trade family history, fuelled by the Internet, by new interests in oral history, and, not least, by modern descendants' growing pride in and affection for their Aboriginal roots, is flourishing as never before. In the 1970s, Sylvia Van Kirk and I (like Harmon when he entered the fur trade—see below) had few people to talk with. Now the networks of conversations can be endless.

As I read the documents that the literati (overwhelmingly men) of the times left behind, I found that I had some favourites among them. Certain traders wrote with unusual detail, perspective, and even sometimes with feeling and introspection. Among the best are Daniel Harmon, George Nelson, David Thompson, and Peter Fidler; these four writers left us some of the richest

[1]Van Kirk, *Many Tender Ties: Women in Fur Trade Society, 1670–1870* (Winnipeg: Watson and Dwyer, 1980); Brown, *Strangers in Blood: Fur Trade Company Families in Indian Country* (Vancouver: University of British Columbia Press, 1980); both have been reprinted and were later co-published in the US by the University of Oklahoma Press.

records we have of traders' experiences and of their relations with their fellow traders and with the Aboriginal people on whom their trade and livelihood depended.

Harmon and Nelson, in particular, tell us more than perhaps any of their peers about the transforming process of becoming a fur trader, leaving home and family to learn about and adapt to a radically different lifestyle, occupation, and physical and social world. They had much in common. Their fur-trade careers overlapped closely (1800–1820 for Harmon; 1802–1823 for Nelson); they both worked mainly for the North West Company; they both acquired Native wives and families in the fur-trade country, and they both brought them east rather than leaving them behind.[2] But the trajectories of their lives were far from straightforward. Getting along in the fur trade, dealing with one's superiors and fellow clerks, and with voyageurs of French or Metis descent, who spoke their own language and had their own ways, while travelling and living among varied Aboriginal peoples, presented considerable challenges and barriers to communication. A fur trade clerk finding his way faced no end of decisions about options, tactics, and obligations and commitments to be assumed or avoided, in the spheres of both work and personal affairs, and he might often find himself without trusted or familiar peers with whom to consult.

In this context, keeping a journal could help to fill the void, as its writer conversed with himself or with distant family members whom he could imagine as eventual readers of his words (both Harmon and Nelson sent letters and other writings home to family members at one time or another). A colleague of mine, Laura Murray, on reading Harmon, was struck by how often he wrote of lacking opportunities for good conversation. She has found that this lack is often a theme in fur traders' writings, evoking the

[2]Nelson's writings were almost unknown before Van Kirk and I began using them. For those that have been published, see Jennifer S. H. Brown and Robert Brightman, *The Orders of the Dreamed: George Nelson on Cree and Northern Ojibwa Religion and Myth, 1823* (Winnipeg: University of Manitoba Press, 1988); and George Nelson, *My First Years in the Fur Trade*, ed. by Laura Peers and Theresa Schenck (St. Paul: Minnesota Historical Society Press, co-published in Montreal by McGill Queen's University Press, 2001).

isolation they felt from home, and from people of their own sort with whom they shared implicit understandings and values. Her study of Harmon's journal offers some insight into why he created it, as a space for talking to himself and his familiars, as his responses to his situation evolved.[3]

For readers interested in fur-trade families, Harmon's all-too-brief journal entries about the woman who became his wife and about his children are among the most poignant and interesting. When the relationship began on 10 October 1805, Harmon was twenty-seven, almost twice the age of Elizabeth, Lisette, or Lizette, as she has been variously called. Her father was Canadian, likely a voyageur, named Duval. Her mother was said to be a "Snare" Indian, a name that has been interpreted as referring to the Shuswap people, currently known as Secwepemc (Murray, 310n27) of the Salishan language family. The language that this woman's daughter Lisette and Harmon had in common, however, was Cree, the lingua franca of the fur trade; Lisette's mother may have lived for some time as a Cree captive before her alliance with Duval. Further research may shed more light on this history. The beautifully decorated leather shot bag that Lisette made, which is now in the Bennington Museum in Vermont, is described as being of Cree style.[4]

Harmon never named his new partner in his journal. But in this he was typical of his times; Nelson never named his Ojibwe wife either, and we must turn to later church and other records for the identities of these and many other women allied with fur traders, if indeed they eventually got baptized and married by church rite. Traders often used terms such as "my woman" or "the mother of my children," a vocabulary reflecting their uncertainty or ambivalence about the standing of such relationships and their knowledge that readers at home would also have doubts about their legitimacy and propriety. I mentioned in the foregoing the transforming process of becoming a trader. These fur-trade

---

[3]Laura J. Murray, "Fur Traders in Conversation." *Ethnohistory* 50, 2 (2003): 285–314.
[4]It is illustrated at http://homepage.mac.com/lynnoel/pubs/Lisettes_ Journey.html. Lynn Noel has extensively researched Lisette Duval's life and has presented her story in song and reenactment.

unions, if they endured, also went through a process of transformation as both partners grew into them and moved to redefine them; they were not static. Elsewhere, I have written about these relationships as processual, and about how some of them played out in practice.[5] A few, notably the fur-trade marriage of William Connolly, led to legal battles, as in 1864 when Connolly's half-Cree son John sued the Montreal woman his father had married after setting aside his Cree wife, for a share in his father's estate. Each family's story was different, and neither a young fur trader nor his Native partner, when they started out, could predict the future course of their relationship or the paths that their offspring would travel.

It is interesting to speculate about certain parallels in Harmon's and Lisette Duval's backgrounds, even if they may not have thought much about them, and even if they seem very different indeed. They both became multilingual and transected several boundaries in their lives, and they challenge efforts to put them in compartments. Lisette is sometimes described as Metis. But she fits that category only if one equates Metis with "mixed-blood," and many people of mixed ancestry never became Metis. She was not part of a Metis community or family in her upbringing or in the course of her life. If Shuswap or Secwepemc through her mother, she must have been brought up at least partially among Cree. Maybe she learned some French from her father, but when she "was offered" to Harmon, Duval was not mentioned and there is no sign he was present. On 20 July 1816, Harmon wrote that Lisette's own language was Cree and that he therefore used Cree in speaking to their children; however, he more frequently used French in speaking with her. In living and travelling among Nor'Westers and voyageurs, both he and Lisette also needed and learned French. Ultimately, she learned still another language, English, when the family headed east.

As for Harmon, he too evidently acquired some proficiency in French and Cree in the context of the fur trade. He is often simply identified as American, but he too had also grown up in a

[5]Brown, "Partial Truths: A Closer Look at Fur Trade Marriage." *From Rupert's Land to Canada*, ed. by Theodore Binnema, Gerhard J. Ens, and R.C. Macleod, 59–80 (Edmonton: University of Alberta Press, 2001).

situation where boundaries were more fluid and contested than is sometimes recognized. His birthplace, Bennington, now in Vermont, was in an area that New York and New Hampshire had both been trying to claim for many years before the American Revolution. Vermont had not existed as a separate American colony, and its course was not yet set when Harmon was born in 1778. During the revolution, both the British in Canada and a good many loyalist Vermonters seriously explored the idea of arranging for this in-between territory to join its northern neighbour. That idea faded as the tide of war turned. But the Vermonters then asserted their own identity by establishing an independent republic, which existed from 1778 to 1791 when they accepted American statehood.[6] Harmon, born to a Bennington innkeeper, grew up in a setting where state and national identities had not yet congealed, and in which many people had ties to and relatives in Canada. Viewed in that light, his heading to Montreal in 1799 to become a clerk in the Canadian fur trade seems less curious than if we interpret it from a later boundary-focused perspective.

Harmon's journal deserves to be better known, and its reprinting is greatly to be welcomed. He repays close reading and study. Reading his words, and reading also beyond them for what he implies or omits, accepting his way of writing both critically and on his own terms, we glimpse a life of unusual scope, stretching from Bennington and Montreal to the far Northwest and back again. His conversations with himself, the efforts he made to set down his thoughts and observations, contribute to our conversations almost two centuries later in ways he could never have foreseen.

[6]Jones, Matt Bushnell, *Vermont in the Making* (Cambridge: Harvard University Press, 1939; reprint Archion Books, 1968).

Preface to the 2006 Edition

The journal of Daniel Williams Harmon is one of the most descriptive accounts of fur-trade life in the Western Canada of two hundred years ago. In 1800 Harmon, a twenty-one-year-old native of Bennington, Vermont, was engaged by the North West Company in Montreal to proceed to Indian Country where he was to spend the next nineteen years. Nine of these were as a seasoned trader in north-central British Columbia, most particularly at the Stuart Lake Post.

In 1805 he accepted the offer of a fourteen-year-old girl of mixed blood to be his "country wife." He intended, when his contract expired, to leave her with "some good honest Man." This was the custom, and although boys were sometimes sent to "civilization" to be educated, children were normally left with their mother. In Harmon's case, when the time came, he could not "leave his beloved children in the wilderness" nor could he "tear them from a mother's love." Thus Harmon in 1819 travelled with his "wife," Elizabeth Duval, and children Polly and Sally to Fort William. He and Elizabeth were legally married there before continuing on to Vermont.

The Journal was first printed in 1820, heavily edited. In 1957, W. Kaye Lamb published the text of the original manuscript, but that volume has long been out of print. Thus I thought it appropriate to republish it this year as a commemorative edition with a scholarly foreword. 2006 is the 200th anniversary of the founding by Simon Fraser of the Stuart Lake Post (now Fort St. James), where Harmon spent so much of his fur-trading life.

Above all, however, the work deserves republication because it is an engaging story. It is lively and conveys vividly the rough and tumble of life where two cultures trade ascendancy on a daily basis. Most fur-trade journals were kept to record business transactions in detail or to chronicle the adventures of de facto explorers. Harmon's is about his often raw, often warm and often reflective life involving conciliation, celebration and near starvation—the latter being a frequent threat.

The initiative of the Fort St. James Historical Society in the 1950s, coupled with local determination, brought about the multi-million-dollar restoration of the fort in 1971 by senior governments. Parks Canada continues to maintain the site in excellent condition.

My proceeds from this edition will be turned over to the Friends of the Fort St. James National Historic Site, a successor society, to further their commitment to the site.

I would like to acknowledge the support and encouragement I have received from such diverse quarters. Elizabeth Hawkins, daughter and executor of the Estate of Dr. W. Kaye Lamb, editor of the 1957 edition, gave permission to publish, the *sine qua non* of the project. Dr. Jennifer Brown's book *Strangers in Blood* and other writings have made a major contribution to understanding the intercultural relations of fur-trade families. Dr. Brown kindly agreed to write the foreword to provide an historical and cultural context that will help the reader understand the world in which Harmon lived. The Friends of the Fort St. James National Historic Site, and its executive member Pat Hampe in particular, provided the liaison with the Elders of the Nak'azdli Band and with Robert Grill, Parks Canada Superintendent of the site. My sincere thanks to all. Finally, I am grateful to my friend and colleague Vic Marks of Hartley & Marks Publishers Inc., whose commitment to doing "good works" in publishing made the project financially possible.

And I thank Daniel Williams Harmon for returning with his family to his roots in Vermont, and later Montreal—and specifically for bringing Polly with him.

Graham R. Ross
Great, great, great-grandson of
Daniel Williams Harmon

Introduction to the 1957 Edition

by

W. Kaye Lamb

I

There is here printed, for the first time, the original text of the greater part of one of the most famous journals of the Canadian fur trade—the diary kept by Daniel Williams Harmon in the years 1800–19, while he was in the service of the North West Company. Hitherto this journal has been available only in the version edited by the Rev. Daniel Haskel and first printed in 1820. Haskel stated frankly in his preface that he had "written it wholly over." This is an exaggeration, for Harmon's own phraseology survives in many passages; but the changes made were numerous and drastic. Few accounts of the fur trade have been quoted more frequently than Harmon's, and the position of authority that his narrative has gained makes it important that an authentic text, and an adequate account of the author himself, should be published.

Harmon came of pioneer New England Stock. John Harmon, his great-great-great-grandfather, who was born in England in 1616, came to America and settled in Springfield, Massachusetts, where he died in 1661. One of this descendants moved to nearby Suffield, in Connecticut, and there the diarist's father, Daniel Harmon, was born in January 1748 (New Style). Daniel in turn moved to Bennington, Vermont, where he married Lucretia Dewey in 1770. About the time of his marriage he built a tavern, which he kept for many years. This was a more important establishment than the word "tavern" now implies. It was in reality a hotel, and a social centre in the community. Pictures show that it was a substantial structure, and it became a well-known and popular stopping-place for travellers.

All eight of the children born to Daniel and Lucretia Harmon —seven sons and one daughter—are believed to have first seen the light in the tavern at Bennington. Daniel Williams Harmon, the fourth child, was born there on February 19, 1778.

The American Revolutionary War was then in progress, and, in August 1777, the father had fought on the American side in the Battle of Bennington, in which the "Green Mountain Boys" of Vermont defeated the British. By an odd coincidence the officers of the defeated Loyalist force included Captain Simon Fraser, who had come to America from Scotland in 1773, and had settled the following year on a farm on the outskirts of Bennington. There his famous son and namesake, Simon Fraser the explorer and fur-trader, was born in 1776. Years later he and Daniel Williams Harmon were to be colleagues in the North West Company.

A few months after the Battle of Bennington Captain Fraser was captured by the Americans and he later died in prison at Albany. When peace was concluded, his widow and children joined the Loyalist migration to Canada. The Revolution did not disturb the Harmons, who prospered quietly in Bennington, and later in Vergennes, to which they moved in 1795. They were active in community life and prominent members of the Congregational Church. Walter O'Meara, who has unearthed many references to them in contemporary records, goes so far as to describe the family as "brilliant and cultured." The eldest son, Argalus, became town clerk of Vergennes and was later elected to the House of Representatives. Martin, the second son, "was a graduate of Dartmouth, a Phi Beta Kappa at the age of nineteen, and a brilliant lawyer until his tragic death at twenty-four.c[1] Calvin, the next son, prospered in business and in real estate. Lucretia, the daughter, married into a prominent Vermont family. Of the three sons younger than Daniel, we know that Stephen was looked up to as a scholar and that Reuben became a physician. Little is known about the youngest child, Joseph, except that he died in 1811.

As Mr. O'Meara remarks, this is not a *milieu* that one would expect to produce "a fur trader, content to remain for almost twenty years in the crude and brutal environment of the *pays d'en haut*..."[2] He suggests that the "family competition" offered by his

---

[1]Walter O'Meara, "Adventure in Local History," *Minnesota History*, 31 (1950), p. 6.
[2]*Ibid.*

clever brothers may have contributed to Daniel's decision to leave home and seek his fortune in the western wilderness. Very likely this was the case; certainly the journal does not suggest that Harmon was either particularly able or ambitious. But there were other reasons. One was innate restlessness—the "roving disposition" to which Harmon refers several times, and to which he himself ascribed his entry into the fur trade. The latter offered action and adventure, and, as the great fortunes then being built up in Montreal showed, it could offer rich material rewards as well. Religion also influenced Harmon's decision. The austere faith to which the family adhered with great sincerity must have produced an atmosphere that Daniel found irksome and confining. It is significant that in his younger days he was evidently not a member of the church. The respect for Christian morality that is reflected so strongly in his diary seems to have been due at first much more to conscience than to conviction. In later life he himself did not consider that he had been a true Christian until the conversion he experienced in 1813, at the age of thirty-five.

Many Canadian travellers had stayed at the tavern in Bennington on their way to Albany or New York; their tales may well have aroused Harmon's interest in Canada. Some time after his twenty-first birthday—in 1799 or early in 1800—he left home and journeyed to Montreal, where he entered the employ of McTavish, Frobisher & Company as a warehouseman. The head of the firm, Simon McTavish, a colourful and commanding personality, was the leading figure in the flourishing Montreal fur trade. He and his associates controlled the North West Company. They purchased its supplies, marketed its furs, and recruited many of its personnel. A young man with a roving disposition could not be expected to remain long in a warehouse, and in the spring of 1800 the new recruits for the North West Company included Daniel Williams Harmon. He joined its service as a clerk for the usual term of seven years. The salary he was to receive is not recorded, but if we may judge from the experience of others, it was probably no more than £20 per annum. Harmon's journal begins on April 29, 1800, the day he left Lachine for the West, travelling in one of thirty canoes, all heavily laden with supplies, and bound for the Company's central rendezvous and depot at Grand Portage, on Lake Superior.

In the next nineteen years, the period covered by his diary, Harmon served the Company in five different trading-areas. His first five years were spent in the Swan River District, which lay to the west of Lake Winnipegosis, in what is now Manitoba and eastern Saskatchewan. The chief posts at which he was stationed were Swan River Fort and Bird Mountain, both on Swan River, and Fort Alexandria, on the upper waters of the Assiniboine River. Harmon travelled to this first assignment by a northern route, but when he left the district he made a great circle to the south, by way of Fort Qu'Appelle, the future site of Winnipeg at the junction of the Assiniboine and the Red, and the Red River itself.

Three shorter spells of duty in three widely separated areas followed. He spent two seasons in the valley of the Saskatchewan—the first (1805–06) at South Branch House, on the South Saskatchewan River, and the second (1806–07) further east at Cumberland House, one of the Company's most important traffic centres. When the time came to assign staff to the various posts for the winter of 1807–08, Harmon was not well. For this reason he was sent to Sturgeon Lake Fort, in the Nipigon District, where Dr. John McLoughlin, then a young medical officer, was to be stationed. By the spring of 1808, Harmon's health had improved greatly, and he was assigned to Dunvegan, on the Peace River, in the famed Athabaska District. There he spent two years and found life very agreeable.

The summer of 1810 was a dividing point in Harmon's career. Hitherto he had served mostly on the prairies. He was now directed to cross the Rocky Mountains and take charge of a post in New Caledonia, a huge ill-defined area corresponding roughly to the Cariboo country and the central interior of what is now British Columbia. This was a new trading-district, for although Alexander Mackenzie had spied out the land beyond the Rockies on his famous journey to the Pacific Ocean in 1793, the North West Company did not begin trading there until 1805. Simon Fraser, Harmon's Bennington-born colleague, built a post that year at McLeod Lake—the oldest continuously-occupied white settlement in Canada, west of the Rocky Mountains. Harmon spent nine years in New Caledonia, and the last pages of his journal describe his journey eastward to Fort William in the summer of 1819, when he finally left the district. For the greater part of his stay he was in charge of the post on Stuart Lake (later renamed Fort St. James), but he spent one long spell of duty, lasting almost two and a half years, at Fraser Lake (Fort Fraser).

No complete record of Harmon's service in the North West Company is known to exist, but a good many details are now available.

His first engagement as a clerk, which it will be remembered was for a term of seven years, expired in 1807. It was then renewed for an eighth year. In July 1808, when he was being sent to Dunvegan, Harmon signed an agreement "to remain at Athabaska at least three years," and his journal states that his salary was to be "one hundred pounds Halifax Currency [the equivalent of ninety pounds sterling] per annum, besides being furnished with Cloathing and victuals &c. &c."[3]

As already mentioned, Harmon remained only two years in Athabaska, and then moved on to New Caledonia in the fall of 1810. His journal shows that he was offered two alternatives at this time: he could assume the superintendency of New Caledonia immediately, or, if he preferred, he could go to the district as assistant to the superintendent (John Stuart), in the expectation of taking over the office in the spring. Harmon chose the latter course, influenced largely, it would seem, by reports that the salmon run in New Caledonia had failed, and his feeling that someone who knew the district well could cope better with the shortage of food and other difficulties that had resulted. This cautious decision was probably best for the Company, but it certainly delayed Harmon's personal advancement. Spring came, but the expected transfer of authority did not take place; Harmon's salary continued at the old rate of £100 Halifax currency per annum. No reference to the change in plan is made in the journal, and Harmon evidently bore no grudge, for he and Stuart became firm friends.

An enormous old North West Company ledger, now preserved in the Archives of the Hudson's Bay Company, throws some light on Harmon's later career. This volume contains the personal accounts of the Company's servants for the years 1811–21. It shows

3*Journal,* July 7, 1808.

that Harmon continued to receive a salary of £100 Halifax currency per annum until 1817.[4] The last credit entry, dated 1818, added a further £50 to his account, being "salary short credited last year." This would seem to indicate that his remuneration was increased to £150 for the year 1817, and the absence of credit entries for later years shows that he became a wintering partner—a fullfledged bourgeois of the North West Company—in 1818. It would be this new and important status (to which, oddly enough, he makes no reference in his journal) that enabled him to travel eastward in the summer of 1819, and to take a holiday sufficiently long to visit his family and friends in Vermont.

2

Accounts of Harmon usually place some emphasis on his domestic affairs. It was customary at the time for the Nor'Westers to take unofficial Indian or half-breed wives, who could afford them some measure of companionship in the wilderness. Harmon's strict upbringing made him hesitate to follow the custom, but in October 1805 he yielded. The girl, Elizabeth Duval,[5] was the daughter of a French Canadian and a Cree Indian mother. The union proved to be an unusually happy one, and lasted all Harmon's days. He and Elizabeth are said to have had fourteen children, but the births of only twelve are on record.[6] Doubtless the other two were stillborn, or died soon after birth. George, the first child, was born in December 1807. Twin sons, both of whom died within a few days, followed in February 1809. Two daughters were born within the period covered by the journal: Mary Patricia (Polly), in April 1811, and Sarah (Sally), in February 1817. George was a bright child, and Harmon decided to send him to his brother Argalus, in Vermont, in order that he might receive better care and an education. At the age of

---

[4]The accounts of the North West Company were actually kept in livres and sous. In the ledger, Harmon's salary is given as 1,200 livres per annum. This was the equivalent of £100 Halifax currency or £90 sterling.

[5]She was probably called "Lizzette." Her surname is sometimes given as "Laval," but "Duval" is used in the official records relating to Harmon's estate.

[6]For a list of the children, with birth and death dates, so far as these are known, *see* John Spargo, *Two Bennington-Born Explorers*, 1950, pp. 122–5.

three years and five months little George began the long trek eastward. He arrived safely, but died after a brief illness in March 1813. His death was perhaps the greatest sorrow of his father's career.

Half-breed wives rarely left the Indian country. When a Nor'Wester retired, it was considered best for all concerned that some modest provision should be made for the woman, and that she should remain in the surroundings to which she was accustomed. But Harmon had no thought of abandoning his Elizabeth, and she and their two daughters accompanied him when he journeyed to Fort William, where they arrived on August 18, 1819. Six days later Elizabeth gave birth to a son, John; and before they continued on their way to Vermont she and Harmon were legally married.

Harmon spent the winter of 1819–20 in Vermont, on furlough from the fur trade. Doubtless he paid visits to his mother and brother Calvin in Vergennes, and to Argalus in Shelburne; but much of his time seems to have been spent in Burlington. There he arranged with the Rev. Daniel Haskel for the publication of his journal, and presumably assisted in its revision. And there, on April 9, 1820, he was admitted to membership in the Congregational Church. Three days later his three children, Polly, Sally and John, were baptized.

Soon after this Harmon returned to the wilderness, but his family remained in Vermont. He was placed in charge of the North West Company's post at Lac la Pluie (Rainy Lake). The long and exhausting struggle between the North West Company and the Hudson's Bay Company was now in its last stages and, while Harmon traded at Lac la Pluie, negotiations for a union of the companies were proceeding in London. Agreement was finally reached in March 1821, and under the terms of the Deed Poll signed at that time, Harmon was one of the wintering partners of the North West Company who were offered commissions as Chief Traders in the service of the Hudson's Bay Company. On July 11, 1821, at Fort William, Harmon duly signed the covenant and received his commission: the original covenant, bearing his signature, is preserved in the Archives of the Hudson's Bay Company.

It is clear that Harmon had for some time contemplated retiring from the fur trade. Although his salary had long been a very modest one, his need for cash had been small, and he had been able to send most of his earnings to his brother Argalus for investment.[7] Shortly before he left New Caledonia, in 1819, he wrote in his journal: "Our worldly affairs have prospered, to as great an extent as we could reasonably expect."[8] Provisions in the Deed Poll made it possible for Harmon to retire in the summer of 1821, while retaining for a period of seven years his share, as a Chief Trader, in the profits of the Hudson's Bay Company. Seizing this opportunity, he left the fur trade; and a letter written to the Company on September 9, shows that by that time he was back in Burlington.

Some years before, Harmon's two surviving brothers, Argalus and Calvin, had purchased a tract of land in northern Vermont, a few miles from the Canadian border. In 1820 Calvin had begun to develop this area, and a town sprang up, known at first as Harmonsville, but soon renamed Coventry. Daniel joined Calvin at Coventry, and the brothers are regarded as the founders of the town. They contributed generously to the building of the first school and gave the land for the town common. Their own enterprises included a general store and a sawmill.

It is evident that the Harmons prospered. In 1822 both Calvin and Daniel built new frame houses to replace the log cabins in which they had first lived in Coventry. Their father had died in 1805, but they were joined by their mother, who lived with them until her death in 1829 at the age of seventy-eight. Daniel moved into a new and larger house in 1830, a step perhaps made necessary by his growing family. Six children were born to Daniel and Elizabeth in Coventry, three sons and three daughters. The last of the six, Abby Maria, was born on July 27, 1838, and it is to her that we owe the preservation of the manuscript copy of her father's journal.

Harmon's last years are shrouded in mystery. All that we know for certain is that his fortunes declined, and that he decided eventually to return to Canada. The move was probably made late in 1842 or early in 1843. Until he could find a permanent place of abode, Harmon is though to have rented a small farm at Sault au Recollet,

---

[7]The North West Company ledger shows that in 1816 he sent 6,000 livres (£450 sterling) to Argalus. This was the equivalent of his full salary for five years.

[8]*Journal*, May 8, 1819.

on the northern outskirts of Montreal. In the spring of 1843 the family contracted smallpox, and four the them died within three months. Two of the children born in Coventry—Frederick and Susan—died in March; Sally, who had been born in far-off New Caledonia, followed in May. The stout old fur-trader himself died on April 23. Montreal had not completely forgotten the great days of the Nor'Westers, and on the 27th his passing was noted in the *Gazette:*—

> At Sault au Recollet, on the 23rd instant, Mr. D. W. Harmon, late partner in the North West Company, aged 65.

The place of Harmon's burial is not known. An inventory of his estate shows that it amounted to the pitiful sum of ninety-six pounds ten shillings and five-pence, and his heirs later renounced all claim to it on the grounds that it was "more burdensome than profitable."

Harmon's wife and six of his children survived him. One son, John, became a merchant in Brooklyn; another, Stephen, was in Indiana when he died at the age of 17. Most of the family died at a relatively early age. Elizabeth Harmon, their mother, lived on in Montreal until February 14, 1862, when she died at the age of seventy-two. Her daughter Amelia may have been living at the time, but it is possible that only her youngest child, Abby Maria, survived her. Maria later moved to Ottawa, where for many years she conducted a popular and fashionable girls' school. She committed suicide by drowning in September 1904.

3

Hundreds of fur-trade journals have survived, but they are almost all official records, kept for business purposes by officers in charge of trading-posts or trading expeditions. Harmon's journal is of special interest because it is a private record, kept purely for his own amusement and information. It reflects his feelings and personal opinions, and gives us a far more vivid impression of many aspects of life in the fur trade than one would be likely to find in a business document.

One is struck, for example, by the loneliness of the life he led. Except at Fort Alexandria, where his inexperience made it impracticable at first to leave him alone, and at Dunvegan, where the staff was large and some sort of community life was possible, Harmon was frequently without any English-speaking companion for weeks and even months at a time. His consciousness of loneliness was intensified by idleness. In 1804, at Fort Alexandria, he noted that "leisure moments" accounted for "nearly nine-tenths of our time";[9] nine years later, at Stuart Lake, he wrote that "few of us here are employed more and many much less than one fifth of our time in transacting the business of the Concern."[10]

To counteract this loneliness, letters were exchanged at every opportunity, and frequent visits were paid to neighbouring trading-posts. The journal records many instances in which Harmon or his colleagues made long and dangerous journeys in the depth of winter for no other reason than to pass a few days in the company of a kindred soul. Books also furnished some solace in the wilderness, particularly to Harmon, and it is interesting to note that the North West Company was aware of this, and took steps to see that some reading matter was available at most of its posts.

Though Harmon refers to them in a very matter-of-fact way, it is evident that the dangers of the life were considerable. Medical attention was rarely available in the event of an accident or serious illness; travel was often difficult and hazardous. The Indians were a constant source of anxiety and danger. In the course of a single journey, in March 1804, three attempts were made to murder Harmon, and two months later he had a very narrow escape from drowning.

Yet it is clear that Harmon got along with the Indians remarkably well, and this in spite of the fact that he dealt with them at a specially difficult time, when the intense competition between the North West Company and the Hudson's Bay Company had led to the prodigal use of liquor in the fur trade. At all the posts at which Harmon served, the normal practice seems to have been to pay in liquor a high percentage of the price the natives asked for their furs. This they proceeded to drink there and then, with devastating results. When drunk, the Indians were a danger to themselves and everyone else;

9*Journal,* April 29, 1804.
10*Journal,* May 13, 1813.

and this fact, coupled with the noise and violence to which the drinking bouts gave rise, gave the traders no rest, and made it necessary for them to be continually on the alert, night and day.

His journal shows that Harmon took much more than a casual interest in the Indians; he even seems to have had some appreciation of their point of view. He tells us that they had given him the name "Big Knife," but unfortunately we do not know why.

The almost constant threat of starvation at the trading-posts is frequently puzzling. Time and again we read that although game was known to be nearby, the hunters from the post were unable to make a kill. Deaths from starvation were not infrequent, and the traders were often reduced to such unattractive fare as tallow and rose buds. Equally surprising is the quantity of food that was evidently consumed at the posts. At Fort Alexandria in 1805 Harmon noted that his "family" consisted at the moment "of upwards of seventy Souls" who required "at least four hundred and fifty pounds of Meat per Day to feed them"—a truly astonishing total.[11] At Stuart Lake, in 1811, he noted that four whole salmon per day was the standard allowance of food per man.[12]

In spite of the hardships, Harmon enjoyed his years in the wilderness. He loved the outdoors and had a keen appreciation of natural beauties. Plant life interested him particularly, and wherever he went he soon made a garden, the progress of which through the seasons is usually noted in his journal. The vegetable garden that Harmon planted in Stuart Lake, in May 1811, is believed to have been the first cultivation of the kind west of the Rocky Mountains on the Canadian mainland.

It was while Harmon was in its service that the North West Company expanded its operations in the West, and extended them first to New Caledonia, and later all the way to the Pacific seaboard. Some of these developments were echoed in his journal, notably the Company's efforts to find a travel route from the posts in New Caledonia to the mouth of the Columbia River over which it would be practicable to transport furs and supplies. Harmon also served through the years when rivalry between the North West Company and the Hudson's Bay Company was most bitter and

[11]*Journal,* February 7, 1805.
[12]*Journal,* October 21, 1811.

most violent; but except for a passage in which he comments upon the massacre at Seven Oaks in 1816, little is said about the struggle in his journal. After 1810 Harmon was in New Caledonia, an area that the Nor'Westers had to themselves, and the matter was thus of relatively small moment to him personally.

4

No less than eighty-three fur-traders are mentioned by name in the journal. They include some of the most influential merchants in the trade, such as William McGillivray and Roderick McKenzie, and such famous explorers as Simon Fraser and David Thompson. But only a few of the eighty-three are of real consequence in Harmon's personal story. He was a friendly soul to whom his intimate friends meant a great deal and it is evident that he had a very special regard for Archibald Norman McLeod, Frederick Goedike, James McDougall and John Stuart.

McLeod had been in the service of the North West Company since 1787, and he was already an important and influential partner when Harmon first served under him in the Swan River District. The post journal kept by McLeod at Fort Alexandria in 1800–01 has been published; it reflects the multitude of cares and business details with which he was concerned, and forms an interesting contrast to Harmon's tranquil personal narrative, kept at the same post at the same time.[13] McLeod treated Harmon with much consideration, and made his adjustment to life in the fur trade much easier and pleasanter than it might have been. In particular, he introduced him to the pleasures and profits of reading, for which Harmon remained grateful all his life. The two men seldom saw one another after McLeod was transferred to Athabaska in 1802, but Harmon's regard for him did not diminish. In 1807, when they met by chance on the White River, Harmon noted in his journal that he had ever been his friend, and that he esteemed him "above any other person I know in this Savage Country."[14]

---

[13]*See* Charles M. Gates (ed.), *Five Fur Traders of the Northwest*, Minneapolis, 1933, pp. 121–85. McLeod's journal covers the period November 15, 1800 to June 4, 1801.

[14]*Journal*, June 16, 1807.

At Bird Mountain, in the fall of 1801, Harmon met Frederick Goedike, a fellow-clerk, and the two soon became firm friends. Goedike's accomplishments included playing the violin. He and Harmon were together in the Swan River District for three years, and for part of the time they frequently enjoyed the company of another kindred spirit, William Henry. "...So well do we agree," Harmon wrote in 1803, "that when People live happily together, it might be said, they live like Henry, Goedike and Harmon!"[15]

A third close friend was James McDougall, a clerk who was a few years younger than Harmon. The two met at the very beginning of Harmon's service, when he was travelling from Montreal to Grand Portage, but they did not become intimate until Harmon was sent to New Caledonia in 1810. After they had enjoyed a visit together at Stuart Lake in 1814, Harmon wrote: "There are I believe few Countries where Friendship is so rightly valued as in this where we meet so seldom."[16] McDougall never rose above the rank of clerk, and after the union of the companies he served the Hudson's Bay Company in that capacity until 1832. It is possible that Harmon met him years later in Montreal, as he lived there until his death in 1851.

Lastly, a word must be said about John Stuart, who was Superintendent for the North West Company in New Caledonia at the time Harmon arrived, and for many years thereafter. He was a Scot, and two of the things that bound him and Harmon together were a preference for serious books and a liking for theological discussion. Stuart is a well-known figure; he was Simon Fraser's second-in-command when the latter founded the first trading-posts west of the Rockies in 1805–07, and he accompanied Fraser on his famous descent of the Fraser River in 1808. Stuart became a partner in the North West Company in 1813, and a Chief Factor in the Hudson's Bay Company in 1821. He was in charge of New Caledonia until 1824, and did not retire until 1839. He then returned to Scotland, where he died in 1847. He was the uncle of Donald Smith, better known to history as Lord Strathcona.

---

[15]*Journal*, December 28, 1803.
[16]*Journal*, August 29, 1814.

The surviving manuscript is a copy of his diary that Harmon sent
to his family in the spring of 1816, when he was completing his six-
teenth year in the Indian country. It concludes with an entry dated
April 15, 1816, in which he explains the circumstances that
prompted him to make the copy. He had just heard that two of his
brothers were dying and that his mother was far from well; "little
except disappointments and Death" seemed certain in his world of
sorrows. He longed to go home on a visit, but that "inexpressible
pleasure" was denied him. As a substitute, he sent the copy of his
journal, so that his "Friends below" might know "how their long
absent Relative has been employed both as to Body and Mind
while in this Savage Country."

A dated note on the manuscript shows that in 1899 it was in the
possession of Harmon's last surviving child, his daughter Maria,
who lived for many years in Ottawa. Presumably she retained it
until her death in 1904. Subsequently it was acquired by Mr.
Guthrie Y. Barber, of New York, who in 1924 lent it to the Public
Archives of Canada, and generously allowed the Archives to make
a photostat copy. The text that follows has been prepared from this
photostat. After Mr. Barber died, in 1941, the manuscript was purchased by his brother, Mr. Courtenay Barber, of Chicago; it remained in his hands until his death in 1951. It then passed to his
son, Mr. Courtenay Barber, Jr., and was sold to Mr. Philip D. Sang,
also of Chicago. In 1955 it found a permanent home when Mr. Sang
presented it to the Library of the State University of Iowa, in
Iowa City.

The manuscript consists of 244 pages, foolscap size, and appears to be written in a single hand. There are some variations, but
interruptions, changes in ink or pen, and fatigue could easily account for these. The copy may well have been made by Harmon
himself, but as no document known to be in his handwriting is
available for comparison, the point cannot be settled definitely.

Haskel probably never saw this copy. His edition was prepared
from the journal itself, in which Harmon had continued to add entries for another three years and more. The last note is dated
August 18, 1819. But the entries for this last period are relatively

few, and the copy made in 1816 represents more than nine-tenths of the whole diary.[17] To complete the story, the printed version of the entries made after April 1816 is here reprinted as a supplement to the text taken from the manuscript.

Haskel's preface (here reprinted) indicates that he found the task of editing the journal a difficult one, and that he was none too pleased with the result. He would have preferred to be given the substance of the diary "in the form of notes and sketches, or by verbal recitals," and to write it up as he saw fit. Instead, he was faced with the task of improving the style of Harmon's narrative, and eliminating material that he felt was uninteresting or superfluous. Whether the style of the printed version is actually superior to that of the manuscript may be a matter of opinion. Harmon's rusticities are in keeping with his character and surroundings, whereas certain characteristics of Haskel's style—notably a plethora of commas—annoy and distract the modern reader. But the integrity of Haskel's intention is beyond question; there is no twisting of the text to suit any purpose of his own. Because he was a clergyman, it has usually been assumed that he either added or expanded the numerous passages in the journal devoted to religious reflections. Comparison of the two versions shows that the contrary was really the case; Haskel shortened many of the passages, and even eliminated some, especially in the latter half of the manuscript.

Harmon returned to the West before Haskel wrote his preface, but a good many of the changes made in the journal are clearly the result of talks between the author and his editor. Figures have been revised; ambiguities have been cleared up; descriptions have been added or elaborated. Much less certain is the part Harmon took in the compilation of the descriptions of Indians and animals that were included in the printed volume. T. W. Field, who in 1873 published *An Essay towards an Indian Bibliography*, felt that they were "evidently written by another hand, perhaps from Harmon's dictation." In substance this is no doubt correct, though "dictation" may be too strong a word, attributing to Harmon a greater share in authorship than he deserves. Many passages in his journal indicate that Harmon was a close and shrewd observer of Indian life and

[17]In the first printed edition the journal occupies 249 pages; the copy parallels 232 of them.

A

JOURNAL

OF

VOYAGES AND TRAVELS

IN THE

INTERIOUR OF NORTH AMERICA,

BETWEEN THE 47TH AND 58TH DEGREES OF NORTH LATITUDE, EXTEND-
ING FROM MONTREAL NEARLY TO THE PACIFIC OCEAN, A DISTANCE
OF ABOUT 5,000 MILES, INCLUDING AN ACCOUNT OF THE PRIN-
CIPAL OCCURRENCES, DURING A RESIDENCE OF NINETEEN
YEARS, IN DIFFERENT PARTS OF THE COUNTRY.

TO WHICH ARE ADDED,

A CONCISE DESCRIPTION OF THE FACE OF THE COUNTRY, ITS INHABITANTS,
THEIR MANNERS, CUSTOMS, LAWS, RELIGION, ETC. AND CONSIDERA-
BLE SPECIMENS OF THE TWO LANGUAGES, MOST EXTENSIVELY
SPOKEN; TOGETHER WITH AN ACCOUNT OF THE PRINCI-
PAL ANIMALS, TO BE FOUND IN THE FORESTS AND
PRAIRIES OF THIS EXTENSIVE REGION.

ILLUSTRATED BY A MAP OF THE COUNTRY.

BY DANIEL WILLIAMS HARMON,

A PARTNER IN THE NORTH WEST COMPANY.

❖

ANDOVER:

PRINTED BY FLAGG AND GOULD.

1820.

Title page of the first edition

SIXTEEN YEARS IN THE INDIAN COUNTRY

The Journal of
Daniel Williams Harmon
1800-1816

Edited with an Introduction
By W. KAYE LAMB
DOMINION ARCHIVIST

Maps by C. C. J. Bond
HISTORICAL SECTION, GENERAL STAFF
ARMY HEADQUARTERS

PIONEER
BOOKS

TORONTO
THE MACMILLAN COMPANY OF CANADA LIMITED
1957

Title page of the 1957 edition

customs, and the printed descriptions were most likely written by someone who talked with him and plied him with questions.

Harmon's journal and Haskel's preface show that both were familiar with Sir Alexander Mackenzie's *Voyages from Montreal...to the Frozen and Pacific Oceans in the years 1789 and 1793* (London, 1801), the most comprehensive account of the fur trade in the Canadian West that had been printed up to that time. Haskel claimed that "the country surveyed" by Harmon was "considerably more extensive" than that dealt with by Mackenzie, and he felt further that his volume included "the most correct map of the interiour of North America, which has ever been published." On several occasions Harmon refers to Jonathan Carver, whose *Travels through the Interior Parts of North-America, in the years 1766, 1767, and 1768,* had been published in London in 1778. Indeed, it is probable that Carver's volume was the model Haskel had in mind when he prepared Harmon's diary for the press. The arrangement of the contents is the same: a journal, followed first by a description of the Indians, and then by an account of the animals of the region to which the journal refers.[18]

Haskel's volume was registered for copyright by Calvin Harmon, Daniel's elder brother, on August 2, 1820, and printed at Andover, Vermont, by Flagg & Gould. The size of the edition is not known. The book attracted some attention and was noticed in the *Quarterly Review* in 1822, but it was not reprinted until the early years of this century. In 1903 the A. S. Barnes Company, of New York, included it is "The Trail Makers," a series consisting of reprints of the journals of such noted explorers and fur-traders as Champlain, La Salle and Mackenzie. Robert Waite contributed a brief introduction. The plates of this edition were used for three later reprints with different preliminary pages. The first was published in Toronto in 1904 by Morang & Company, which rechristened the series "Classics of American History." In 1911 the Courier Press, of Toronto, published the journal in "The

---

[18]Two other narratives published before Harmon's journal dealt with the fur trade in parts of the country in which he served. These were John Long's *Travels and Voyages as an Indian Interpreter and Trader* (London, 1791), and *Travels and Adventures in Canada and the Indian Territories, between the Years 1760 and 1776* (New York, 1809), by Alexander Henry the elder.

Trailmakers of Canada" series; in this edition the note by Robert
Waite was replaced by a new introduction by W. L. Grant. The
journal, with Grant's introduction, was reprinted in 1922 by the
Allerton Book Company, of New York, the series title on this occasion being "American Explorers."

6

In preparing the new version of the journal for printing, three lib-
erties have been taken with the text: the date entries have all been
given the same form; every sentence has been made to begin with a
capital letter and end with a suitable punctuation mark, and the
names of the North West Company and the Hudson's Bay Company have been written out in full. Except for these changes, which
make the journal easier to refer to and easier to read, the text of the
manuscript is followed exactly. Generally speaking, Harmon's
style is simple and straightforward, but three or four oddities of expression occur throughout the text. He usually notes that he "sat
off" (instead of "set off") on a journey; he travelled "a horse back"
instead of "on horse back," and the Rockies are referred to in the
singular as "the Rocky Mountain." The expression "John Smith
&c." means "John Smith and his party."

A careful check indicates that when the day of the week given in
a date entry does not agree with the date, the weekday is more
likely to be right. In such instances the correct date is given in
square brackets.

Footnotes have been kept to a minimum, and simple corrections and identifications have been inserted in the text, in square
brackets. In order to make the edition as complete as possible, all
passages in Haskel's version that add anything of special interest or
significance to the manuscript have also been added within square
brackets.

The whole of the supplementary material in Haskel's edition
has been reprinted with the exception of the vocabularies of the
Cree and Carrier Indian languages. These are of interest only to the
specialist, and in any event are now of little value.

In preparing this introduction I have drawn freely upon the
work of two writers who have spent much time investigating

Harmon's life and career. In 1950 Mr. John Spargo, Director-Curator of the Bennington Historical Museum and Art Gallery, published his findings in a volume entitled *Two Bennington-Born Explorers and Makers of Modern Canada* (Bradford, Vt., The Green Mountain Press). This is a study of Daniel Williams Harmon and of Simon Fraser. The same year Mr. Walter O'Meara contributed an interesting article entitled "Adventure in Local History" to the March issue of *Minnesota History*, in which he noted many details about Harmon and his family that he had discovered in the course of a personal pilgrimage through Vermont. In 1951 he published *The Grand Portage* (Indianapolis, The Bobbs-Merrill Company), a fictional account of the romance of Daniel and Elizabeth Harmon. Mr. O'Meara very kindly placed some of his unpublished notes at my disposal.

I am indebted to the Governor and Committee of the Hudson's Bay Company for their courtesy in allowing me to consult records in the Company's Archives that relate to Harmon, and in particular his personal account in the ledger of the North West Company.

As already noted, the original manuscript of Harmon's journal is now in the Library of the State University of Iowa, in Iowa City. The copper plates from which the engravings of Harmon's map and portrait were made for Haskel's edition of the journal have also survived and are with the manuscript. Mr. Frank S. Hanlin, Curator of the Rare Books at the University, very generously furnished me with a fresh impression of the portrait, made from the original plate, for reproduction in this volume.

Preface to the 1820 Edition

by

Daniel Haskel

Having prepared the following work for the press, I have a few things to say respecting it, and the part in regard to it, which I have performed.

The author of these Voyages and Travels, had no thought, while in the N.W. Country, of making publick his Journal. It was commenced and continued, partly for his own amusement, and partly to gratify his friends, who, he thought, would be pleased to be informed, with some particularity, on his return, how his time had been employed, during his absence. When he returned to civilized society, he found that curiosity was awake, in regard to the state of the country which he had visited; and the repeated questions, relating to this subject, which he was called upon to answer, together with the suggestions of some persons, in whose judgment he placed much confidence, that such a publication might be useful, first determined him to commit the following work to the press.

Had he carried into the wilderness a greater stock of general information, and expected, on his return, to appear in this manner before the publick, his inquiries would undoubtedly have been more extensive, and the result of them would be more satisfactory, to men of science. Had literary men been in the habit of traversing the regions which he has visited, he would have left it to them, to give an account of them to the publick. Having remained nineteen years in the interiour of North America, without visiting, during that time, the civilized part of the world, and having, many times, changed the place of his residence, while there, he has had an opportunity for taking a wide survey of the country, and of its inhabitants; and if the information which he has collected, be not equal to his opportunities, it is such as no other existing publication will fully afford.

McKenzie's Voyages give some account of a considerable part of the country which is here described. His residence in it, however, was much shorter than that of the authour of this work, and his personal acquaintance with the different parts of it, was much more limited. It is not intended, by this remark, to detract from the reputation, which that respectable traveller and his work, have deservedly gained. By his toilsome and dangerous voyage to the North Sea, and by leading the way, through the Rocky Mountain, to the Pacific Ocean, he has richly merited the commendation which he has received. By comparing the following work with that of McKenzie, it will appear, that, though the geographical details are less minute, the country surveyed, if we except the voyage to the North Sea, which is wholly out of the sphere of this publication, is considerably more extensive; and the information, in regard to the inhabitants, is much more particular. Considerable additions are here made, to the existing stock of geographical information, particularly as it respects the country beyond the Rocky Mountain. The basis of the map, here given to the publick, is that of Sir Alexander McKenzie, drawn by Arrowsmith. That map has received many corrections, and to it many important additions have been made, by the authour of this work; so that it is presumed now to be the most correct map of the interiour of North America, which has ever been published.

Literary men have recently taken much interest in comparing the different Indian languages, spoken on this continent, with each other, and with other languages, particularly with those anciently spoken on the other continent. A very considerable vocabulary of the one which is spoken, with a little variation of dialect, through the long tract of country, from a little back of Montreal to the Rocky Mountain, and one less extensive of the principal language spoken beyond it, are here given. Sir Alexander McKenzie has given a vocabulary of the first, which will be found, on comparison, to be somewhat different from that, which is contained in this work. Two reasons may be assigned for this. In the country about the Athabasca Lake, where McKenzie principally resided, the Cree or Knisteneux language is, in some measure, a mixed dialect; and it is far less pure than that which is spoken by the inhabitants of the plains. The words, also, are spelled by McKenzie, much according to the French sound of the letters, which is frequently calculated to mislead an English reader. Thus, the name of God, or the Good

Spirit, which McKenzie spells Ki-jai-Manitou, is here spelled Kitche-e-mon-e-too. The above remark will account, in a great measure, for this difference; and for that which will be found, in the spelling of many other words. This is the native language of the wife of Mr. Harmon, (for so I may now call her, as they have been regularly married) and great pains have been taken to make this vocabulary correct, by making the nice distinctions in the sound of the words, as derived from her repeated pronunciation of them. With this language he is, also, well acquainted, since it has been daily spoken in his family, and by himself, for many years.

The education of the authour of this work was not classical; and had it been more extensive than it was, a residence for more than half of his life, since he has arrived to years of understanding in a country where the English language is rarely spoken, would have poorly qualified him to give to this publication, a suitable English dress.

The editor undertook the business of preparing this work for the press of the time, that could be allowed him for the performance of it, and the numerous avocations of the gospel ministry, which would leave but a part of that time at his own command. For undertaking it at all, in such circumstances, his only apology is, that, in the opinion of the authour, there was no other person, conveniently situated for personal intercourse with him, who would be willing to undertake it, whose circumstances would be more favourable. It is by the particular request of the authour, and not because I suppose that I have performed the office of an editor, in a manner creditable to myself, that I have consented to connect my name with this publication.

The following work was furnished to my hand, fully written out; and though I have written it wholly over, I should have been much better able to satisfy myself, with respect to its style, if I could as fully have possessed the materials, in the form of notes and sketches, or by verbal recitals. Every man's own mind is the mould of his language; and he who has attempted to vary that of another, if he be at all accustomed to writing, must have found the task more difficult than original composition. The style of this work is not properly my own, nor that of Mr. Harmon, but something between both.

There is one subject, on which I wish especially to address a few remarks, through the medium of this preface, to the christian publick, and to all who feel any regard for the welfare of the Indian tribes, whose condition is unfolded in this work. As Mr. Harmon has returned to the interiour of North America, and, therefore, the observations which follow, will not be submitted to his inspection, before they are made publick, the editor alone must be made accountable for them.

In surveying the widely extended trade of the North West Company, we perceive evidence of an energy and perseverance, highly creditable to the members of it, as men of business. They have explored the western wilds, and planted their establishments over a tract of country, some thousands of miles in extent. They have made the savages of the wilderness tributary to the comforts of civilized society; and in many instances, they have exhibited a surprising fortitude, in exposing themselves to hardship and to danger.

The souls of the Indians are of more value than their furs; and to raise this people in the scale of intellectual existence, to surround them with the comforts of civilization, to rescue them from the gloom of superstition, to mould their hearts to christian kindness, and to cheer their dying hour with a well founded hope of immortal glory and blessedness, constitutes an aggregate of good sufficient to call forth exertion for their relief. The time is rapidly coming, when christian benevolence will emulate the activity and perseverance, which have long been displayed in commercial enterprizes; when no country will remain unexplored by the heralds of the cross, where immortal souls are shrouded in the darkness of heathenism, and are perishing for lack of vision. The wandering and benighted sons of our own forests, shall not be overlooked. They are not a race abandoned by God, to inevitable destruction; though the idea has, strangely, gotten possession of some minds. In proportion to the efforts which have been made, perhaps no missions to the heathen have been crowned with greater success, than those to the American Aborigines. To this fact, the fruit of the labours of Elliott, of the Mayhews, of Brainerd, of the Moravians, and, especially, of the recent establishment among the Cherokees, will bear abundant witness.

The Indian tribes, whose condition is unfolded in this work, have claims upon christian compassion; and some facts, which the authour has disclosed to me, have led me to suppose, that a missionary establishment might be made, with reference to their instruction, with a fair prospect of success, and with less expense, than ordinarily attends such operations.

In the numerous establishments of the North West Company, there are from twelve to fifteen hundred women and children, who are wholly, or in part, of Indian extraction. Women have, from time to time, been taken from among the Natives, to reside in the forts, by the men in service of the company; and families have been reared, which have generally been left in the country, when these men have retired to the civilized parts of the world. These women and children, with a humanity which deserves commendation, are not turned over to the savages; but they are fed, if not clothed, by the company. They have become so numerous, as to be a burden to the concern; and a rule has been established, that no person, in the service of the company, shall hereafter take a woman from among the Natives to reside with him, as a sufficient number, of a mixed blood, can be found, who are already connected with the company. There are, also, in the N.W. country, many superannuated Canadians, who have spent the flower of their days in the service of the company, who have families that they are unwilling to leave; and having nothing to attract them to the civilized world, they continue under the protection of the company, and are supplied by them, with the necessaries of life.

A plan has been in contemplation, to provide for the future maintenance of these people, and for the relief of the Company from an increasing burden, which is, to establish a settlement on the Rainy Lake River, where the soil is excellent, to which the people, above mentioned, may resort. To enable them to make a beginning, in the cultivation of the land, and in the erection of mills, &c. the Company propose to give them fifteen or twenty thousand dollars, and to appoint one of the Partners to superintend the affairs of the settlement, for three years, or for a longer time, if it shall be necessary.

It appears highly probable that a settlement might thus be formed, which, in a few years, would secure to those who should belong to it, the comforts of life, as the fruit of their own industry; and should they prosper, so far as to raise a supply beyond their own necessities, it might, with mutual advantage, be disposed of to the Company.

The Partners and Clerks of the North West Company, who are in the Indian country, as well as some of those who reside in Canada, and elsewhere, have subscribed several thousand dollars, toward the establishment of a school, either at the Rainy Lake, or at Fort William, for the instruction of the children, connected with their establishments. Some of these children are the offspring of parents, who survey their comparative degradation, with the deep interest of a strong natural affection, who are able to bear the expense of their education, and who would cheerfully contribute, in this way, to raise them to increased respectability, comfort and usefulness. Should this school be established, such persons would be required to support their children, who should belong to it; while the children of the poor, would be taught gratuitously.

These facts have opened to my mind a prospect, to which I wish to direct the eye of christian benevolence. I would ask, with deep interest, some one of the institutions, whose object is the diffusion of civilization and christianity among the Indian tribes, whether a missionary establishment might not be formed, in concert with the North West Company, which would, with much less trouble and even expense to them, accomplish the object which the Company have in view, than any establishment which they could independently make; and which would, at the same time, have a most auspicious bearing upon the religious interests of the tribes of the N.W. Country.

A school for the instruction of children in the arts of life, and in the rudiments of science, as well as in the principles of the christian religion, forms the basis of the most efficient missionary exertions among the Indians. The school among the Cherokees, is a most interesting object to christian benevolence; and as the fruit of it, the light of science, and the still brighter light of the Sun of Righteousness, is shedding a cheering radiance over many minds, that would otherwise have been shrouded in intellectual and moral darkness. The school has received the unqualified approbation of men of all descriptions who have visited it, among whom are many persons of the most distinguished character and rank in civil life. If such a school were established, at a convenient place in the N.W. Country, it would be as the day spring from on high to a region, now overspread by an intellectual and moral midnight.

Men, occupied as the gentlemen of the North West Company are, in the overwhelming cares of a vast commercial concern, would find it difficult to bestow all that attention on a school for the instruction of the children and youth, now in their establishments, whom they might think it proper to educate, which would be necessary to secure its proper management. Could this care be entirely taken off their hands, by men of known and approved characters, acting under a responsibility to some respectable society; by men who would feel all the interests which christian benevolence can create in the welfare of the children and youth committed to their care, it does appear to me, that they would gladly cooperate with them.

As the North West Company from motives of interest, as well as from more noble considerations, would contribute something to the support of such an establishment, should it meet their approbation, the expense of it would, of course, be less to the society that should embark in the undertaking than is commonly incurred, in establishments of this sort.

The children and youth above mentioned, might be instructed in the arts of civilized life, in science and in christianity, with much greater ease than the children of the Natives, even if they could as easily be obtained; and when instructed, they would be equally promising, as the instruments of spreading civilization and the religion of the gospel, among the Indian tribes. They have always been habituated to a life, in a great measure settled; and they would, therefore, endure confinement, better than children who have lived among the wandering savages. They are partially civilized by an intercourse with those, who have carried into the wilderness many of the feelings and habits of civilized society. They would not be liable to be withdrawn, at an improper time, from the place of their education, by the whims and caprice of unstable parents. At the same time, being familiarly acquainted with the manners and customs and feelings of the savages, by a frequent intercourse with them, being able to speak their languages, and having some of the Indian blood circulating in their veins, they would, when properly instructed, be as well qualified to gain access to the Natives, and to have influence over them, as if they had originally been taken, directly from their families.

As this establishment could probably be made, with the greatest convenience, within the British dominions, it might, perhaps, be undertaken with the surest prospect of success, by some society in Great Britain. The Society in Scotland for Propagating Christian Knowledge has, heretofore, contributed to the support of missionaries among the American Indians; and might, perhaps, be willing to engage in this undertaking. The Society in Massachusetts for Propagating the Gospel among the Indians of North America has, in some instances, if I mistake not, acted in concert with the Society in Scotland, above mentioned; and might, perhaps, conveniently do it, in this instance. Every association, however, who may become acquainted with the facts here disclosed, will be able themselves, to judge most correctly, of their own resources, and of their own duty.—At Fort William, on Lake Superior, a very considerable number of the partners of the North West Company assemble annually, about the middle of June, at which meeting, many important arrangement are made, respecting the business of the Company. At such a meeting, an agent from some benevolent association, might ascertain their feelings, in regard to such an establishment as I have proposed.

The Aborigines of America, are capable of being exalted in the scale of existence, and of arriving, even at eminence, in the arts and sciences. The native oratory of some of them, is proverbial in civilized countries, and has caused them to be enrolled among the sons of genius. Many of them afford proof, that they possess acute and comprehensive minds; and as a people, their mental capacity is certainly respectable. Nor, perhaps, can a people be found on the earth who are not raised above them by superiour cultivation and means of improvement, who possess greater elevation of feeling, and who appear more majestick in ruins. Their virtues and their vices too, are not those of ignoble minds. Let their condition be improved by the arts of civilized life, their minds be enlightened by science, and their hearts be softened by the genial influence of christianity, and they will assume a respectable rank among the nations. Could we hear some of their superior geniuses unfold to their countrymen the wonderful scheme of redeeming mercy, with the brilliancy and pathos, which have characterised some of their speeches, on the interests of their tribes,—with a brilliancy, rendered more splendid by cultivation, and a pathos, made doubly tender by the softening influence of the gospel, who would not listen to them with admiration and with pleasure? Might we not hope that, by the blessing of God, they would be made the honoured and happy instruments, of turning many of their countrymen, from the errour of their ways to the wisdom of the just. Could numbers of them be brought to concert plans for the extension of the gospel, in the North Western wilds, with the skill, and to execute them with the fortitude and perseverance, which they display in warring upon each other, the happiest results might be expected.

Whether the suggestions here made deserve consideration or not, I cheerfully submit to the wisdom and benevolence of those, for whom they were especially intended. Such has been by own view of the importance of the subject here presented, that I should have charged myself with a culpable neglect, if I had failed to improve this opportunity, to hold it up to the attention of the christian publick.

Burlington, Vt.
August 2, 1820

Harmon's Journal
1800-1819

Copy of A JOURNAL OR NARRATIVE of the
most material circumstances occurred to, and
some thoughts and reflections by

DANIEL WILLIAMS HARMON

during the space of Sixteen Years while in the

North West or Indian Country.

JOURNEY TO THE WEST: 1800

Montreal to Grand Portage

April 29, 1800, Tuesday. La Chine. I yesterday in company with
several other Clerks left Montreal for this place, and am thus far on
my way to the Indian Countries, there to remain at least Seven
Years, as for that space of time I am under an engagement to the
North West (or McTavish Frobisher &) Coy. and here is where the
Goods intended for the Interior or Indian Country are put aboard
Canoes (made of the Rind of the Birch Tree) which will carry about
five Tuns burden each, and manned by eight or nine Men, who are
mostly [French] Canadians, and are said to answer the purpose
better than People of any other Nation.

April 30, Wednesday. Pointe Claire. Rainy evening and I for the
first time am to pass the night in a Tent. In the fore part of the Day
I was employed at marking Bales of Goods to be sent to the Grand
Portage, but about twelve embarked aboard one of the Canoes destined for the above mentioned place, and in all there are thirty and
in the one I am, there is a Mr. Joseph Pangman (a fellow Clerk). The
whole squadron is divided into three Brigades, and in each Brigade
there is one or two Guides or Pilots who serve in a double capacity
of pointing out the best way to steer, and have also at the same time
the charge of the Canoes & Property on board, and it is them

likewise who command the Men, in short they are the same in their Brigade as a Captain is to his vessel & Men on board. Those voyagers [voyageurs] I am told have many of the Sailors customs, and the following is one of them:—from all who have not passed certain places they expect a *treat* of some thing to drink, and should you not comply with their whims, you might be sure of getting a Ducking which they call *baptizing*, but to avoid that ceremony I gave the People of my Canoe a few Bottles of Spirits and Porter, and in drinking which they got rather merry and forgot their Relations, whom they had but a few Days before left with heavy hearts and eyes drowned in tears. After being encamped, an Irish Gentleman invited me to go and take a cup of Tea at his House which was nigh bye.

May 2, Friday. Chute du Blondeau.[1] We have a strong head wind, however since yesterday morning we have come about Sixty Miles and passed two Rapids, where the most of the Property was taken out of the Canoes and carried across the Portages on the Peoples backs. [The printed text adds: "The young men, who had never been in the Indian countries, now began to regret that they had enlisted into this service, which requires them, as they say, to carry burdens like horses, when, by remaining in their own country, they might have laboured like men."]

May 4, Sunday. We have had so strong a head wind that we could not march, and I have passed the Day in reading the Travels of James Massey,[2] and in angling with Mr. John Clarke, another fellow Clerk.

May 5, Monday. Fine weather, and we are now about 120 Miles from Montreal. This afternoon our People killed a Deer with their setting Poles as he was crossing the River.

May 6, Tuesday. The Three Kettles.[3] In the fore part of the Day we passed a Beautiful Fall, where the *Riviere au Rideau* or Curtain River falls into this (which is the Otaway [Ottawa] River). The

---

[1]Chute à Blondeau, on the Ottawa River. Harmon consistently overestimates distances. From Pointe Claire to Chute à Blondeau by water is less than 40 miles, not 60 miles, as he suggests. The rapids at his point were drowned out when a dam was built across the river near Carillon.

[2]A translation of the volume entitled *Voyages et Avantures de Jaques Massé*, first published in Paris in 1710. The book was actually written by

former is about ten rods wide and the Waterfall perpendicular about forty feet, and is of an equal depth from one side to the other and when beheld at a little distance forms a pleasing scene. William McGillivray Esqre. &c. passed us this evening in a *light* canoe,[4] and are like ourselves bound for the Grand Portage also. We are now about one hundred and fifty Miles from Montreal, and the land all along on either side of the River lies very level & the soil appears to be excellent.

May 8, Thursday. Au Chat [Portage des Chats]. We now begin to see Indian Huts or Tents.

May 9, Friday. Here we arrived early in the morning, where the North West Coy. have a small Establishment, and I have passed the afternoon in shooting Pigeons.

May 10, Saturday. Grand Calumet, which is a Portage of about two miles long[5] and over which the People carry both Canoes and Ladings, and here stands a House [trading-post] which however has been abandoned for several years, by People who came here to traffic with Indians who then hunted hereabouts but are now gone farther Northward, where Beaver are more plentiful. Behind the House I found a small Bark Canoe into which I embarked alone to go and shoot Ducks, but when I had got some distance from the shore the canoe upset & I Gun and all of canoe fell into the Water, and as I had my Great Coat upon me, it was with not a little difficulty that I reached dry land, but left my Gun in the bottom of the River, which however I was loth to leave, therefore I stripped

---

Simon Tyssot de Patot. The first edition in English was published in London in 1733.

[3]Harmon had reached the spot where the City of Ottawa now stands. The mouth of the Rideau River and the Rideau Falls are within the city limits. By "The Three Kettles" Harmon meant the three Chaudière portages. The first of these (643 paces long, according to Mackenzie) was round the Chaudière Falls, which are on the Ottawa River between the cities of Ottawa and Hull; the second (700 paces) was at the Little Chaudière Falls, a short distance upstream; the third (740 paces) was at the Deschenes Rapids, about five miles farther up the Ottawa. At the falls the water rushing into a deep hole in the river-bed gave the impression of a boiling kettle or cauldron—hence the name Chaudière.

[4]A canoe carrying passengers only, in contrast to the heavily laden freight canoes that made up the brigade on which Harmon was travelling.

[5]The longest portage on the Ottawa River—2,035 paces, according to Mackenzie.

off my clothes and went to dive for it but to no effect, the water being too cold to remain long in it. I shall therefore leave my Gun where it is and thank God I did not remain with it, neither do I think I shall very soon embark in a small Canoe alone to go a shooting Ducks.

May 11, Sunday. We are encamped on a small Island opposite to where the North West Coy. have a Fort [Coulonge][6] and the Person who has it in charge came to invite my fellow travellers and me to go to sup with him, to which invitation I readily agreed (but my companion chose to remain with the Canoes) and was treated with all the politeness of which a Canadian is master (which is not a little) and they in that, as well as in many other respects resemble their ancestors the French.

May 12, Monday. Encamped on a large Sand-bank. My fellow traveller & I have had a few words together, arising from his proceedings of last night while I was absent. When I set off for the Fort I gave him the Keys of our travelling Box and Basket that he might find wherewith to make his supper, and at my return I was not a little surprised to find not only him but several of the common men much intoxicated & the keys lost. And for such unbecoming conduct I gave Mr. Pangman a pretty severe reprimand, and told him that if ever I found him again in the condition he was last night, I should be under the disagreeable necessity of informing our Employers of his conduct as soon as we reached Head Quarters. Hereupon he promised never again to be guilty of the like behaviour, yet as his Mother was a *Squaw* (and it is in the blood of the Savages to be fond of Spiritous Liquor) I can place but little confidence or dependence in his promises or resolutions. We barter Biscuit with the Natives for Sugar, of which they appear remarkably fond, as well as of Pork Beef and Spirits &c.

May 13, Tuesday. We are encamped on a Rocky Bank where it is impossible to find a place large enough to pitch our Tent, and therefore make our bed between two large rocks. On the North side of the River are Mountains that appear almost destitute of Timber of any kind.

[6]As the name indicates, this was originally a French post, founded about 1650. At the time of Harmon's visit some of the last buildings erected by the French were probably still standing.

May 14, Wednesday. Fine weather. We shall again sleep where we did last night, as the People have been employed all Day in repairing their Canoes, which become leaky. Towards the evening Messrs. Clarke Pangman & myself walked to the other end of the Portage to see Mr. Alexander Henry (another fellow Clerk) who had just arrived & was pleased to see us. With him I had formed some acquaintance before we left Montreal. He is a son of Alexander Henry Esqre. of the above mentioned place.

May 15, Thursday. Roche Capitaine Portage, so named from there being a large Rock that rises a considerable distance above the water in the middle of the rapid, and to Day we have come up several difficult ones, where many People have been drowned either coming up or going down them and for every such unfortunate Person (whether his Corpse is found or not) his surviving Companions erect a Cross, agreeable to the custom of the Roman Catholics, and here I see no less than fourteen! Which melancholy sight makes me reflect on the obstinacy & folly of man in persisting to follow a road which has lead so many of his fellow creatures to sustain [so] unfortunate and premature an end! and all through the hopes of gaining a little money! which at the longest cannot serve us but a very few years yet we are willing to run the risque of loosing our lives to gain what we tho' wrongly conceive will add greatly to our happiness.

May 16, Friday. Came up a Rapid where only a few years since two Canoes with twelve men in them were broken and every soul drowned.

May 17, Saturday. Roderick McKenzie Esqre. [and party] passed us who are on their way to the Grand Portage.

May 18, Sunday. The Lazy Portage [Portage des Paresseux]. We have left the *Otaway* [Ottawa] River on our right hand side, and come up a small one [the Mattawa River] that falls into it. About twelve we passed a Cave in the side of a high hill, which I am told is spacious but we were in too great a hurry for me to go to see it, of which the Natives know many remarkable tales to relate.

May 19, Monday. The Pines. Came up several bad Rapids but have been so fortunate as not to meet with any untoward accident. The Banks on either side of the River for a considerable distance are a perfect natural Wall, formed of smooth stones & about one hundred feet high.

May 20, Tuesday. La Vase.[7] All Day we have been crossing Small Lakes & Ponds.

May 21, Wednesday, Lake Nipisanque [Nipissing]. After coming over a number of Portages & crossing several Ponds & descending a small River [the Rivière de Vase], we arrived at what is called the Meadows & where we find several Indians, who let us have Sugar &c.

May 22, Thursday. Sailed a part of the Day in the above mentioned Lake, but toward noon the wind was so high as to oblige us to encamp on a small Island almost destitute of wood.

May 23, Friday. The lost Child, which place took its name from the following circumstances:—The natives several years since being encamped here, where they lost a Child for whom they made great search, but all in vain. However they imagined they heard his lamentations in the bowels of the earth, so they set adigging, but to no purpose for the Child could not be discovered, but as they suppose [had been] taken away by the Devil, or bad Spirit as they call him. In the morning we left Lake Nipisanque and fell into what is called the French River.

May 24, Saturday. Lake Huron [Georgian Bay]. Here we find low Cranberries very plentiful, and in the after part of the Day we passed a narrow place in the French River, and where a number of years since many of the abandoned Natives used to hide themselves behind the Rocks in the bank of the River, till the Voyagers were passing, when they would fire upon them, and then run & butcher the remainder & go off into a distant part of the Country with their booty. But the better sort of their Countrymen would not join them in such cruel and unprovoked actions. At length the Good Indians said that those Murderers were a nuisance to their society, and of course made war upon them till the greater part were destroyed & the few that survived went into a distant part of the Country & have never been heard of since. But the good Indians for their becoming behaviour were handsomely recompensed by the North West Coy. The Canadian Voyagers when they leave one stream to follow another have a custom of pulling off their Hats and making the sign of the Cross, and one in each Brigade if not in every Canoe repeats a short Prayer. The same ceremonies are

---

[7] A muddy or miry place.

also observed by them whenever they pass a place where any one has been buried or a Cross erected, consequently those who are in the habit of voyaging up this way are obliged to say their prayers perhaps oftener than when at home, for at almost every Rapid that we have passed since we left Montreal, we have seen a number of Crosses erected, and at one I counted no less than thirty! It is truly melancholy and discouraging when I seriously reflect on the great number of my fellow creatures who have been brought to untimely ends by voyaging up this way, and yet notwithstanding such dismal spectacles which are almost constantly before our eyes, we with all the eagerness of youth press forward to follow the same route, and all in hopes of gaining a little Gold!

May 25, Sunday. In the after part of the Day the Canoe in which is my old friend Mr. Clarke, overtook us, and our Guides say we have since morning sailed Sixty Miles.

May 26, Monday. So high a wind that it has prevented us from sailing much of the Day. We are encamped on an Island, of which there are many in this Lake, and on one of them it is said the Natives killed a Snake that measured thirty-six feet, the length and size of which they engraved on a large smooth Rock, which we saw as we passed bye.

May 28, Wednesday. St. Josephs or the New Fort, & where the British came and built when the Americans took possession of Mackanu [Mackinac; i.e., Michilimackinac].[8] Here there is one Captain, one Lieutenant, an Ensign & thirty-nine Privates. The Fort is built on a beautiful rise of Ground, that is joined to the main Island by a narrow neck of land, but as it is not long since People came to settle here, they have only four Dwelling Houses & two Stores on the other parts of the peninsula, and the inhabitants resemble people in exile. The North West Coy. have a House & Store here, in the latter they make Canoes for sending into the Interior or down to Montreal. Vessels also of about Sixty Tons burthen come here from De Troit, Mackanu [Mackinac] & Sault St. Maries. The whole Island is computed to be about twenty Miles in

---

[8]The Americans took over Michilimackinac, in what is now Michigan, in 1796; the same year the British moved their military post to St. Joseph Island, now part of Ontario. The North West Company's post on the island was built in 1783.

circumference & the soil is said to be good, and [it] lies nearly nine hundred miles from Montreal & forty-five from Mackanu and nearly in the 47° of North Latitude.[9] Rum here is sold for Six Dollars per Gallon & other things in proportion.

May 29, Thursday. Duncan McGillivray Esqre. (one of the Agents for the North West Coy.) came in the morning to St. Josephs from Mackanu, and soon after we embarked aboard our Canoes to come to this small Island, and as it is a fine calm [night] my fellow traveller and I intend to sleep in our Canoe.

May 30, Friday. Sault St. Maries. Rained all Day. Here the North West Coy. have another Establishment on the North side of the Rapid, and on the opposite shore there are a few Americans, Scotch and Canadians, who carry on a small traffic with the Natives, who are Sauteux (Saulteaux, a division of the Chippewa] and here the North West Coy. have built Locks for taking up loaded Canoes, to prevent them from carrying them, for the currint is too strong to be stemmed.[10] They are also building a Saw Mill.

May 31, Saturday. We shall sleep again where we did last night. Several of us have paid a visit to the People who are on the other side of the Rapid, where we saw the Indians Dance. Here is where the Water of Lake Superior runs into Lake Huron, on each of which the North West Coy. have a Vessel, one goes to Grand Portage and the other to De Troit &c.

June 1, Sunday. Pointe au Pin [Pointe au Pins], in Lake Superior, and here we find the Vessel that voyages between this & the Grand Portage. I went on board & the Captain told me she would carry about ninety-five Tons & generally makes four trips every Season to the Grand Portage. I left the Sault in company with three hundred Men who are in thirty-five Canoes.

June 2, Monday. Pointe aux Arable [Erables; i.e., Maple Point]. We now form four Brigades in which there are Six Clerks viz:— Messrs. Kenneth McKenzie, John Clarke, Alexander Henry, Joseph Pangman, Seriphin & myself.

[9]As usual, Harmon over-estimates the distance he had travelled. Sault St. Marie is 616 miles from Montreal by rail. The southern tip of St. Joseph Island is just north of the 46th parallel.

[10]A lock of this canal, built in 1797–8 and just sufficiently large to accommodate the largest freight canoes of the time, is still in existence.

June 3, Tuesday. High wind. In the morning we attempted to sail, but soon found that our weak Crafts could not stand it, therefore we made for Land, and are encamped within a hundred rods from where we were last night.

June 4, Wednesday. As it has Rained and Snowed all Day accompanied by a high wind, we have not been able to leave our encampment. Monsr. St. Germain who has charge of a small Fort belonging to the North West Coy. not far from this,[11] paid us a visit and brought us a few necessaries.

June 6, Friday. We have come on well all Day, and are encamped nigh a large Rock, on which the Natives as they pass this way throw an Arrow or some other article of little value which they say they do to appease & prevent the Devil or Muchimerutou as they call him from doing them harm.

June 8, Sunday. In the course of today we have passed several Islands which as well as the main land appear covered with Little else than Moss, with here & there a shruby Spruce.

June 9, Monday. In the morning we passed another Fort[12] which as well as the others we have seen belong to the North West Coy.

June 10, Tuesday. We anchor our Canoes by the side of a small Island in order to pass the night in them, for the country all about is on fire, but whether intentionally or by accident I cannot learn. However our People who pass this every Summer say that the fire passes over the Country almost yearly, and [it] is as may be supposed almost destitute of Animals of any kind.

June 11, Wednesday. High wind which obliged us to encamp rather early on a small Island. I am troubled with a seve[re] headache.

June 12, Thursday. Sugar Point, and is within thirty Miles of the Grand Portage. Our People say we have sailed at least ninety miles since morning. I now have a fit of the Ague and fever upon me.

June 13, Friday. Grand Portage, where we arrived late this evening. This place I am informed lies in the 48° North Latitude and is said to be about nine hundred Miles from the *Sault St. Maries* and eighteen hundred from Montreal.[13] The Fort which is twenty-four

[11]Probably Fort Michipicoten, at the mouth of the Magpie River.
[12]Probably Fort Pic, on Heron Bay.

Rods by thirty is built in a Bay at the foot of a considerable Hill or Mountain. Within the Fort there are a number of Dwelling Houses, Shops & Stores &c. all of which appear to be temporary buildings, just to serve for this moment. The Bay is so shoal that the vessel must be almost light before she can approach the shore, and directly opposite the Fort there is a considerable Island, which shelters the vessel from feeling the wind from off the Lake, and therefore makes this a tolerable convenient harbour. There also is another Fort which stands within two hundred Rods of this belonging to Parker, Gerard, Forsyth, Richardson, Ogilvy & Coy. [the XY Company],[14] but who have been in this Country only three years & have not as yet met with much success, and it is said they must fail for want of *Capital.* As this is the Head-Quarters or General Rendezvous for all who commerce in this part of the World, therefore every summer the Proprietors and many of the Clerks who Winter in the Interior come here with the Furs that they have been able to collect in course of the last Season, and I am told this is the time when they generally arrive, but some of them are already here. Those who bring the Goods from Montreal go no farther than this, except a few who takes Goods to the Rainy Lake, intended for Athabasca, as that place lies at too great a distance from this, for the People of that quarter to come this far & return before the Winter sets in—and those who bring the Goods from Montreal on their return take the Returns of the North.

June 14, Saturday. Mr. J. Clarke & I are placed in the General Shop where we deal out to the People Dry Goods, Rum, Flour, Sugar, Butter & Meat &c. &c.

[13]Mackenzie estimated the distance "coastaways" from Sault Ste. Marie to Grand Portage to be 160 leagues, or 480 miles. The distance by rail from Montreal to Fort William is 989 miles; Grand Portage is about 35 miles from Fort William.

[14]The reference is to the "New North West Company," popularly known as the XY Company. It was formed in 1798 by the union of the fur-trading firms of Forsyth, Richardson & Company, and Leith, Jamieson & Company. John Ogilvy and John Mure, representing Parker, Gerrard & Ogilvy, joined the XY Company in 1800, and Sir Alexander Mackenzie joined in 1802. The XY Company existed only until 1804 when it was absorbed by the North West Company in which it was given a quarter interest. Mackenzie, however, was excluded from the amalgamation. Harmon refers to the union of the companies in the entry dated February 19, 1805.

June 15, Sunday. I have another fit of the Ague & Fever. The People here pass the Sundays like the Natives, with this only difference, *we* change our Cloathes but *they* do not. The labouring People have all Day been employed in making & pressing Packs of Furs to be sent to Canada. To me who has never been accustomed to see People labour on the Sabbath it appears very wrong, but I perceive that those who have been any length of time in this Savage Country pay but little regard to it. However I hope that I shall never forget the Sabbath is the Lords Day.

June 24, Tuesday. I along with several other Clerks am busily employed in marking Packs—and almost every Day for some time past People have been flocking in from the Interior with the Returns of the Season.

June 28, Saturday. Last night while drunk a Squaw stabbed her Husband, who soon expired, and this afternoon I went to their Tent, where a number of Indians (of both sexes) were drinking and crying over the Corpse, to whom they would often offer Rum and try to turn it down his throat supposing that he when dead was as fond of Spiritous Liquor as when alive.

July 4 [Friday]. In the Day time the Indians were allowed to Dance in the Fort, & to whom the Coy. made a present of thirty-six Gallons of Shrub &c.[15] and this evening the Gentlemen of the place dressed & we had a famous Ball in the Dining Room, and for music we had the Bag-Pipe the Violin, the Flue & the Fife, which enabled us to spend the evening agreeably. At the Ball there were a number of this Countries *Ladies,* whom I was surprised to find could behave themselves so well, and who danced not amiss.

July 6, Sunday. In the morning Messrs. Clarke and Henry, sat off for Athabasca,[16] but where I shall pass the ensuing Winter is not

---

[15]Shrub: "A prepared drink made with the juice of orange or lemon (or other acid fruit), sugar, and rum (or other spirit)."—*Oxford English Dictionary.*

[16]The dates given in the printed version of Alexander Henry's journal differ considerably from those in Harmon's manuscript. According to Henry's journal he left Grand Portage on July 19, arrived at Rainy Lake Fort on August 2, and at the mouth of the Winnipeg River on August 14. Harmon states that Henry left Grand Portage on July 6, that he himself set out on July 15, that Henry was at Rainy Lake when he arrived there on July 24, and that he saw Henry again at Bas de la Rivière on August 7 or 8.

yet known. However as I now am in The Shop where the Fort Des Prairies[17] People are equipped I expect to go to that quarter.

July 9, Wednesday. Monday last Messrs. Robert Stuart and James Grant (both Clerks) arrived who are directly from Scotland which Country they left the 21st of March last and came by way of New York. They understand as little French as myself and we are all in the same Room, and as far as I can judge from the short acquaintance I have had with then, they are sober decent young Gentlemen.

July 13, Sunday. Yesterday Mr. Alexander Ferguson Thomas Gray & myself &c. went to Fort Charlotte, which is at the other end of this Portage and is nine Miles over. I went there to send off a number of Canoes bound for Fort des Prairies, and the others sat off for their Winter quarters, one for Swan River Department and the other for Fort des Prairies.

GRAND PORTAGE TO FORT ALEXANDRIA

July 15, Tuesday. In the morning William McGillivray, Alxr. Norman McLeod,[18] John McDonald Esqre. & myself &c. left the Grand Portage, all for our Winter quarters except the former Gentleman. He Returns to Montreal as soon as the business at head quarters is transacted—and Mr. McDonald whom I accompany goes to Fort des Prairies & Mr. McLeod to Swan River Dept. and about three of the OClock P.M. we left Fort Charlotte aboard two Canoes, which will carry about a Tun and a half burden each & Manned with Six Men. Although we have come but a very short distance yet we have passed several short Portages.

July 16, Wednesday. The long Cherry Portage. Our way has been over small Lakes & Ponds and down a small River. We met two Canadians who were not under an engagement to any one, therefore Mr. McLeod hired them to accompany him to Swan River Dept.

[17]This name was applied at different times to different posts on the Saskatchewan River. In the present instance, Fort George appears to have been meant.
[18]Archibald Norman McLeod is meant. Harmon makes the same mistake in his first name in later entries—which is surprising, as McLeod and he became close friends.

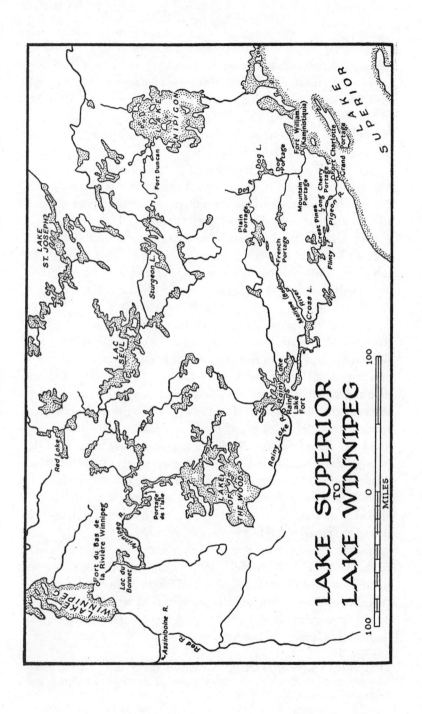

LAKE SUPERIOR
TO
LAKE WINNIPEG

July 17, Thursday. We are encamped at the north end of what is called the New Grand Portage.[19]

July 18, Friday. Great Pines. We have come over what is called the Flinty Lake which takes its name from the Stones that are to be found on its shore, which will strike fire equally well as the common Flint. Almost every day I have a fit of the Ague & Fever but not so violent as when it first took me.

July 21, Monday. For several days passed we have been coming over small Lakes & Ponds & down a small River & this morning we came down a place which was not more than ten feet broad and all the Canoes that go into the Interior are obliged to pass there.

July 22, Tuesday. Late this evening Mr. Charles Chaboillez &c. over took us, and are on their way to the Lower Red River. Also came here three Canoes Manned by Iroquois, who are going to hunt the Beaver for the North West Co. in the vicinity of the upper Red River.

July 24, Thursday. Rainy Lake Fort, where we find Messrs. Roderick McKenzie, John Finlay, John Clarke & Alexr. Henry &c. thus far on their way to Athabasca. [The printed version includes a description of the surroundings of the fort: "This is built about a mile and an half down river, from the entrance to the Lake, where there is a considerable fall. Here the soil is better than any we have seen, since we left the Ottawa River. The timber, also, is of a very good size. The Lake and River are said to contain excellent fish, such as sturgeon, white-fish, &c. In the vicinity, a considerable quantity of wild rice is gathered, by the Natives, who are Chippeways. This is thought to be nearly as nourishing as the real rice, and almost as palatable. The kernel of the former, is rather longer then that of the latter, and is of a brownish colour."]

July 25, Friday. In the fore part of the Day we over took Messrs. Alexander McKay, John McDonell, William Monroe & [François Victor] Mayotte [i.e. Malhiot], all bound for the Upper Red River except the former Gentleman he is going to the English River. I have passed the greater part of the night in copying papers to be forwarded to the Grand Portage by the Athabasca People whom we expect every

---

[19]This was a major obstruction. Mackenzie gives its length as 3,100 paces, "over rough ground, which requires the utmost exertions of the men, and frequently lames them...."

moment to meet—and the others pass the evening in *Chat* about this that and the other thing, for when People meet in this Country as it is so seldom not a moment is to be lost, but improved by keeping up an agreeable (if possible) conversation, and in smoking the sociable Pipe.

July 26, Saturday. In the fore part of the Day we met twenty-four Canoes from Athabasca loaded with twenty-five Packs of Furs & a nine-Gallon keg of Castorum each. They say they starved much on their way out, and for four Days ate nothing at all. To each we gave a reasonable Dram which made them almost forget their late misery. Mr. James McDougall a young Gentleman who has been in this Country two years accompanies them out to the Rainy Lake.

July 27 [28], Monday. Sleep on an Island without putting up our Tents but am much troubled by Musquitoes.

July 28 [29], Tuesday. Have come down several rapids at one of which last year a Canoe was broken and a Man drowned, and the Canoe came very nigh filling. We are now in Rainy Lake River which is about one hundred and twenty Miles long & twelve or fifteen Rods broad. The land on either side appears to be good but the Timber is small, for I have not seen many Trees that would measure more than a foot in diameter, which are Burch, a species of Pine, Hemlock, Poplar, Aspin & Cedar &c.

June 29 [30], Wednesday. Passed a Rapid where last year three Men were drowned in coming down it. One of our People fired at a Black Bear but missed him.

July 30 [31], Thursday. Passed a number of Mirey Portages—and the place where three years since, the Natives fired upon our People as they were passing, but done no injury. However Mr. McLeod &c. went and took one of them intending to bring him to the next Fort and then to punish him as he deserved, but after they had come some distance & near a Rapid, the Indian jumped out of the Canoe into the River, in hopes as was supposed of swimming to the opposite side and then run off, but the Current was too strong for him to gain the Shore, therefore he went down the Rapid and was never seen after.

July 31 [August 1], Friday. Bottom of the River Ouinipick [Winnipeg] Fort,[20] and where the Hudsons Bay Coy. have a Fort also.

[20]Frequently referred to as "Bas de la Rivière Winipic" in documents of the time; later known as Fort Alexander. The neighbouring Hudson's Bay Company post had just been established.

The latter People fell into our road in a small Lake that we came over yesterday. Both People [the Hudson's Bay and North West companies] have miserable buildings. I am encamped a little below the Fort in a small Plain, to have a convenient place to dry the Goods which yesterday got wet coming down the Rapids. [The printed text adds: "A few miles above this, there is a small lake, called Lac de Bonne (Lac du Bonnet), from which the Hudson Bay people leave our rout, and proceed toward the Albany Factory. The soil is good; and among the fruit, I observe the red plum. The grape, also, grows well in this vicinity. In the neighbouring woods, a few moose and deer are found; and the Lake and River are well supplied with fish."]

August 1 [2], Saturday. In the Morning Messrs. McLeod & McDonald came down to wre [where] I was (for they had Passed the night at the Fort) and told me they had got news from Swan River, and that it would be absolutely necessary to make another Establishment in that quarter, and as there was no one to take charge of it, they thought it requisite that I should be the person. I of course returned to the Fort along with Mr. McLeod to wait for his Brigade which is still behind, but Mr. McDonald proceeded on to his Winter quarters. In the after part of the Day I went to shoot Pigeons, for at this Season they are plentiful hereabouts there being such an abundance of Berries of various kinds. Here also they have Grapes and Red Plumbs, which as I am told are not to be found at many other parts of this Country. The land lies low and the soil appears excellent.

August 2 [3], Sunday. Fine weather. Part of the Day I have passed in reading Camelia or the Picture of Youth, and the remainder in shooting Pigeons and gathering Berries. This is the first Day I ever past (since my infancy) without eating either Bread or Biscuit, but as a substitute for them we now have what the Natives call *Pimican* [pemmican], which is a compound of lean Meat dried and pounded fine & then mixed with melted Fat, and then put into Bags (made of the Skins of Buffaloe &c.) and when cold becomes a solid body and if kept in a dry place will preserve good for years, but if in a damp place it soon becomes musty. Our people like it much better than Milled Indian Corn & then boiled as it is cooked in this Country & I although not accustomed to it, find it very palatable and it is said to be very nourishing & healthy Food. This is what the common Men live upon from their Winter quarters to the Grand Portage, as well as part of their way back again.

August 3 [4], Monday. The most of the Day I have been employed in copying papers for Mr. McLeod, who is till [still] here, but towards the evening I paid the Hudson's Bay Gentleman (Mr. Miller) a visit who told me [that] to go to Albany Factory, where they get their Goods, generally takes them about forty Days, but twice that time to return from thence, as they come against the current. The Factory he says lies nearly North of this [at the mouth of the Albany River, on James Bay].

August 5 [6], Wednesday. This morning Mr. J. McDonell (whom we left along the way) arrived, and inform us that one of his Canoes broke in coming down the Rapids and one of Men drowned & the most of its lading lost.

August 6 [7], Thursday. In the morning, Mr. McLeod sat off for Swan River, but as I am to remain here to wait the arrival of Messrs. Hugh McGillis & A. Ferguson, who are behind with the main Brigade. At eleven A.M. Messrs. R. McKenzie and Donald McTavish passed this, the former bound for Athabasca & the latter for the English River, and in the evening Messrs. McGillis & Alexr. Henry Junr. cast up, the former going to the Red Deer River & the latter To *Riviere au Painbinas,* or Cranberry River [Fort Pembina, on the Red River].

August 7 [8], Friday. In the after part of the Day Messrs. John Finlay, Clarke & A. Henry &c. arrived, also soon after Messrs. A. McKay & Robert Stuart going to the English River, and in the evening Monsr. Mayotte [Malhiot] took a Woman of this Country for a Wife or rather Concubine, and all the ceremonies (as I am informed) attending such a circumstance is, when a person is desirous of having one of the Natives Daughters to live with him, he makes a present to the Parents of the Damsel, of such articles as he may suppose that will best please them, but Rum always forms a principal part of the donation, for this is what Savages in general are most fond of, and should they accept the articles offered, the Girl remains at the Fort with her lover, and is clothed after the fashion of the Canadians, with a Shirt, short Gown, Petticoats & Leggins &c. and the most of them I am told are better pleased to remain with the White People than with their own Relations. But should the newly joined couple not agree, they are at full liberty to separate whenever either chooses—however no part of the property that was given to the Girls Parents will be refunded.

August 9 [10], Sunday. Entrance of Lake Ouinipick [Winnipeg] and about a Mile from the Fort, where in the morning at long last Mr. Ferguson &c. arrived, and soon after Mr. McGillis & myself embarked to accompany them here. Our People killed a Dog to eat, the flesh of which they say is excellent, but they are of a different species than those I have seen in the Civilized part of the World, these have a greater resemblance to Wolves, and it is said that their flesh has a different flavour.

August 10 [11], Monday. Early in the morning we embarked & hoisted Sails, but the wing [wind] soon after bluie so high as to oblige us to encamp on a point of land that makes out far into the Lake, and not long after a number of the Natives paid us a visit to whom we gave a little Rum & Tobacco &c.

August 16 [17], Sunday. Entrance of Riviere Dauphine [Dauphin River], where we leave Lake Ouinipick [Winnipeg] to go up the above mentioned River, which is so shoal that our People are obliged to leave half of their ladings here, and take the remainder a certain distance up the River, where there is more water, and then will come back for the rest.

August 18 [19], Tuesday. Last night the wind blew so high that it drove the water in the Lake to such a distance up the beach that we were under the necessity of removing our Baggage three times farther into the Woods. But this morning our people came back for the remainder of the property and as the water is low Messrs. McGillis, Ferguson & myself, walked along the beach to where our people made the first trip & then embarked as there was no want of water and the River about ten Rods broad and the Country lies level.

August 19 [20], Wednesday. Lac St. Martin, through which passes the river that we have just left, and here we see Swans, Bustards, Ducks & Pilicans plentiful.

August 21 [22], Friday. In the morning we left Lac St. Martin & entered the Mudy Lake [the upper portion of Lake Manitoba], and here again we find Fowls plentiful.

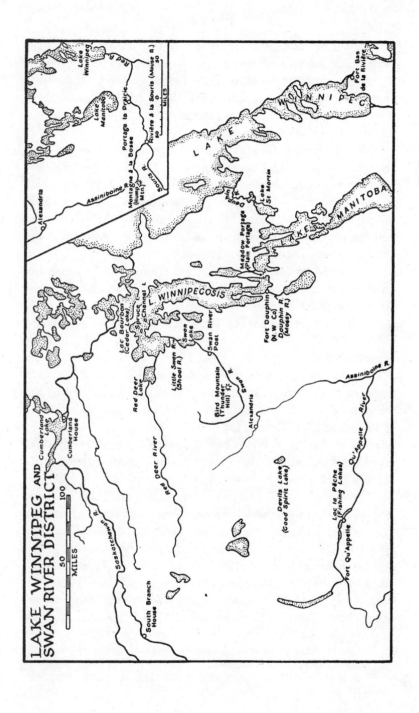

August 22 [23], Saturday. North end of the Plain Portage,[21] which is about two Miles over, but through a beautiful Country.

August 23 [24], Sunday. Little Lake Ouinipick [Lake Winnipegosis], and where we overtake Mr. McLeod &c. & a number of the Natives, (who are Sauteux) encamped about him, waiting our arrival to get Rum to drink.

August 24 [25], Monday. Still where we slept last night—and have been busy all Day in making out an Outfit for the Establishment at the entrance of Riviere Dauphine [Mossy River], which place lies but a few Miles from this—and is where a French Missionary a number of years since, resided to instruct the Natives in the Christian Religion, but I am told did not meet with much success, for he did not remain long enough among them.

August 26 [27], Wednesday. Early in the morning I in company with four Canoes sat off to Swan River but soon after the wind blew so high we were obliged to encamp.

August 27 [28], Thursday. In the fore part of the Day Messrs. McLeod & McGillis &c. overtook us, & soon after the wind blew so high that we encamped.

August 29 [30], Saturday. Encampment Island [Lake Winnipegosis],[22] where we in the fore part of the Day arrived & ever since have been busy in making out an Outfit for Mr. McGillis to take to Red Deer River. That Gentleman made me a present of a Brass Barreled Pistol. We are now as I am told near the north end of the Lake which may be about 150 Miles long and from five to thirty broad. The Country lies low.

September 1 [2], Tuesday. A Canadian in a small Canoe arrived from Red Deer River, which is about a half a Days march from this, and late at night Mr. McLeod &c. embarked for Lac Bourbon [Cedar Lake], where the Company have an Establishment.

September 2 [3], Wednesday. In the morning Mr. [Hugh] McGillis & all of the People except one Man sat off for the Red Deer River, but I shall wait Mr. McLeods return, as well as for several Canoes that are still behind. Here we take what is called White Fish and are excellent.

[21]Meadow Portage, between the northern end of Lake Manitoba and the southern end of Lake Winnipegosis.
[22]The identity of this island is uncertain. It was probably either Spruce Island or Channel Island.

September 3 [4], Thursday. I have past the Day in reading the Bible and in meditating on my present way of living, which appears to me to resemble too much that of a Savage.

September 6 [7], Sunday. Late this evening Mr. McLeod &c. returned from Lac Bourbon [Cedar Lake], and this morning they again embarked for Swan River, and left me here with two Men & as many Women to wait the arrival of a number of Canoes that we expect Daily.

September 8 [9], Tuesday. Part of the People for whom I have been waiting are arrived whose ladings I have examined.

September 9 [10], Wednesday. Sent those who arrived yesterday to Red Deer River—also came people from Swan River for the Goods that were remaining here.

October 6 [5], Sunday. North end of Little Lake Ouinipick [Lake Winnipegosis]. Ever since the 29th August I remained on Encampment Island waiting the arrival of People who were left behind and who owing to having had almost continually high winds as is customary I am told at this Season did not make their appearance till the 4th Inst. During the long space of time I remained on that unpleasant Island we had little or nothing to eat except the Fish we took out of the Lake with our Nets, and at times we would take very few, especially when the wind was high, but for eight Days successively we did not take a Fish, as the wind in the night blew so high that it took the only Canoe we had to the other side of the Lake. However on the eighth Day Providence sent an Indian to where we were encamped and he lent us his Canoe to go for ours which our People found not the least injured on the other side of the Lake, which is a distance of at least five Miles. But while we had no Canoe we were under the disagreeable necessity of living upon the Fish we had (when they were plentiful) left on the beach, and by that time had become almost putrefyed. However they did not last long & then we had nothing at all, till Kind Providence sent a black Bear near our Camp, at which one of our Men fired & killed him, and was a blessing for which we endeavoured to be thankful, as we looked upon it as a favour from Heaven, although I could not pretend to think we were deserving it,—but it Rains on the unjust as well as on the just. Yesterday it Snowed the most of the Day, which prevented us decamping, but early this morning we with little reluctance left the solitary Island, where I past many a moment of *ennui*—and during my stay there for the want of any other Book I read the greater part of the bible. This afternoon we met two Men in a small Canoe from Swan River loaded with provisions for the People of Red Deer River, but we did not let slip so good an opportunity unimproved, without taking a sufficiency of the Staff of life to bring us to where there is more.

October 8 [7], Tuesday. Little Swan River [Shoal River]. Yesterday on account of high wind we could not leave our encampment, but early this morning we embarked and at twelve left the Lake to come up this River, which is nearly ten Rods wide, very shallow and full of Rapids. Therefore I debarked and walked along the beach about four Miles in the Snow, Mud & water, and the People also for want of a sufficiency of water were obliged to debark & drag their Canoes up the shoal places, but now we are encamped around a rousing fire, and none of us think much on the fatigue & trouble we had in the course of the Day. To make a place to lie down the people scraped away the Snow & lay down a few Branches of a species of Pine we find every where in this part of the World, and then upon the top of that, a Blanket or two, and where after a Day of hard labour I am persuaded a person will sleep as sound as if on a Feather Bed.

October 9 [8], Wednesday. Swan River Fort. In the morning we crossed Swan Lake, which is nearly eight Miles long and then entered, what is called Great Swan River (to distinguish it from the other of the same name) and is about eleven Rods wide, & plenty of water, an[d] no Rapids to this Fort which stands about twelve Miles from its entrance. The Country lies flat and low & I am told that the soil is excellent. Here we find a Monsr. Perigné in charge of the Fort, where they have a tolerable Kitchen Garden. [The printed text adds: "The Hudson Bay people, once came here; but it is several years since they abandoned the place. As they have nothing to expect from the Company, but their salaries, they seem, so far as I can learn, to make but little exertion to extend their trade, and thereby, to benefit their employers."]

October 10 [9], Thursday. Fine weather for the Season. All Day I have been busy in settling the affairs of this place & in making out an Outfit for Mr. Perigné, who is with Six common labouring Men to go and build a Fort about one Days march up this River where they will pass the ensuing Winter. I am informed that a few Miles up this River there is a Salt Spring the water of which when boiled down makes tolerable Salt, however it is not so strong, as that which comes from Canada, but it preserves Meat &c. well.

October 11 [10], Friday. The People whom I arranged yesterday I have sent off to build their Fort, but I am to remain here till People come from Alexandria where I shall pass the ensuing Winter with Mr. McLeod, or go and build by the side of the Hudson's Bay People who are about three leagues from where he is. But not to be idle, till then I shall read the adventures of David Simple.

October 12 [11], Saturday. As I am soon to leave this place I have taken an Inventory of every thing here.

October 14 [13], Monday. Our People have been a shooting & killed a few Hares[23] & Ducks.

October 16 [15], Wednesday. We take a few Fish with Nets out of the River and this evening two Men on Horseback arrived from Alexandria who delivered me a Letter from Mr. McLeod desiring me to accompany them to where he is.

October 18 [17], Friday. Second crossing place in Swan River. In the morning we left the Fort and the Country we have come over lies low & the Timber small, consisting of Poplar, Aspin, Burch, Willow, and an inferior species of the Maple Tree, of the sap of which they however make tolerable Sugar, but not so good a quality as that produced of the real Maple.

October 19 [18], Saturday. In the course of the Day we have traversed several small Plains, where we saw Cranes & Pheasants &c.

October 20 [19], Sunday. Bird Mountain,[24] and where Mr. Perigné &c. are building. The most of the Day our walk has been over Plains, and this afternoon I saw eight Red Deer (which are about the size of a common Cow) and fired at them but missed my mark.

October 21 [20], Monday. Again to Day we have passed over Plains but I should think the soil not good for it appears to be a yellow Sand.

---

[23]Misprinted *horses* in the printed version.
[24]The present Thunder Hill, Manitoba. In earlier times it was known variously as Bird, Thunder and Thunderbird Mountain.

October 22 [21], Tuesday. The Foot of a high Hill & near a small Lake, whose water has a Sulphurious taste. In the morning we left Swan River, and to cross it we were obliged to make a Raft—and ever since the country appears to be more hilly but almost destitute of Timber of any kind.

October 23 [22], Wednesday. Alexandria, where we this after-noon arrived, and am happy to find myself at long last at the end of my Journey, and where I hope to pass at least a five [few] months in quietness. The Fort is built on a small rise of ground on the Bank of the Upper Red [Assiniboine] River, which separates it from a beau-tiful Plain about ten Miles long and is as level as a House floor. Just behind the Fort are small Groves of Burch, Poplar, Aspin and a species of the Pine Tree, which renders it a delightsome place. The Fort is twelve Rods by Sixteen & the Houses well built, plastered inside & out & washed over with white Earth, which is plentiful hereabouts and answers nearly as well for whitewashing as Lime. Mr. McLeod is goin [gone] to Fort Dauphin on Horse-back, which place over land lies only four Days march from this—yet it is about two months since I passed there in a Canoe.[25]

[25]The North West Company's Fort Dauphin was then situated at the mouth of the Mossy River (*see* entry for August 24, 1800, above). The dis-tance from Fort Alexandria, as the crow flies, was about 120 miles.

FORT ALEXANDRIA

October 26, Sunday. This evening the People of the Fort danced (all Days appears to be the same to them) and the Women danced full as well as those of the lower Class in the Civilized World.

October 28, Tuesday. Mr. McLeod &c. returned from Fort Dauphin, and whom after so long a separation I am happy to see, and he appears pleased to find me here. Since he left me at the Encampment Island I have had no one with me who could speak English and I cannot as yet understand much of the French Language. However I read it tolerably well.

November 8 [9], Sunday. On the 30th Ult. I in company with four Men on Horse back sat off for Swan River, and the Day we left the Fort it Snowed & Rained, which made us pass a disagreeable night, as we had nothing but our wet Blankets to cover ourselves. The People went down for Goods and as there is no one there who can read and write I went to give out such articles as are wanted here.

November 16, Sunday. Fine weather. Last Wednesday, came twelve Families of Crees & Assiniboins from the large Plains and let us have Furs & Provisions & who have been drinking ever since, both Men & Women, which occasions them to make an intolerable noise, for they talk, Sing & cry all at the same time. Our own Men play at Cards on the Sabbath the same as on any other Day, and for such improper conduct I once spoke to them, but their answer was that there is no Sabbath in this Country, and their behaviour but too plainly shews that they think as they speak, and it is a lamentable fact that the most of those who are in this wild part of the World, lay aside the most of Christian and Civilized regulations, and behave but little better than the Savages themselves. It is true we have it not at all times in our power, however much we may be inclined, to keep the Sabbaths as we aught, for the Natives come to our Establishments as often on the Lords Day as on any other, and when they are there we must attend to & let them have their wants. We are also often obliged to travel about on Sundays as well as week Days, yet it is true again, let our bodies be employed as they will, our minds if so disposed may almost wholly be taken up on things Heavenly, therefore after all I must acknowledge that we have no reasonable excuse for breaking the Sabbaths as we all do.

November 19, Wednesday. Last night there fell about four Inches of Snow, and yesterday came eight Families of Crees, and while drinking one of their Women who had a knife about her, fell down (by accident) and drove the point of it nearly two inches into her side, but the wound is not thought mortal. To behold a House full of Drunken Indians, as it generally consists of Men, Women & Children, is truly an unpleasant sight, for they in that condition often quarrel, fight and pull each other by the hair, and at times you will see ten or twelve or more (of Both sexes) all by the ears at one and the same time, till at last they all fall flat on the floor, one upon the top of the other, some spilling Rum out of a Kettle or Dish which they have in their hand, while others are throwing up what they had just drank. And to add to this uproar a number of Children, some on their Mothers shoulders and often laying hold of them, are constantly bawling out & I must confess makes a very unpleasant chorus to the brutal noise kept up by their Drunken Parents who are engaged in the squabble.

November 30, Sunday. This being St. Andrews Day, and therefore a *Fate [fête]* among the Scotch, and our *Bourgeois* Mr. McLeod belonging to that Nation, the People of the Fort agreeable to the custom of the Country early in the morning presented him with a Cross &c. and at the same time a number of others who were at his door let off a volley or two of shot, and soon after they were invited into the Hall, where each got a reasonable Dram, and then Mr. McLeod made them a present of a sufficiency of Rum to keep them merry during the remainder of the Day (which they drank in their own Houses) and in the evening they were invited to dance in the Hall where they got several Flaggons of Spirits in the course of the evening, and who behaved themselves with much propriety till about eleven of the OClock, when their heads became too much heated by the great quantity of Spiritous Liquor they had drank in the course of the Day & evening. Of course some of them became quarrelsome, as is generally the case with Canadians when intoxicated, and from high words they soon came to blows & we had two famous Battles, but they put an end to our *truly genteel* North West Ball!

December 2, Tuesday. As yet we have only a few inches of Snow. Yesterday morning I accompanied by Six Men a [on] Horse back went to our Hunters Lodge—the People for meat & I to have a ride and see the Country, and we arrived where the Indian was encamped just as the Sun was sinking below the horizon & when the Hunter was going to take a sweat, as I am told is their custom often to do & in the following manner:—The Women make a kind of Hut of bended Willows, which is nearly circular, and if only for one or two persons not more than fifteen feet in circumference & three or four in height, over which they throw skins of Buffaloe &c. and in the centre of the hut they place heated Stones. Then the Indian goes in perfectly naked with a Dish of water a little of which he now and then throws on the hot Stones that the heat may be greater, which soon puts him in a great perspiration, and there he will remain about an hour, but a person who is not accustomed to so great a degree of heat would suffocate in half that time. They say they sweat themselves in this manner, in order that their limbs may become more suple & alert to pursue the Animals they wish to kill. The Country we past through in going there is a large Plain with here & there a Grove to be seen, and this evening we returned to the Fort, the People Horses loaded with the Flesh of Moose & Deer. The Buffaloe are still a considerable distance farther out into the spacious Plains and nothing but severe cold weather, will drive them into the more woody part of the Country.

December 4, Thursday. Two Men arrived from Lac Bourbon with Letters.

December 10, Wednesday. One Mr. Sutherland a Clerk for the Hudson's Bay Coy. paid us a visit. He has built a Fort about eight Miles down this River. He is an Orkney man, & I am told that the greater part of the Hudson's Bay Coy's Servants are from the Orkney Islands.

December 21 [20], Saturday. There is now about a foot of Snow on the ground, and I on the 11th Inst. with Seven Men sat off for Swan River Fort. Each man had a Sledge drawn by two Dogs loaded with one hundred & fifty pounds wight [weight] of Furs, and Provisions for Man & beasts to perform the trip, and on our return they were loaded with Goods, and this afternoon we reached this Fort [Alexandria] where I am happy to find Mr. Hugh McGillis (who appears to be a worthy Man) on a visit from Red Deer River, also two men with Letters from Fort des Prairies. The former place lies about five Days march from this & the latter ten & in nearly a North direction.

December 24, Wednesday. Yesterday I went down to the Hudson's Bay House on business, and where I was agreeably surprised to find that Mr. Sutherland's Woman a native of this Country could speak the English Language tolerably well and I understand can both read and write it also. She likewise speaks the Cree & Sauteux tongues, and with her I had a long conversation, who appears to be a sensible Woman, but her Husband is a great Drunkard and when in his cups a perfect mad-man.

1801

January 2, Friday. Severe cold weather as it has been for some time. Yesterday being the first Day of another year and agreeable to the Canadian custom, either in Canada or in this Country, they on that Day always get drunk if possible, therefore yesterday they drank from morning till night, and in the evening danced in the Hall, but no scratching nor fighting! This evening there was to be seen a large light on either side of the Moon and two others which appeared to run through it, which phenomenon struck me as well as all those who beheld it with some surprise.

January 4, Sunday. In the morning the greater part of our People (Men, Women & Children) were sent to go and pass the remainder of the Winter in the Plains about two Days march from this, and where they will live upon the flesh of Buffaloe which they will kill themselves, and during their stay there, their Dwellings Will be Tents or Lodges made of the Skins of either Buffaloe, Moose or Red Deer after being dressed or tanned & then sewed together, one of which contains from ten to twenty of those Skins and when erected assume the form of a Sugar-Loaf, and in one of those tents ten or fifteen persons will find sufficient space, for when they are there they are always either seated or lying down.

The Indians who come to this Establishment are *Crees* &

Assiniboins, and I am told both of them are numerous Tribes. The former generally remain in the strong or thick Woods and hunt the Beaver, Moose & Red Deer &c. but most of the latter live out in the spacious Plains and hunt the Wolves (of different species) Foxes, Bears & Buffaloe &c. As both Tribes often meet their customs & manners are nearly the same, however there is no resemblance in their Dialects. Neither of them want for Horses but the *Assiniboins* are the best Horse-Men, for they never go any distance a foot, and with those Animals they often run down & kill the Buffaloe with their Bows & Arrows, which they find full as convenient for that purpose as fire arms, but the *Crees* alway when they can purchase them [and] make use of the latter to kill their Game. Their Cloathing consists of a pair of Leggins, a kind of Shirt or Frock, with a Robe of dressed Buffaloe Skin which they wrap about their bodies and tie around their waists. Last evening I wrote Letters to my old fellow travellers from Montreal, Messrs. Henry & Clarke which will be taken them by the Winter Express that leaves this tomorrow and is to pass by the way of Fort des Prairies, from thence to the English River and then directly to Athabasca. And I am informed that there is an Express that every year leaves Athabasca in the Month of December and passes throughout the whole Country called the North West and reaches *Soult St. Maries* towards the latter end of March, and thus the Gentlemen who come up in the Spring from Montreal get the news of the preceeding Summer much earlier than they would otherwise have done and [this] often is of great service to them and attended with a very little expense to the Concern.

January 15, Thursday. Beautiful weather. On the eleventh I accompanied Six of our People to our Hunters Lodge, and the Day following they returned to the Fort with their Sledges loaded with Meat, while I remained there to go farther into the Plains along with the Hunter, and where I am sure I saw in different herds at least a thousand Buffaloe grazing, and [they] would allow us to come within a few Rods of them before they would leave their places. At this Season they are very tame and harmless, and it is not at all dangerous to go among them, but in the fore part of the Summer at their rutting season it is quite the reverse for then as soon as they perceive a human being they will pursue & should they overtake him will trample him under their feet or run their horns through his body. The Meat of the Buffaloe (that is the male) when fat will weigh from one thousand to fourteen hundred pounds & the Female from Seven hundred to a thousand,[26] and is excellent eating, but is not however looked upon by the most of people [as] so delicious and palatable as that of the Moose.

February 11, Wednesday. On the 1st Inst. I accompanied by eight of our People & one of the natives (who served as Guide) sat off with a small assortment of Goods to go and trade with about fifty Families of Crees & Assiniboins and in going to their Camp or Village we were three Days always in a Plain Country. The first night after we were encamped there came a terrible Storm of Snow accompanied by a strong & cold north wind and we were encamped in the open Plains, with nothing to shelter us from the Storm, but in the morning we found ourselves buried under about a foot of Snow, and very cold weather, but our People were not long in harnessing the Dogs, when we sat off to try to warm ourselves by running, but which we had hard work to do for we had a strong head wind that prevented us from going fast. The Day following after we had encamped our Guide killed a fat Buffaloe, which served as food for both ourselves & Dogs and while eating it around a rousing fire, we almost forgot the hardship we had suffered by the cold the preceeding night & morning and if we were not thankful for the *blessing* bestowed upon us, we were at least *glad* to enjoy it. When we got within a Mile of the Natives Camp, ten or a dozen of their Chiefs and most respectable Men, came a Horse back to meet & conduct us to their dwellings, and immediately after our arrival there, one of the Chiefs sent his Son to invite me & my Interpreter to go to his Lodge and as soon as we were seated, the old Man caused Meat and Berries &c. (in short the best of everything he had) to be set before us, for Savages pride themselves in being hospitable to Strangers, but before we had ate much, we were sent for to go and do the same at another Lodge, and from his to another, and so on till we had been to more than half a dozen at all of which we ate a little (and smoaked our pipe) for (as my Interpreter informed me) they would think we dispised them, and

[26]In the printed version the figures are given as 1,000 to 1,500 pounds for the male and 800 to 1,000 pounds for the female buffalo.

look upon it as an affront should we not taste of every thing they sat before us—in fact during several Days that we remained with those People, we met with more real politeness (in this way) than is often shown to Strangers in the civilized part of the World, and much more than I had expected [to] meet with from *Savages* as the Indians are generally called, but I think wrongfully.

While I was at the Indians Camp I went to see them Dance where there might have been about thirty Men all Clothed with Skins of *Cabri* or jumping Deer [antelope] and which were nearly as white as Snow, and their Dance began as follows:—A Man nearly forty years of age rose with his Tomyhawk in his hand & made a long harangue when he recounted all the noble & manly exploits he had achieved in the several War-parties where he was engaged with his enemies, and he mentioned of two whom he had killed and taken off their Scalps, for each of which he gave a blow with his Tomyhawk against a Stake that was set up for that purpose in the centre of the Lodge, & now the Music began which consisted of Tambourines & the shaking of Bells accompanied with singing. Soon after the Man who made the harangue began to dance, then another arose and shortly after a third and so on one after the other till there were about a Dozen up who all danced around a small fire that was in the middle of the Lodge and continued so doing for about an hour, then they sat down & others rose and took their places, but their Dance to me appeared always nearly the same. Therefore after having remained there about two hours, I returned to my Lodgings but how long they continued jumping about I cannot say.

In our excursion we saw Buffaloe in abundance, and when on a small rise of ground I may with truth say that we could see grazing in the Plains below at least five thousand of which Animals we killed what we wanted for ourselves & Dogs, and this evening returned to the Ford loaded with Furs & Provisions without having received the least affront or the smallest injury from the Natives, notwithstanding the most of them were intoxicated with the Rum we gave them.

February 17, Tuesday. Clear and cold. We now have about a foot and a half of Snow. Mr. Montour accompanied by two Canadians arrived from Fort des Prairies who brought Letters from

Gentlemen in that quarter. This morning one of our People killed a Buffaloe in the Plain opposite the Fort & another came within ten Rods of the Fort Gate but the Dogs pursued him & he ran off.

February 19, Thursday. This Day I am twenty-three years of age, and how rapidly does it now appear that that space of time has past away! For it seems as if it was but yesterday that I was a Child! In fact the time is so short that we remain in this fleeting world that a person can scarcely begin to live ere he must *set his House in order to Die!* And of this truth we are all well convinced, yet are continually laying plans as though we expected to always live. But Man is so made that he cannot be idle, if not doing good a doing harm. However we always ought to strive to be so employed as to be useful to ourselves as well as to others while here below and then we may with some reason have cause to hope that hereafter we shall be happy.

February 20, Friday. All last night I sat up trading with Drunken Indians, one of whom has his own Daughter for a Wife & her Mother also at the same time! However incest is a crime of which the Indians are not often guilty, but when such a thing does take place among them they are looked upon by the others as People void of sense.

March 14, Saturday. On the 6th Inst. I accompanied by eighteen of our People left this to go to Swan River Fort. They had thirty Sledges some hauled by Horses and others by Dogs, which were loaded with Furs & Provisions, and on the 12th we reached the lower Fort and this evening returned to this. The greater part of the Snow is now dissolved.

March 17, Tuesday. Sent four men to Swan River to make Sugar.

SWAN RIVER FORT

April 4, Saturday. Swan River Fort, where I this afternoon arrived and am come to pass the remainder of the Spring here. During the time I was at Alexandria I past those Days agreeably in the company of Mr. McLeod, who is a sensible Man & an agreeable Companion, but he like most others also gives in too much to the ways and customs of the Country he is in and therefore does not lead so moral a life as I am persuaded he would were he in the civilized part of the World. Yet truth as well as gratitude obliges me to say this much in his behalf that he appeared desirous of instructing me in what was most necessary for me to know concerning the affairs of this Country as well as what would make me more virtuous and good—and it was also from the example he sat me that I became fond of reading and for which I hope & trust I shall ever have a grateful heart, as well as for the many other favors he was pleased to shew me. But now I am as it were alone there being not a person here able to speak a word of English and as I have not often been in the Mens company I cannot as yet speak much of their Language. However fortunately I have a few Books here and in perusing them I shall pass most of my leisure moments.

April 6, Monday. I have taken a ride a Horse back to where our People are making Sugar & my path lead me over small Plains & through the wood, where I saw a great variety of Birds that were straining their tuneful throats as it were to welcome the return of another revolving Spring, and also small Animals running about in the wood or skipping from Tree to tree and at the same time were to be seen Swans, Bustards & Ducks &c. swiming about in the River and Ponds and all together rendered my ramble beyond expression delightful.

April 10, Friday. Fine pleasant weather. This afternoon I took a solitary yet a pleasing walk to the ruins of a Fort which was a few years since abandoned by the Hudson's Bay People to whom it belonged,[27] but now they do not come into this part of the Country. After examining for some time where the Fort stood but now most of the Houses are fallen to the Ground, I could not help reflecting on the short duration of every thing that is in this perishable & fleeting World, and after I had thus meditated for a considerable time, I then went to visit a piece of Ground where a number of their People had been interred far from their Native Country, their Friends and Relations! And while lamenting their sad fate I must acknowledge my blood chilled as I thought that what had happened to them might in all probability befall me also! For I am following the same path and leading the same life as they were! But let

---

[27]According to A. S. Morton, this post had been built in 1790, and was situated about an eighth of a mile upstream from the North West Company's fort.

my earnest prayers ever be that our merciful God will in due time restore me to my Friends & Relations in good health and an unblemished Character.

April 19, Sunday. On Friday last there fell nearly a foot of Snow, which however soon dissolved and caused the River to overflow its Bank to such a distance as to oblige our People who were making Sugar to leave the Woods & come to the Fort.

April 21, Tuesday. All the Snow had now left us & we are again blessed with fine weather and last night the Ice in the River broke up.

April 27, Monday. It has Snowed all Day & fell about Six Inches. I now begin to feel the want of Books having brought but few with me, and him who has for several years last past had charge of this Fort was a Canadian and being not able to read himself as is the case with the most of his Countrymen who come into this Country for they are of the lowest class, he therefore did not desire to have Books in his possession. At Alexandria Mr. McLeod has a tolerable good collection of moral and some religous Books, but I thought it not worth the while to bring many with me for the short time I was to remain here.

May 2, Saturday. Rained all Day & is the first we have had since last Autumn. Having little business to attend to I pass the greater part of my time in reading the Bible & studying the French language.

May 10, Sunday. It has for three successive Days Rained constantly, which caused the water in the River to rise since yesterday four feet. Yesterday one of our Men went a shooting Ducks, but lost his way and therefore was under the necessity of passing the night in the wood, with nothing to cover himself from the cold & Rain that poured down in the torrents. However he in the morning by chance (or had by all-protecting Providence) fell upon a small foot path which brought him straight to the Fort where he arrived not a little pleased and I presume is not much inclined to make another such ramble.

May 13, Wednesday. The late Rains we have had has caused this River to overflow its banks to such an uncommon distance, that this morning when I arose I was not a little surprised to find Seven Inches of water on the first floor, which is what the oldest person here does not remember to have seen before, and we are obliged to leave our Fort and Pitch our Tents on a small rise of Ground no great distance off, and where we shall remain till the deluge is past.

May 15, Friday. Sent five Men in a Canoe two Days march up this river for Mr. McLeod &c. as the face of the Country lies under water.

May 20, Wednesday. The water has left the Fort and we with pleasure quit our Tents to occupy our former Dwellings—and this afternoon Mr. McLeod &c. arrived & are thus far on their way to the Grand Portage.

May 26, Tuesday. Yesterday our People finished making our Furs into Packs that weigh ninety pounds each (and two or three of them make a load for a Man to carry in the Portages) and this morning they embarked aboard five Canoes for Head Quarters—and to Mr. McLeod I delivered a packet of Letters to be forwarded to my friends who reside at Vergennes in the State of Vermont and tomorrow I shall set off for Alexandria & there God willing pass the ensuing Summer, and have the affairs of that place and this place to superintend till next Autumn.

SECOND SOJOURN AT FORT ALEXANDRIA

June 1, Monday. Alexandria, where I accompanied by two Men arrived this afternoon, and find Six Families of Crees encamped about the Fort—& here I am to pass a long Summer, but have with one Clerk, two Interpreters & five labouring Men, Six Women & thirteen Children belonging to our People, also a number of Women & Children belonging to the Natives, whose Husbands have gone to war upon the Rapid Indians (a Tribe who remain a considerable distance out into the large Plains and near the upper part of the Missisours [Missouri] River).[28] In short there are nearly one hundred mouths to be filled out of our Store for the greater part of the Summer—but we have two good Hunters & Moose & Deer are not scarce, but the Buffaloe are gone to the large Plains again.

June 11 [10], Wednesday. As we have been informed that the Rapid Indians intend to form a war party and come against the

---

[28]Harmon was mistaken. The Rapid Indians were so named because their usual place of abode was in the vicinity of the falls or rapids on the Saskatchewan River.

Indians of this quarter, (and if they come this way they will as soon fall upon us as upon the Natives themselves, for we furnish them with fire arms which they do not like) I have therefore thought it proper to set our People to build Block Houses over the Fort Gates and put the Bastions in order, so that we may be prepared to defend ourselves in case of attack.

June 14, Sunday. This afternoon a number of the natives danced in the Fort and as follows:—Two Stakes were drove into the Ground about twenty feet asunder, and as one beat the Drum the others Men & Women danced around those Stakes, but the Men had a different step from the Women, the latter placed both feet close together, first moving their heels forward & then their toes, and so they went round the Stakes, while the Men rather hoped [hopped] than danced & therefore went round the above mentioned Stakes twice in the same span of time the Women took to go once—but have excellent ears consequently keep exact time to the music.

July 9, Thursday. Cam [came] here an American who when quite a Child was taken from his Parents (who then lived in the Illinois Country) by the Sauteux and with whom he has remained ever since and speaks no other language but theirs. He may now be about twenty years of age and is looked upon as a Chief, neither does he like that any one should speak to him about his Relations but he in every respect except his colour resembles the real Savages with whom he lives & is said to be an excellent Hunter, and remains with an old Woman who soon after he was taken from his Friends adopted him for her son & he appears to be as fond of her and she of him as if she actually was his Mother.[28a]

July 30, Thursday. The different kinds of Berries are now ripe, such as Strawberries, Raspberries & Paires &c. The latter both in shape and taste resemble what in the New England States are called Shad-berries, and they when properly dried by the Sun are excellent to mix with Pimican [pemmican], but the Natives generally boil them in the Broth of fat Meat, and serves them as one of their most dainty Dishes at all their Feasts. [The printed text adds:

[28a]It is generally assumed that this young man was John Tanner, who later returned to civilization and told his story in a volume entitled *A Narrative of the Captivity and Adventures of John Tanner* (New York, 1830; new edition, Minneapolis, 1956).

"When they are found in the prairies, they grow on bushes, four or five feet high; but in a thick wood they often reach to the height of fifteen or twenty feet. Of this wood, the Natives always make their arrows."] Mr. A. N. McLeod has a son here named also Alexander[29] who is about five years of age & whose Mother is of the Tribe of the Rapid Indians, and I in my leisure moments am teaching him the rudiments of the English Language. He speaks the Sauteux & Cree Dialects well for a Child of his age, and makes himself understood tolerably well in the Assiniboin & French Languages. In short he is like the most of the Children in this Country blessed with a retentive memory and apt to learn. We have made about ten tuns of Hay to serve our Horses that work during the winter season, but the others pass that part as well as all the rest of the year upon Grass which they find in the Plains by taking away about a foot and a half of Snow, for I am told they seldom have more hereabouts, and on the hills the wind soon takes the greater part into the valleys.

August 28 [20], Thursday. All the Provisions that we now have in Store consists of only about fifteen pounds of Pimican [pemmican], and when or from whince we shall be able to procure a supply God only knows, for all our dependence is on the success of our Hunters, and it is now some time since they have killed an Animal, yet Moose & Deer are plentiful hereabouts.

August 25, Tuesday. Yesterday three of our People arrived from the Grand Portage & delivered me Letters from Mr. McLeod &c. which inform me that the above mentioned people as well as another Man who is on his way from Swan River, were sent off from Head Quarters earlier than usual with an assortment of Goods in case we might stand in need of some articles before the main brigade can arrive.

September 6, Sunday. This is the third Day it has Rained without out the least cessation. There is five Families of Crees encamped about the Fort who have been constantly drunk during the last forty-eight hours, and now begin to be troublesome, as they have nothing to trade, yet would wish to drink longer. Just arrived an

[29]As already pointed out, McLeod's own first name was Archibald, not Alexander.

Indian who made one of the War party that left this last Spring. When he arrived his face was painted entirely black (as I am told is ever their custom when they return from such an expedition) and as he drew nigh the Fort he began to sing a War Song. He says that his party (Crees & Assiniboins) have made great slaughter among their Enemies (the Rapid Indians) and are bringing a number of their Women & Children home Slaves, while he was sent ahead to inform us of what they think as glorious news.

September 7, Monday. More of the Indians who have been to wage War are arrived & brought several Slaves and a few Scalps, and this afternoon they danced & sung their war Songs, and to whom (agreeable to the custom of the Country) I gave a few trifling articles, not for having been to war, but because they done us the honour (as they think) of dancing in the Fort.

September 29 [27], Sunday. Snowed and Rained by turns all Day, and this afternoon Mr. McLeod &c. arrived from the Grand Portage & delivered me a number of Letters from my friends below, and I am happy to learn they left them all blessed with good health, which is news highly grateful to my feelings, than which nothing could give me half the real satisfaction, while thus *self-banished* in this dreary Country an [and] at such a great distance from all I hold dear in this World. I also received several Letters from Gentlemen in this Country.

BIRD MOUNTAIN

October 2[7], Wednesday. Montagne D'Oiseau or the Bird Mountain. In the morning I a Horse back left Alexandria & this evening arrived here, where I am to pass the ensuing Winter, and have with me three Interpreters—and Six labouring Men & two Women. The Fort is built on the bank of Swan River and about fifty Miles from where it runs into Swan Lake. The Indians who frequent this Establishment are Sauteux, Crees and Muscagoes. Moose and Deer are plentiful hereabouts.

October 17, Saturday. Received a Letter from Mr. J. Clarke of Athabasca, and also another from Mr. McLeod, as well as a Horse as a present from the latter Gentleman. My People are building me a House.

October 29, Thursday. On the 22nd Inst. Mr. McLeod & ten Men all a Horse back arrived & the Day following I accompanied them to the lower Fort, where I saw Mr. William Henry brother to Mr. A. Henry who last year came up to the Grand Portage with me but the latter came up this Season. Mr. McLeod also brought in another Clerk by the name of Frederick Goedike. This evening Messrs. McLeod Henry and myself returned but left our People behind whose Horses are loaded with Goods for this place & Alexandria.

October 30, Friday. Early in the morning the two above mentioned Gentlemen set off for Alexandria where they intend passing the ensuing Winter.

November 3, Tuesday. Fell about three Inches of Snow and is the first we have had this Season.

November 19, Thursday. For several Days past I have been much troubled with a swollen Throat and a high fever, which made it impossible to swallow anything but liquids. Fell about a foot & a half of Snow.

December 23, Wednesday. Clear and cold. On the 16th Inst. I left this for Alexandria, where I passed several Days agreeably in the company of Messrs. McLeod, Henry & Goedike, and the evening before our separation we had a Ball or rather a Dance, and Mr. Goedike played the Violin. We now have more Snow than at any time last year, and on my return my right leg became stiff, owing to an excruciating pain I had in my knee, and therefore was obliged to get myself hauled on a Sledge.

December 25, Friday. This being Christmas Day, and agreeable to the custom of the Country I gave our People a Dram and a pint of Rum each.

December 28, Monday. Payet one of my Interpreters, has taken one of the Natives Daughters for a Wife, and to her Parents he gave in Rum & dry Goods &c. to the value of two hundred Dollars, and all the cerimonies attending such circumstances are that when it becomes time to retire, the Husband or rather Bridegroom (for as yet they are not joined by any *bonds*) shews his Bride where his Bed is, and then they, of course, both go to rest together, and so they continue to do as long as they can agree among themselves, but when either is displeased with their choice, he or she will seek another Partner, and thus the Hymenial [Hymeneal] Bond, without any more ado is broke asunder—which is *law* here & I think reasonable also, for I cannot conceive it to be right for a Man & Woman to cohabit when they cannot agree, but to live in discontent, if not downright hatered to each other, as many do.

1802

January 1, Friday. This being the first Day of the year, in the morning I gave the People a Dram or two & a pint of Rum each to drink in the course of the Day which enabled them to pass it merrily, although little or nothing to eat, for our Hunters say they cannot kill.

January 9, Saturday. Several Days ago I sent a number of my Men to Alexandria for Meat (as our Hunters do not kill anything yet there are no want of Moose & Deer hereabout) but they have just returned with nothing and say that the Buffaloe owing to the late mild weather have returned a considerable distance out into the large Plains—therefore we are obliged to live upon pounded Meat or dried choak Cherries which are but little better than nothing at all, and when we shall be in a better condition God only knows but *hope* which seldom abandons a person makes us believe that ere long we shall be out of wants reach.

January 17, Sunday. Last evening our People brought home from our Hunters Lodge the Meat of a Moose, the sight of which caused every one to put on a joyful countenance and rejoiced to find that kind Providence had not wholly abandoned us, but on the contrary favoured us with one of its richest blessings, and for which I wish we were as *thankful* as we are *glad* to receive it. Although we are twelve persons in all, yet for the last fifteen Days we have subsisted on what would scarcely have been sufficient for two people! In short they were the darkest Days I ever experienced in this or any other Country.

January 19, Tuesday. I have taken a walk accompanied by Payet a short distance from the Fort, where we found Hazle nuts so plentiful still on the Bushes, that a person might gather at least a Bushel in the course of a Day, and I am told that they do not all fall off till the Month of May when sheltered from the wind.

February 1, Monday. For several Days last past it has been exceedingly cold weather, but this in my opinion has been the coldest

Day I ever experienced—in fact the cold is so intence that our Hunters do no like to leave their Lodges, and of course kill nothing yet they as well as ourselves have little to eat.

February 7, Sunday. During the three last Days we subsisted on tallow & dried Cherries, but this evening two of my Men returned from Alexandria with their Sledges loaded with Buffaloe Meat— and how thankful are we or rather how happy are we at the sight of it! *Thankful* we are all ready to acknowledge we ought to be, for such disinterested & as unmerited favors—yet we must as readily acknowledge that few if any are sufficiently grateful for such inestimable blessings. Had the last been withheld from us only a few Days longer we must have ended our Days by dying a miserable Death! And how little prepared to meet such a change! God is merciful and long suffering.

February 8, Monday. All the Indians of this place except my Hunters are gone to pass a couple of Months (as they are wont yearly to do) on their beloved food—Buffaloe Meat.

February 19, Friday. At present thanks be to God we have a pretty good stock of Provisions in the Store and therefore may expect not to want again this Season. I find that another year is already past and gone since I was twenty-three years of age! And when I take a retrospective view of my transactions during that space of time I am both surprised & grieved to find that I have done so many things which I ought not and left so many others undone which I ought to have attended to, and as I now am convinced that hitherto my life has been too heedless & careless I therefore now am determined on a reformation.

March 6, Saturday. I am just returned from paying my friends who are at Alexandria a visit & where I passed four Days pleasantly in conversing in my Mother Tongue—which is a satisfaction as no one knows except those who are situated much like myself—that is alone as it were the greater part of my time, or at least with people with whom I cannot speak fluently—and if I could, what conversation would an illiterate ignorant Canadian be able to keep up. All of their chat is about Horses, Dogs, Canoes and Women, and strong Men who can fight a good battle.

March 20, Saturday. The most of our Indians are returned from the Plains, and as they have brought little with them to trade, I of course give them as little, for we are at too great distance from the Civilized World to make many *Gratuities,* yet the Indians were of a different opinion, and made use of some unpleasant language. However we did not come to blows, but all are preparing to go to rest, and I am persuaded nearly as good friends as civilized People and Savages generally are for that friendship seldom goes farther than *their* fondness for our property and *our* eagerness to obtain their Furs—which is I am persuaded (with a few exceptions only) all the friendship that exists between the Traders and Savages of this Country.

April 1, Thursday. On the 27th Ult. Mr. Wm. Henry accompanied by Sixteen Men, arrived from Alexandria, their Sledges loaded with Furs & Provisions, and the Day following I joined their party & went to the lower Fort where Mr. Henry is to pass this Spring as I did the last, but the People return back from whence they came.

April 21, Wednesday. The most of the Snow is now dissolved & this afternoon the Ice in the River broke up. For several Days the greater part of our Indians have been encamped about the Fort, but are now off to hunt the Beaver—and while they were here they made a Feast, at which they Danced, cryed Sung and houled &c. in short made a terrible Savage noise. Such Feasts the Crees are accustomed to make at the return of every Spring, and some times at other Seasons of the year, and by so doing they say they appease the anger of the Evil Spirit or Devil, and thus prevent him from doing them harm. They also have certain places where they put part of their property, such as Guns, Kettles, Bows & Arrows &c. as a sacrifice to the same Spirit—whereas to the Supreme Being Creator & Governor of the World or as they call Him *Kitchemonetou* ie:— Great Spirit they say there is no necessity of their paying Him any devotion for they add, that He is a good Spirit and therefore would not wish to do any one an injury but the Devil as they think (and I believe rightly) is malicious and it is therefore proper and right that they should strive to live upon good terms with him. The above mentioned Feast was made by their Chief whose name is *Kâ she we ske wâte* and who previous to the entertainment, neither ate nor drank for the long space of forty-eight hours! [The printed text continues: "At the commencement of the feast, every person put on a grave countenance; and the Chief went through a number of ceremonies, with the utmost solemnity. After the entertainment was over, every Indian made a voluntary sacrifice of a part of his property to the devil, or as they call him, Much-e-mon-e-too."]

May 2, Sunday. A beautiful Day. I with one of my Interpreters have been to take a ride to a place where I intend building a Fort the ensuing Summer, which is on the border of a pretty spacious Plain, surrounded by a range of small Trees and at different places of the Plain there are small Groves of Burch & Poplar &c. a Rivulet also passes along the edge of the Wood, which forms beautiful cascades, and all together renders the place convenient & delightful. Of Animals that we have hereabouts are the Moose, several kinds of Deer, five Do. [ditto] of Bears, two Do. of Wolves, the Wolverine, the Cat [lynx], the Beaver, the Otter, the Mink, the Fisher, the Martin, the Badger, the Musk Rat & several kinds of Foxes &c. and of Fowls we have the Swan, the wild Goose, the Bustard, the Crane, the Cormorant, several kinds of Ducks, the Water-Hen, the Pigeon, the Patridge & Pheasants &c. &c. and most of the above mentioned Fowls we have them plentifully in their Seasons—Autumns & Springs, but a few remain with us all Summer while the others go farther North to brood and then towards the fall they return again, but before the Winter sets in they go to the Southward.

May 6, Thursday. In the morning one of Mr. McLeod's Men arrived with a Letter from him which informs me that a few nights since the Assiniboins (who are noted Thieves) run away with twenty of his Horses. [The printed version adds: "Many of this tribe, who reside in the large prairies, are constantly going about to steal horses. Those which they find at one fort, they will take and sell to the people of another fort. Indeed, they steal horses, not unfrequently, from their own relations."]

May 12, Wednesday. Snowed and Rained all Day. On the 7th Inst. I went to Alexandria to transact some business with Mr. McLeod, and during my jaunt it Rained almost continually, and I in crossing this River drowned my Horse, which last fall cost the Company Goods to the value of 100 Dollars.

May 17, Monday. Mild. This afternoon Mr. McLeod &c. past this and are on their way to the Grand Portage but I am to pass another Summer *in-land* and have the superintendence of the lower

Fort [Swan River Fort], this place and Alexandria, but shall remain the greater part of my time at the last mentioned place.

May 20 [18], Tuesday. All of the Indians have come in with their hunts which are good & to recompense them for their industry I Cloathed two of their Chiefs and [gave] a certain quantity of Rum to the others which kept them drunk all last night and I of course was not able to shut an eye, and in all this bustle I am writing my friends below as well as to a few people in this Country. But I am pleased to find that my transactions of last Winter meets with Mr. McLeods approbation, as it is a great satisfaction for a person who wishes to do his duty towards or gain the good will of his Employers.

May 23, Sunday. Snowed all Day & fell about six inches. I am now waiting the arrival of Mr. Henry to come and take charge of this Post when I shall set off for Alexandria. A couple of Women brought me a few Hazle Nuts which they gathered to day from off the Bushes.

Third Sojourn at Fort Alexandria

May 31, Monday. Alexandria where I with two Men arrive this afternoon, but in crossing Swan River I was so unfortunate as to drown another Horse, and therefore was under the necessity of performing the rest of the way on foot and nothing to eat. However thanks be to the Bestower of all good, here I find a tolerable stack of Provisions. Mr. F. Goedike is to pass the Summer with me also two Interpreters & three labouring Men besides a number of Women & Children—who all together form a *snug* Family.

June 23, Wednesday. On the 16th Inst. I accompanied by two Men sat off for Swan River a Horse back and the first night we slept at the Bird Mountain & the Day following arrived at the lower Fort, and from where on my return I came in one Day which is a distance of ninety miles. However I exchanged Horses at the Bird Mountain, but I left my People along the road one of whom arrived this evening and says he has drowned his Horse at the same place where I lost two this Spring, & I cannot help reflecting how unfortunate I have been in the Horse way since last Winter. It is true they did not belong to me, but to the Company however I had them in charge. On my arrival here those to whom I had left the Fort in charge had nothing to offer me except boiled Parchment Skins which is little better than nothing at all, and will hardly deserve the naim of food, therefore I have sent part of our People to try to take a few Fish out of a Small Lake which is about ten Miles from this,[30] and if they should not succeed & our Hunters to be not more fortunate than they have been for some time past I really do not know what will become of us. But where there is *life* there is generally *hope* also, therefore we do not despair but place all our dependence on Providence and hope a speedy relief from our truly sad condition.

July 2, Friday. For Six Days after I sent the People to Fish at the above mentioned Lake, we at the Fort lived on Parchment Skins, Dogs & herbs and a few small Fish which we took out of the River opposite to the Fort, but now we get them more plentiful. One of our best Hunters has been in and told me what he thought the cause was why we could not kill. He told me that when he went a hunting he generally soon fell upon the tracks of some Animal which he followed, but as soon as he came nigh him, he heard the voice of an evil Spirit, which frightened bothe him and the Animal, and the latter of course would run off and then the chase would be at an end. Hereupon I told him I had a certain medicine that if he done with it as I should direct him, it would not only frighten the evil Spirit in his turn, but would also render him Speachless & in the end cause his death. Therefore I took several Drugs & mixed them together, which I wrapped in a piece of Paper & tied it to the butt end of his Gun & told him to go in search of a Moose or Deer, and as soon as he heard the voice of the evil Spirit, to throw what I had given him behind him in the air & it would fall into the evil Spirits mouth, as he was pursuing him—and the effect would be as above described. However I warned him not to look back in case he should be too much frightened at the sight of so monstrous a creature as the Devil was, but pursue the Animal which he [would] undoubtedly kill. The same Day he went a hunting, fell upon a track, which he had (as he says) followed but a short distance before the evil Spirit began his horrid cry, however he done with the medicine as I had directed him, and of course heard no more of the

[30]The printed version adds: "called by the Natives Devil's Lake."

frightful voice, but continued following the Animal till he came nigh him, then fired and killed a fine fat Red Deer—and since then several others, consequently not only him but all the other Indians hereabouts have great confidence in my Medicines. What will not imagination aided with not a little superstition make a person believe? It often makes a person hear & see what only exists in his deranged brain!

July 4, Sunday. Mr. Wm. Henry &c. arrived from the Bird Mountain and say they are starving there. Therefore they will all come to pass the remainder of the Season here, where we now have Provisions plentifully. Also came two of the Hudson's Bay Coy's People here, who say they are eight in all who have come to reestablish the Fort they last Spring abandoned but as it has by some evil disposed person been burnt they say that they have a mind to come & build along side of us.

July 6, Tuesday. I accompanied by Collin (one of my Interpreters) have taken a ride down to see what the Hudson's Bay People were about, and we found them busily employed at building another Fort where the other stood, therefore I have some thoughts of sending some of our People to remain along side of them.

July 25, Sunday. We are again poorly off as to Provisions, owing to the number of People from the Bird Mountain, whom we have to feed. However I hope and expect that ere long we shall be in a better condition, for I have sent Seven Men several different ways in search of the Natives, whom should they find will be able to relieve us from want, as this is the best season to make Provisions, as it is now that almost all kinds of Wild Animals are fat.

It is a lamentable fact but owing to the nature of the Country, that it is wholly out of our power to observe the Sabbath Days the same as in the Civilized world for all Days being alike to the uninlightened Savages and consequently they as often come to our Forts on that the same as on any other Day of the Week. However they do believe in the existance of a Supreme Being, Creator & Governor of *this* World, but I could never learn that they paid Him any kind of worship for they say that He by nature is too good and well disposed towards His Creatures to do them the least harm, but to the Devil (as I have elsewhere observed) they pay all their Devotion or rather adulation. They also believe in the immortality of the

Soul and think all those who (according to their ideas of what is right & what is wrong) lead a good life while in this World, will when that part which never dies is separated from the Body, go immediately into another place of existance and where it will meet with its friends and relations who had left this world before him, and where they fully believe that they shall be much happier than while inhabitants of this Earth, as that Country where they go will be better supplyed with Animals &c. than the one they leave. And they also believe that all those who live bad or wicked lives while here below, will when they meet their dissolution be immediately conveyed into the middle of a spacious Swamp or Marsh (which is their Purgatory) and where they will for a considerable time be obliged to wander about alone in search of their Deceased Friends, but whom after having suffered greatly by the cold & hunger will find them inhabiting a pleasant Country, and where they have all their wants supplyed them, attended by very little or no labour—which is the *Heaven* of the Savages!

July 29 [30], Friday. There are at present hereabouts such an incredible number of Grass-hoppers as I never before saw at any place, and (when fair weather) between eight & ten OClock A.M. (the only part of the Day when many of them leave the ground) they then are in such astonishing numbers flying about in the air that they almost hide the Sun from our sight, the same as when a light Cloud when it passes before it. They also devour every thing before them, scarcely leaving a leaf on the Trees or a blade of green Grass in the Plains—neither does our Potatoe Tops &c. in the Garden escape their all-devouring appetites.

August 4 [3], Tuesday. The most of the Mosquitoes and Horse Flies, which are so troublesome to both Man & Beast are leaving us, for the nights now begin to be cool. Yesterday Six Families of Crees came in & have been drinking ever since, and one of them had a few wrangling words with a Woman belonging to another Band, to whom he also gave a slight beating but their Chief, who is a friend to the other Indian, thought the Woman was giving his Friend too abusive language, he therefore stepped towards them and gave the Woman such a severe beating with a Club on her head that soon made her give up the Ghost. And this morning the Women buried her Corpse, and her death is no more taken notice of than if it had been a Dog they had killed, for her relations are in another part of the Country & at a considerable distance from this.

August 8, Sunday. We now have a considerable quantity of Provisions in the Store and for such a blessing we endeavour to be thankful as well as may be after having passed the most of the Summer so miserably in regard to that necessary article of life. What a merciful God we have! who is constantly bestowing upon us His richest blessings, while we like the Children of Israel of old, who when their *Bellies* were not full were ever ready to complain and deny their God! Would to God that I could be sufficiently thankful for the favours I am Daily and hourly receiving from the hands of an ever bountiful Providence, but my heart is so depraved that I cannot set the right value on such infinite blessings. But by whom was it thus corrupted? or was it in this forlorn condition when I first entered into this World? or has it been brought to its present depraved state by my own wiked deeds? The latter most assuredly is the case! Then since I have been able to change my heart from good to bad: why shall I not be able to bring it back to its original state? I have it most undoubtedly in my power.*

[*When I wrote the above I could not conceive the necessity of a Saviour: but thought all depended on my own natural exertions, whether I should be Saved or Damned!! What a deluded and unhappy condition! surely the most deplorable that a person could possibly be in, but thanks be to our Merciful God who has been graciously pleased to cause my deluded eyes to be opened that I might behold the awful condition I was then in.]

August 11, Wednesday. On the 9th Inst. a Chief among the Crees came to the Fort accompanied by a number of his relations who appeared very desirous that I should take one of his Daughters to remain with me, but to put him off I told him that I could not then take a Woman however in the fall perhaps I might for I added that I had no dislike of her. But he pressed me to keep her at once as he said he was fond of me and he wished to have his Daughter with the white people and he almost persuaded me to accept of her, for I was sure that while I had the Daughter I should not only have the Fathers hunts but those of his relations also, of course [this] would be much in the favor of the Company & perhaps in the end of some advantage to me likewise—so that interest (and perhaps a little natural inclination also) I find was nigh making me commit another folly, if not a sin,—but thanks be to God alone if I have not been brought into a snare laid no doubt by the Devil himself.

August 28, Saturday. I have sent Primault (one of my Interpreters) with a Letter about Six Days march from this where I expect he will meet Mr. McLeod &c. on their way in from the Grand Portage. Two of our People who a few Days since I sent into the Plains are just returned, and inform me that Buffaloe are plentiful within two Days march of this, and the Natives during the two Days they remained with them killed eighty Buffaloe by driving them into a Park which they had made for that purpose.

October 3, Sunday. Yesterday there fell a little Snow and is the first we have had this Season. And we now begin to think that some untoward accident has happened to our People on their way in, as they do not make their appearance as soon as usual.

October 4, Monday. One of our Men just arrived from the Grand Portage & delivered me a Letter from Mr. McLeod informing me that he is going to Athabasca and Mr. Hugh McGillis is coming to take his place here. The Canoe in which the above mentioned Man came left Head Quarters alone, some time before the main Brigade was ready to come off. I also received several other Letters from Gentlemen in this Country.

October 21, Thursday. This afternoon Mr. H. McGillis accompanied by one Man a Horse back arrived, who informs me they were stopped by the Ice about fifteen Miles below Swan River Fort, and from whence they will be obliged to bring the Goods on Sledges.

October 25, Monday. A large Band of Indians have been in and continually drinking for the last forty-eight hours, but they are just off however another Band has just cast up, and we of course must pass another night or two sleepless, for when the natives are at the Fort and have wherewith to pay they would wish to drink bothe Day & night. Mr. McGillis has returned to the lower Fort in order to get the Goods brought there.

October 30, Saturday. Several of our People arrived from Swan River and delivered me Letters from home, and in perusing them I have infinite satisfaction as I find they left them in the full enjoyment of good health. Samuel Holmes a Clerk and Countryman of mine has left us to go & join our opponents the X. Y. People.[31] Messrs. Angus McGillis (brother of H. McGillis) and Augustus Rolin &c. who have passed the greater part of the Summer with me, have sat off for their Winter quarters Fort Dauphin.

November 1, Monday. I accompanied by my Interpreter have taken a ride down to see the Hudson's Bay People—one Mr. Miller & fifteen labouring Men are now there, the greater part of whom are just returned from their Factory [Albany].

SECOND SOJOURN AT BIRD MOUNTAIN

November 11 [9], Tuesday. Bird Mountain where I am come to pass another Winter and have with me one Interpreter & Six labouring Men—and thus I am continually shifting about from one place to another and when I shall have a home of my *own* God only knows. However I hope the Day *will* arrive when I shall have it in my power either to be settled down where I can pass the remainder of my Days in quietness or in travelling about in the different parts of the Civilized World.

November 19, Friday. I am just returned from the lower Fort where I have been with part of my People for Goods, & here I find a Band of Indians who have been waiting my arrival to get such articles as they stand in need of to enable them to mak [make] a fall hunt. [The printed text adds: "The Indians in this quarter have been so long accustomed to use European goods, that it would be with difficulty that they could now obtain a livelihood, without them. Especially do they need fire arms, with which to kill their game, and axes, kettles, knives, &c. They have almost lost the use of bows and arrows; and they would find it nearly impossible to cut their wood with implements, made of stone or bone."]

December 25, Saturday. Severe cold weather. This being Christmas Day the People have passed it as is usual for them, that is

---

[31]A note inserted in the printed version adds: "Soon afterwards, he left the service of the last mentioned company, and went to live with the Natives, the Assiniboins, by whom a year or two after, he was killed, while he was on his way from the Red River to the River Missouri."

in drinking & fighting. How different from the way this Day ought to be kept! [The printed version adds: "Of all people in the world, I think the Canadians, when drunk, are the most disagreeable; for excessive drinking generally causes them to quarrel and fight, among themselves. Indeed, I had rather have fifty drunken Indians in the fort, than five drunken Canadians."]

1803

January 3, Monday. On the first Inst. Mr. Wm. Henry &c. arrived from Alexandria & remained with us till this morning when they sat off to continue their route to the lower Fort.

January 27, Thursday. I am just returned from Alexandria and where I past six Days much to my satisfaction in the company of Messrs. H. McGillis, Henry & Goedike &c. and while there wrote Messrs. McLeod, A. Henry & J. Clarke, which will be taken to Athabasca by the Winter Express.

February 19 [20], Sunday. Yesterday morning one of our Indian's Women came to the Fort, and said her Husband was determined to kill her, therefore she thought proper to leave him to go to Alexandria where she would be out of his reach, but after her arrival here she altered her mind, and desired my Interpreter to put an end to her life—which he of course refused doing, then said she I will do the business for myself, for to live any longer with my Husband added she I will not. However we did not believe she would lay violent hands on herself. Then she went a short distance from the Fort into the Woods and laid down the load of things she had on her back and struck up a fire, into which she threw the most of her little property, and when nearly consumed, she took a little bag of Powder & put it into her bosom, than set fire to it which burnt the most of the hair of her head, and her face very much injured and also rendered her perfectly bling [blind], and now she began to run about to try to catch her Dogs being determined to burn them next, but when she began to call out for them we went to see what she was about (for we did not then know what had befallen her) and really she had more the appearance of a Ghost than a human being. However we brought her into the Fort, where she remained very quiet till our People were a bed & asleep, which opportunity she took to return again to the woods, when she tied a Cord about her neck & then to the limb of a Tree, but fortunately for her the branch broke and down she fell into the Snow, where she remained till this morning when we found her nearly lifeless, and after examining her we found that she had run a long Needle its full length into her right ear. However we brought her again into the Fort but her head is very much swollen & her face as black as coal, and whether she will recover God only knows, but if she does I presume she will not be in a hurry to hang herself the second time. [Several years after I saw her & she was in as good health as formerly.][32]

March 10, Thursday. Mr. Angus McGillis &c. arrived from Alexandria where he has been to pay a visit to his Brother, and is now on his way home, [to] Fort Dauphin. He brought me a friendly Letter from Mr. A. N. McLeod.

March 27, Sunday. Mild pleasant weather, and the most of the Snow has left us. On the 22nd Inst. Mr. Henry accompanied by twelve Men arrived from Alexandria who are going to the lower Fort with Furs & Provisions, & whom I accompanied there to give them out such Goods as will be wanted at Alexandria for the ensuing Summer, where I shall God willing pass that Season.

FOURTH SOJOURN AT FORT ALEXANDRIA

May 4, Wednesday. Alexandria, where I accompanied by Six Men arrived yesterday.

May 19, Thursday. Yesterday the most of our People sat off for the Grand Portage & today Mr. McGillis &c. followed them, but I am to pass another summer here and have with me Mr. F. Godike [Goedike], one Interpreter & several labouring Men, besides Women & Children. As Mr. Goedike will be absent from the Fort the greater part of the Summer, I shall as it were therefore be left alone, for the ignorant Canadians make very indifferent Companions, and with whom I cannot associate. However fortunately for me I have *dead* Friends (my Books) who will never abandon me, till I first neglect them.

[32]This note appears in the manuscript; presumably it was added when the text was copied from the original journal.

June 2, Thursday. Our People are making a Garden which they surround with Palisads in the same manner as our Forts are built. The X. Y. People are building a Fort about five Miles up this River. One of our Men gave me his Son (a Lad of about thirteen years of age) whom I in the name of the North West Coy. agree to feed and furnish with Clothing until he becomes able to earn something more. His Mother is a Sauteux Woman & he is to serve me as Cook &c.

June 21, Tuesday. This afternoon we had a heavy Shower of Hail and Rain. Yesterday I sent Mr. Goedike accompanied by two Men, with a small assortment of Goods to go about a Days march beyond where the X. Y. People are building, where they will remain till the Natives return from their hunting excursion, therefore I now have with me only two Men and a Woman, which renders this a solitary place, & nothing but the perusal of the Book we fortunately have here, could keep up my drooping spirits. At such moments as these I cannot help reflecting how happy I should be were it possible for me to pass a few Days or even hours in the company of my Friends below! Ant [and at] such melancholy seasons I almost regret having left my native land & all I hold dear in this World, and where I might if I had not had such a roving disposition been comfortably situated and happy in the enjoyment of the company of that Society of Friends and Relations from whom I now am at such an immense distance *self-banished!* But Providence has brought me into this Wilderness, and it therefore now becomes me to bear up under my lot with resignation, perseverance & fortitude, hoping in the mean time that Day is not far distant when I shall have it in my power to return and mingle once more in that happy circle of Friends on whose conversation I so highly and so justly lay so much value.

June 27, Monday. Mr. F. Goedike &c. are returned to the Fort but much sooner than I expected them. Also Mr. Ferguson &c. arrived from Fort Dauphin & are come on a visit, and they brought me several Letters from Gentlemen in that quarter.

July 1, Friday. In the morning I accompanied Mr. Ferguson &c. as far as the Hudson's Bay House where we spent a few hours in the company of Mr. Miller, & then Mr. F. &c. sat off to continue his route to Fort Dauphin and I to return home. Mr. Ferguson is of

Irish extraction, but was born in Canada, and he like the most of his Countrymen is always laying what he thinks deep plans or in other words builds Castles in the air! And he like the most of the People in this unfortunate Country, yields too easily to the bad customs and ways of it—but he has a tolerable good education & blessed with good natural parts. However he is too volitile to listen to sound reason.

July 30 [31], Sunday. I am just returned from an excursion out into the large Plains, and was accompanied by two of my Men, however in all of our ramble we did not see an Indian, the most of whom (as they are wont to do every Spring) are gone to War again. But we Saw, run down and killed Buffaloe, and we also saw Red Deer & Cabri (the latter is a species of the Deer and about the size of a Sheep) bounding a cross the Plains, as well as Bears & Wolves roving about in search of prey, and in the small Lakes & Ponds, that are to be met with here and there all over the large Plains, were Fowls tolerable plentiful, and of which we killed with our Guns, what we wanted for our Daily consumption. Although it Rained the greater part of the time we were absent from the Fort, yet as the great variety of different objects which alternately presented themselves to our view, served to keep up our spirits and made our ride both agreeable & pleasant. One night we slept at the very same place where a few Days before a number of the Rapid Indian Warriors had been encamped, who were as is supposed in search of their Enemies, the Crees & Assiniboins, but it was fortunate for us that we did not see them, for had we met, there is little doubt but they would have done our business for us—as they look upon us as there enemies also, for furnishing the Crees & Assiniboins with fire arms, while they have few or none, having as yet had but little intercourse with the White People. They are few in number, but uncommonly brave, and excellent Horse Men.

August 8, Monday. We are thirty People in the Fort, and not Provisions for two Days, our Hunters again not being able to kill, although there are no want of Moose and Deer. Here it is not as in the Civilized World. There, when people are out of Provisions, they can go else where and purchase what they may stand in need, but here we must wait till Providence sends us aid & some times we think it rather tardy.

August 18, Thursday. An Indian just arrived and says that forty Lodges of Crees & Assiniboins who last Spring set off on a War party along with forty others, are returning home. They separated at Battle River (which lies about half a Months march from this) the others crossed the River to go and make Peace with their Enemies, the Rapid & Black Feet Indians, for both parties begin to be weary of such a bloody War as has for such a length of time been kept up between them, and are therefore much inclined to patch up a Peace on almost any terms whatever. Thus ruinous Wars for ambitious People are constantly kept up in almost every corner of the World, both by uncivilized as well as Civilized People, which renders a great part of its inhabitants miserable if not wretched.

August 22, Monday. Sent a Man to take a letter to Mr. Hugh McGillis whom I expect he will meet at Fort Dauphin on his way from the Grand Portage.

October 16, Sunday. This afternoon there fell a little Snow and the first we have had this fall. It is now several Days since the X. Y. People arrived from the Grand Portage, but give us no news of Mr. McGillis &c. neither would they let their conditions be ever so bad—for so *well* do we agree, that neither Company will convey the other the least news that can [in] any way concern their affairs in this Country. In a word the North West Co. look upon their opponents the X. Y. Co. as encroachers of *their* territories, while the latter People consider that the former have no better right to commerce in this part of the World than they themselves have, but if the truth must be told, as they are weaker, that is have not been in this country long enough to gain much footing, *we would wish to crush them at once,* before they have too much strength, when it will be more difficult if not impossible. And this jarring of interests keep up continual misunderstandings and occasions frequent broils between the two contending parties, and some times the enmity that exists between them rises to such an unbecoming height as to cause bloodshed, and in several instance's even lives have been sacrificed! But I am of the opinion that those who have committed Murder in this Savage Country, would if a favorable occasion had offered been guilty of the like horrid crime in the Civilized part of the World—yet there are many in this Country who appear to be of a different opinion. Here it is true they have one advantage if indeed it may be thought one, that they have not below, is: here a Murderer escapes the Gallows, as there are no human laws that can reach or have any effect on the People of this Country. However I understand they are, in England about passing laws which will equally affect the People of this Country as those in the Canadas or any other part of the British Dominion[33]—and it is high time it should be so, or the most of us soon should have cut one anothers throats!

October 19, Wednesday. Fell about Six inches of Snow. Mr. McGillis &c. arrived from the Grand Portage and delivered me Letters from home, which as usual give me great satisfaction, by informing me they left my friends in good health, and enjoying the most of the blessings of his life.

October 22, Saturday. This afternoon one of our Men (an Iroquois) departed this life, and it is thought that what hurried him out of this World was, his having forced too much in carrying in the Portages on his way in—a circumstance that occasions the death of many of our People yearly.

November 6, Sunday. On the 28th Ult. we sent eight of our Men a Horse back into the Plains to look for Buffaloe, and this evening they returned with their Horses loaded with the Flesh of those Animals and inform us that they are plentiful within three Days march of this.

December 25, Sunday. This being Christmas Day our people pay no further attention to Worldly affairs *than to Drink all Day.* Notwithstanding I now am in a Savage Country, yet I cannot forget that in my earlier Days I was *taught to believe* that this Day ought to be kept as a Day of thanksgiving in commemoration of the Birth of a Saviour who suffered & Died for us Sinners—yet for all that I cannot flatter myself that I do observe the Day *very* different from my associates. [Then the greater was my guilt—for all had not the pains taken with them to instruct them that *my* Parents took with me.][34]

[33]The *Canada Jurisdiction Act* (43 Geo. III, c. 138), passed in 1803, under the provisions of which Justices of the Peace could be appointed in the "Indian Territories" and crimes committed there could be dealt with by the courts in Upper and Lower Canada.

[34]This note is in the manuscript. Harmon evidently added it when he prepared the copy of his journal that he sent home to his family in 1816.

December 28 [27], Tuesday. As Messrs. Henry & Goedike my Companions & Friends are both absent on excursion in two different parts of the Country, I as might be expected pass now & then a solitary hour, but when they are here, they being such agreeable mesmates [messmates] the moments glide away unperceptably by either of us, and so well do we agree, that when People live happily together, it might be said, they live like Henry, Goedike & Harmon! But when we are separated I pass the greater part of my time either reading or writing, and now & then take a ride about the Fort, or to see our neighbours, frequently a Horse back, but some times in a *Cariol* [carriole], drawn by a Horse when there is not much Snow, but when the depth is too great by Dogs, the latter being light do not sink much into the Snow, and in the above mentioned vehicle I this afternoon accompanied Mr. McGillis to pay a visit to our X. Y. Neighbours.

1804
LAC LA PÊCHE

February 22, Wednesday. Lac la Pêche or Fishing Lake,[35] which lies about two Days march out into the Plain from Alexandria, which place I left on the 15th Ult. accompanied by a dozen of our people and am come to pass the remainder of the Winter here along side of the X. Y. People, and one Mr. Allen McDonell has the charge of their Fort. For some time after our arrival we subsisted on *Rosebuds!* which we gathered in the fields, but they are neither very nourishing nor palatable, yet they are much better than nothing at all, but where to procure anything better I knew not, for the Buffaloe at that time were a great distance out into the Plains & my Hunters could not kill, either Moose or Deer. However we hoped and therefore expected the dark Cloud that then hung over our heads would soon pass away and that we should live to see better Days, for we could not believe that the benign Being who created us, would allows us to starve to Death, notwithstanding our demerits which we knew to be great. However now thanks be to our merciful God we have Provisions in abundance and for which blessing we endeavour to be thankful to the bestower of all Good.

[35]The Fishing Lakes, on the Qu'Appelle River.

On the 11th Inst. I took one of my Interpreters & ten labouring Men and went with them several Days march farther into the Plains, where we fell upon a Camp of thirty Lodges of Crees & Assiniboins, and with them we made a good trade of Furs & Provisions. They were encamped on the summit of a Hill, from whence we have an extensive view of the surrounding Country, which lay low & level and not a Tree to be seen, but thousands of Buffaloe were grazing in the different parts of the Plain—and to kill them the Natives in large Bands mount their Horses run them down & then kill what number they choose, or drive them into Parks, & there kill them at their leisure. In fact those Indians who reside in the large Plains are the most independent and appear to be the happiest and most contented of any People upon the face of the Earth. They subsist on the Flesh of the Buffaloe and of their Skins they make the greater part of their Cloathing, which is both warm and convenient.

March 1, Thursday. Es qui un a wâcha, or the last Mountain, or rather Hill for there are no Mountains in this part of the Country, and where I arrived this evening, having left Lac la Pêch on the 28th Ult. along with my Interpreter & Seven common Men, but ordered the latter to encamp a short distance from this, and come early in the morning to find me, as it is more convenient (especially in the open Plains) to trade & give the Natives to drink in the Day time than at night. On our arrival we were invited at several of the principal Indians Lodges to eat and Smoak our Pipes, for all Savages pride themselves in being hospitable to Strangers until they have long been acquainted with Civilized People, when they adopt many of the manners and customs of the latter, but in many respects they are by no means gainers!

March 5, Monday. On the second, the remainder of our people arrived, and soon after I gave the Natives to drink which they continued doing all that Day & the night following—and we of course did not shut an eye, for Indians often when drunk are like madmen or so many Devils and if not narrowly watched might do some injury, which they as soon as sober would be sorry for, (but it would be then too late) as they are naturally well disposed towards white People. This morning I sent Six of my People loaded with Furs and Provision to the Fort, and for another supply of Goods, to enable us to go and trade with another large Band of Indians who are about two Days march farther into the Plains.

March 6, Tuesday. North side of the Devils Lake[36] (as called by the Natives) and as I had nothing particular to attend to during the time our people would take to make the trip to the Fort, and being desirous of seeing my friend Henry who is as I understand about a half a Days march from where I now am—I therefore in the morning, accompanied by an Indian Lad who serves as Guide, sat off for this place and after walking all Day without finding Wood or water & but a little Snow, and as the Sun was leaving us to give light to the other half of the World we thought we descryed a small Grove at a considerable distance, but directly before us and as long as the light remained with us we steered our course for that object but soon after we had nothing to guide us except the Stars, which however answered very well till it became cloudy, and even then we thought it best to continue our march, for we were loth to lie down with not much of any thing to cover us to keep us from freezing, and there was no wood to make a fire or water to drink & for the want of the latter we suffered much, as we had nothing to eat but very dry Provisions, which excited thirst. Neither would it have been safe to have encamped without a fire, for in so doing we should run much risque of being trampled upon by the large herds of Buffaloe that are constantly roving about in the Plains or devoured by the Wolves that ever follow the Buffaloe. And after making the above reflections, we were determined to continue our march, yet we could not expect to keep a direct course. However after we had wandered about for some time without knowing where we were going, all on a sudden the two Dogs that hauled my Sledge past by us as though they had perceived some uncommon object straight before us, and their motion we did not try to prevent, but followed them, till they took us to where we now are—and it is almost incredible the distance that the Dogs smelt this Camp for we walked a good pace no less than four hours after they past us—but here we are happy in finding fifteen Lodges of Crees & Assiniboins, who want for none of the *dainties* of this Country—and I as usual meet with an hospitable reception. The Woman of the Lodge where I

[36]The present Good Spirit Lake, about 25 miles northwest of Yorkton, Saskatchewan.

am, unharnessed my Dogs and put my Sledge &c. into her Lodge & then gave my Dogs to eat, which I attempted to do, but she told me, to remain quiet & smoak my Pipe and not in the least be uneasy about my things which she added should be taken good care of & would be as safe in her hands as they could be in my own. Notwithstanding its being near midnight when I arrived, yet most of the Indians arose & many of them at that late hour invited me to their Lodges to eat a few mouthfulls & smoak the sociable Pipe, but now as all those ceremonies are over I am glad to lay myself down on Buffaloe Robes along the side of a warm fire expecting to get not a little repose after so long and fatiguing a Days march—and if ever I was thankful for any thing, it is to see myself here, after expecting to pass the night in walking about in the Plains.

March 7, Wednesday. Canadian's Camp, so named on account of a number of our People having past the Winter here, as there is a good road from where I slept last night. I left my young Guide there and came alone—and all along the way I was constantly meeting Indians who are going to encamp at the Devils Lake. Here I came in hopes of passing a Day or two with my friend Henry but I am informed that he yesterday morning set off to return to Alexandria! How disagreeable it is to be so disappointed! Had he supposed I was on my way to see him, there is not the least doubt but he would have deferred his jaunt a few Days longer—and all the consolation I can have after meeting with such a disappointment is the pleasing hopes that we soon shall meet at the Fort. Here I find Six of our Men who have past the greater part of the Winter hereabouts, and live upon the Flesh of Buffaloe which animals are plentiful—and the People appear to be happy, for when a Canadian has his belly full of fat meat he can be contented any where.

March 9, Friday. North side of the Devils Lake or in language of the Natives, *Muchemonitou, Sa ky i gan.* In the morning I left the Canadian's Camp and this afternoon arrived here, where I find my young Guide waiting my return. He is the Son of a Chief among the Crees & Assiniboins, whose Father was a Monsieur Florimaux a Frenchman and who past a number of years in the Indian Country and when he went to Canada he took his Son (the Father of my young Guide) along with him as far as Quebec intending to send him to France, but the Lad who then was thirteen years of age, did not like to leave his Native Country, therefore after remaining some time in Canada, deserted and returned to this part of the Country, where he became in time a famous Warrior and at length a Chief among his Relations by whom he is greatly beloved, and I may say even respected & revered by his numerous Family to whom he is a kind Father—therefore I do not know but it was fortunate for him that he did not go to France, for I am persuaded he could not have been happyer in any part of the World, than he is here, in this independent Country, which is abundantly supplyed by Providence with all the necessaries and many of the luxuries of life.

March 10, Saturday. In the middle of an extensive Plain early in the morning I accompanied by my young Guide left our last nights lodging, to go where I expect to find My People, which is about two Days march farther into the Great Plain than where I left my Interpreter on the 6th, and after walking all Day without finding either Wood or Water, we at 8 OClock lay ourselves down in hopes of getting a little rest, although we knew we run much risque of being destroyed by wild Beasts, but I could not close my eye, owing to the reflections I was continually making on my present unpleasant condition. I thought that, had I been of a different disposition that is not such a roving mind, I might have lived, if not happy at least contented in my native land and where I could have enjoyed the company of my worthy Relations, by whom I am convinced I am beloved. Such were the reflections that kept me from sleep the whole night—but it is only at such moments, that I make those melancholy reflections, and then it never has a long duration for as soon as fortune in the least changes in my favour such unpleasant thoughts vanish like smoke in the air—and I pass the greater part of my time not altogether unpleasantly & I hope in the end to reap some advantage from thus having separated myself from my Friends.

March 11, Sunday. Ca-ta-buy-se-ps or the River that calls [Qu'Appelle], so named by the Natives who imagine a Spirit is constantly going up and down the River, and its voice they say they often hear, but it resembles the cry of a human being. As soon as the light of the Day made its appearance, we left the place where we had lain down the preceding evening, and happy we were that the wild Beasts had not fallen upon us. It has Snowed accompanied by a high wind all Day. Here I find my Interpreter and Eighty Lodges or about two hundred Men & their Families. Along the banks of this River there is a little timber consisting principally of the inferior species of the Maple Tree, but out in the Plain there is not a Shrub or a tree to be seen. Here again as usual I met with an hospitable reception—but those Indians seldome come so far out into the Plains as where they now are, for this part of the Country belongs to the Rapid Indians, but a White Man was never before known to come into this part of the Country.

March 14, Wednesday. Last evening our People returned from the Fort, and the Natives of course drank all night, and when drunk being such a number of them together made a terrible noise. However they did not attempt to do any further injury than to steal a small Keg of Rum from us. [The printed text gives a different version: "They stole a small keg of spirits from us, and one of them attempted to stab me. The knife went through my clothes, and just grazed the skin of my body. To day I spoke to the Indian who made this attempt, and he cried like a child, and said, he had nearly killed his father, meaning me, and asked me why I did not tie him, when he had lost the use of his reason."] My People tell me there is little or no Snow for three Days march from this, but after that there is plenty all the way to the Fort.

March 16, Friday. About twelve we left the Indians Camp, but being greatly loaded considering there is no Snow and our property is hauled by Dogs on Sledges, we therefore get along but slowly. After we were encamped, we sent out Dogs (twenty two in number) after the Buffaloe, and they soon stopped one of them, when one of our People wnt [went] and killed him with an Axe, for we have not a Gun with us, and yet among Savages so far into the Plains.

March 17, Saturday, North West end of the Devils Lake, extremely warm for the Season, and the Country around us is all on fire, but fortunately for us we have a swampy place to encamp in. When the fire passes over the Plains, which takes place almost yearly, great numbers of Horses & Buffaloe are destroyed by that element, for those Animals will not move when they see they are surrounded by fire, but allow themselves to be burnt to death. This evening we killed another Buffaloe the same as yesterday.

March 18, Sunday. Still warm, and here we see many Grasshoppers, which is early for them to make their appearance, even in this part of the Country. As I found we were coming on too slowly loaded as the people were, about twelve OClock I left our property in charge of three Men & am going to the Fort with the others for Horses to come for it. This afternoon we met several of the X. Y. Coy's People in search of Indians, but for the information they got from us they thought them at too great a distance and therefore will accompany us to the Fort. This evening again we have been as fortunate as were the two preceeding Days in killing another Buffaloe—in fact in those Plains where Buffaloe are generally plentiful it is not customary neither is it necessary for People who are travelling over them to take Provisions along with them, for those who have fire arms can always kill a sufficiency for the Day.

March 22, Thursday. Lac la Pêche—and where we arrived this afternoon, and happy am I to have reached a place where I can take a little repose after so long and fatiguing a jaunt, yet it has not been altogether disagreeable but far from being unprofitable. The Country I travelled over is beautifully situated, and covered as it were with Buffaloe and various other kinds of Animals as well as many other delightful objects, which were constantly presenting themselves to our view, made the Days pass away almost unpreceptably. However I must acknowledge there were moments, when my condition was not the most agreeable, but they were of short duration, and I have all cause to be pleased that we have been so fortunate and ought (as I do) return my grateful thanks to kind Providence for our safe return to our homes and families.

[The printed text continues: "At three different times, while performing the tour above described, I was in great danger of losing my life, by the evil machinations of the Natives. One escape has been already mentioned, when one of them attempted to stab me. While I was dealing out spirits to the Savages, at the last mountain, on the night of the 5th inst. an Indian who was much intoxicated, told me, that I should never see another sun arise; and he, unquestionably, intended to kill me. The night following, after I arrived at the north side of the Devil's Lake, I was well received by the greater part of the Natives there; but as I have since been informed, one of them resolved to take my life. And yet, this villain invited me to his tent, and I visited it, without suspicion. He was prevented from executing his purpose by my host, who was acquainted with his purpose, and told him that he must first despatch *him;* for, he added, 'Kitch-e-mo-cum-mon' (that is Big Knife, which is the name that they give me,) 'is my brother, and has taken up his lodging with me, and it therefore becomes me to defend him and his property.' No Indian will suffer a stranger, if he be able to defend him, to be injured, while in his tent, and under his protection. Therefore, he who had intended to massacre me, thought it best to remain quiet. This hostile Indian had nothing against me, but that I was a friend to a person who he considered had injured him; and as this person was at a great distance, and therefore beyond his reach, he was resolved to avenge the affront upon me. It is the custom of all the Savages, not to be very particular on whom the punishment of an offence falls, whether the guilty person, or a relation or friend of this person. The first of these whom he happens to meet, becomes the object of his vengeance; and then his wrath is appeased, and he will not even lift his hand against the person who has offended him."]

March 24, Saturday. Yesterday Mr. Goedike &c. arrived from Alexandria and delivered me a letter from Mr. McGillis, who requests me to abandon Lac la Pêche & go with all my people to Alexandria—therefore in the fore part of the Day, all hands of us left the above mentioned place—and we have a Woman belonging to one of our Men with us who has walked all Day in the Snow and water, but this evening brought forth a Son! The mother says I am his Father.

FIFTH SOJOURN AT FORT ALEXANDRIA

March 27, Tuesday. Alexandria, and where we this afternoon arrived bag & baggage. The Woman who was delivered of a Child on the 24th the Day following took him on her shoulders and continued her march as tho' nothing uncommon had occured. It is really a happy circumstance that the Women of the Country are blessed with such strong constitutions otherwise many of them would be miserable, obliged as they are to undergo all kinds of hardships, and with little or no medical assistance to mitigate their pains.

April 9, Monday. Yesterday the Ice in this River broke up & to day we sent off four Men in a Boat loaded with Pimican [pemmican]—which they will take as far as the entrance of Ouinipick [Winnipeg] River. All the Country round us appears on fire.

April 29, Sunday. Yesterday the most of our people left this for Swan River, and to Day Mr. McGillis &c. set off for the same place, and are on their way to the Grand Portage, or rather the New Fort [Fort William], which stands about forty five miles north west of the above mentioned place—and I shall pass another Summer at this place and am happy in having with me my two friends Messrs. Henry & Goedike, also are here one Interpreter and several labouring Men besides Women and Children. We are preparing a piece of ground for a Garden & where I hope to pass many an agreeable hour in the company of my two companions. As Mr. Goedike plays the Violin well, he now and then will give us an air to enliven our spirits, and thus make the minutes pass away more pleasantly than they otherwise could. However the most of our leisure moments (and which is nearly nine tenths of our time) will be spent in reading, conversing on what we have read & meditation. We have the same neighbours as last year.

May 22, Tuesday. The Seeds that we put in the ground on the 10th Inst. are up and grow remarkably well.

May 29, Tuesday. For eight and forty hours it has constantly Rained, and in the same space of time I think I never saw so much water fall and which has caused the River to overflow its banks to a much greater distance than I ever before knew it to do, and the most of our Garden lies under water.

May 31, Thursday. In the morning Mr. Goedike, Collin a Boy & myself, wet off to go and pay our X. Y. neighbours a visit, and in leaving the Fort we had the River to cross, which from the late Rains is about Sixty rods broad, and as we had no other Craft, we crossed in a Canoe made of the Skins of Buffaloe, but that being not very good, before we reached the other side it let in water fast, however we drew it ashore mounted our horses and went up to see our neighbours and about three OClock P.M. returned to where we had left our Canoe, which we repaired a little and then embarked to come to the Fort. But we soon perceived it let in water very fast, yet we continued paddling in hopes of reaching the opposite Shore before it would fill. However when we had come about a third of the way, it actually filled but did not immediately upset. Here we had about five feet of water and a strong current that soon took us to where we could not find bottom, then the Canoe upset and threw us all into the Water. But we all clung fast to the Canoe, and in this condition drifted a considerable distance until the Canoe was stopped by a few Willows whose tops just reached above the water. And now I had a moments time to reflect on our sad and truly precarious condition, and how to extricate ourselves out of it occupied all my thoughts, but when we stood in the greatest need of assistance, the most benevolent God who is ever as ready to help all those who rightly call upon Him for aid, put devices in my head which I immediately set about to put in execution, which were in the first place to try to gain the Shore to take off my cloths as I could not do it where I then was. In doing which I found much difficulty, for I had a Great Coat, a heavy Poignard and Boots upon me, which very much hindered me from swimming, and as I already had had some time in the cold water, I had become benumbed, so that before I had reached one third of the way across I sunk, but soon rose to the surface of the water when I continued to exert myself as much as possible. However I soon sunk a second time, and now I thought I must absolutely drown, and nothing in this world took any part of my reflections, yet I did not think that I was afraid to meet my dissolution [for I was ignorant as to my miserable state concerning spiritual affairs & therefore could not have a just idea of the awful change I had every reason to believe I as about to make].[37] Notwithstanding I was apprehensive that all was lost, yet I gave a few struggles more which fortunately took me to a small Tree (which stood on what is usually the bank of the River but now several Rods from dry land) which I eagerly lay hold of, where I remained some time to recover my strength, and then set off again to gain the dry land, and as soon as I had effected that desirable object I with earnestness offered my sincere prayers to my Gracious Deliverer & preserver, Who had as it were snatched me out of the jaws of death! I was now safe on shore but my unfortunate

[37]This note is in the manuscript. Harmon means that the incident took place before his conversion, which occurred in 1813. *See* entry dated September 1 of that year.

companions were still struggling to keep themselves from sinking to the bottom of the River. They still had hold of the Canoe which just kept their heads above the water. Unfortunately we have no other Craft to go upon the water, neither were any of our people who were standing on the beach (as melancholy spectators of their friends sad condition) able to swim or give them the least assistance. Therefore I took off my cloths and threw myself a second time into the River in order to go and try to give those who were in the water, if possible some aid, and when I reached the place where they were I told the Boy to lay hold the hair of my head, and I took him to a Staddle [tree trunk] that stood no great distance off and told him to lay hold of it by which means he could keep the greater part of his body above the water. I then returned to the Canoe & took Collin to a similar place, but Mr. Goedike had alone reached a small Staddle & would have been able to swim a shore had not the cramp taken him in one of his legs. My next business was to try to take the Canoe ashore, but found it was impossible of myself alone. I therefore swam to the opposite shore caught a Horse, which I mounted and made swim to the Canoe, at one end of which I tied a Cord and held the other in my hands, and in this manner after drifting a considerable distance down the current, I reached dry land, where I repaired the Canoe a little, and then embarked to go and find my three wretched fellow creatures, who by this time had become nearly lifeless, for they had been in the cold water at least two hours! However with the aid of kind Providence I at length brought them all ashore, where we joined in offering up our sincere and hearty thanks to our Great Preserver for His kind aid in delivering us from such a horrible dissolution—and none of us will I presume attempt soon to embark in a leaky Canoe.

July 1, Sunday. We now begin to have Straw-berries—and to all appearance they will be plentiful.

July 17, Tuesday. On the eighth Inst. Indians ran away with three of our Horses, and the following morning Mr. Goedike & myself mounted two others, to pursue the Thieves, whom we followed two Days, but then finding they had so much the start of us and went at such a rate that it would be impossible for us to overtake them till they reached their Camp, which is Six or Seven Days march from this, we therefore left following them, and directed our course another way, in hopes of seeing Buffaloe, but found none. However we killed as many Fowls in the small Lakes, as we stood in need of for our Daily consumption—and all things considered had a pleasant ride & this evening returned to the Fort. We already have had so hard a frost as to injure many things in the Garden.

July 20 [25], Wednesday. An Indian arrived with Six horses who says he is directly from the Blackfeet Indians lands, who he says have made Peace with the Crees and Assiniboins, and that the forty Lodges of the latter Tribes who went in that quarter two years ago are on their way home & will be here before the Winter sets in.

September 1, Saturday. This afternoon Mr. Ferguson &c. arrived from Fort Dauphin, and informs us that all the Indians who were wont to remain in that quarter are gone to the Great Ouinipick [Winnipeg] Lake.

October 4, Thursday. This afternoon Mr. François La Roque arrived from Montagne a la Basse (Montagne à la Bosse, or Hump Mountain)[38] (which place lies about seven Days march down this River) who delivered me letters from home, as well as several from Gentlemen in this Country. One of the latter from Mr. Charles Chaboillez informs me that this place this Season will get its supply of Goods by the way of the Red River, and of which Department he has the superintendence—therefore as I am to pass the ensuing Winter here he desires me to accompany Mr. La Roque down to the Montagne a la Basse, and receive such Goods as will be required for the Post. I am also informed that Mr. Hugh McGillis has gone to the South end of Lake Superior, and at no great distance from the source of the Missisippi River.

October 26, Friday. Agreeable to Mr. Chaboillez's instructions I on the 6th Inst. in company with Mr. La Roque & an Indian who served as Guide, left this place a Horse back to go to Montagne a la Basse, our course being nearly South over a Plain Country and on the 9th we reached Riviere Qui Appelle [Qu'Appelle River] where the North West & X. Y. Coys. have each a Fort and where we passed one night with Monsr. Poitras who has charge of the Post, and the next morning we continued our march, always in beautiful Plains

[38]About three miles north of the town of Routledge, Man., which is on the main line of the Canadian Pacific Railway, 40 miles west of Brandon.

till the eleventh in the afternoon when we arrived at Montagne a la Basse where we found Messrs. C. Chaboillez & Charles McKenzie &c. &c. This is a well built Fort and beautifully situated on a very high bank of the Red River [the Assiniboine River is meant], and the Country all around a level Plain, but as the Fort stands on a much more elevated place than the Country on the opposite side of the River we can from the Fort Gate (as I am informed) at almost all seasons of the year see Buffaloe Grazing or Deer & Cabri bounding across the Plains. All of which cannot fail to render this a very pleasant situation. And here I past eight Days in the company of the above mentioned Gentlemen, and had not a little satisfaction in their conversation. At all times all of us would mount our Horses to take a ride out into the Plain, and frequently try the speed of our Beasts. However on the 19th I left that enchanted abode, accompanied by Messrs. Chaboillez & McKenzie &c. & the Day following arrived at Riviere qui Appelle, where we found our People waiting our arrival—and as the Canoes go no farther up the River, owing to the shallow water at this Season, the Goods intended for Alexandria will be taken there on Horses backs. We therefore gave out such things as we thought necessary and sent the People off—and the Day following Mr. Chaboillez &c. returned home and I accompanied by Mr. McKenzie, and Mr. Allen McDonell (my X. Y. Neighbour) set off for this place where we arrived this afternoon, after making a pleasant jaunt of twenty one Days. Here I have to pass the Winter with me, Mr. Goedike two Interpreters, twenty labouring Men fifteen Women & as many Children.

November 24, Saturday. A Man arrived from Montagne a la Basse, with a Letter from Mr. Chaboillez which informs me that two Captains Clarke & Lewis & one hundred & eighty Soldiers[39] had arrived at the Mandelle [Mandan] Village on the Missisouri [Missouri] River—who invite Mr. Chaboillez to go & pay them a visit (which is only a distance of five or Six Days march from where

[39]This was the famous American exploring expedition, led by Captain Meriwether Lewis and Captain William Clark, sent out by President Jefferson to survey a route to the Pacific Coast by way of the Missouri and Columbia Rivers. Lewis and Clark left St. Louis in May, 1804, reached the mouth of the Columbia River in November, wintered there, and arrived back at St. Louis late in 1805. *See* Nicholas Biddle, *History of the Lewis and Clark Expedition,* edited by Elliott Coues, New York, 1893.

he is). It is said that on their arrival there they hoisted the American Flag and told the Natives that they were not come among them to traffic, but merely to see the Country, and that as soon as the navigation was open they should continue their route across the Rocky Mountain & then down to the Pacific Ocean. They also made the Natives a few trifling presents, as well as repaired their Guns & Axes &c. gratis. Mr. Chaboillez writes that they behave remarkably honourably towards his people who are there to traffic with the Natives.

December 31, Monday. Mr. Ferguson &c. arrived from Swan River.

1805

January 22, Tuesday. For nearly a Month we have subsisted on little els [else] than Potatoes! But thanks be to kind Providence, last night two of my Men returned from the Plains with their Sledges loaded with the flesh of Buffaloe, and bring us the pleasing news that those Animals are now plentiful within a Days march of this and they could not come at a time when they would be more wanted, for our Potatoes also are getting low. About a Month since I sent Mr. Goedike accompanied by ten of our People into the Plains, hoping they would be so fortunate as to fall upon some of the Natives, who would be able to assist us, but of whom we have not yet had the least tidings, and what can have detained them so long I am at a loss to conjecture, for I did not imagine they would be more than ten Days absent from the Fort.

February 7, Thursday. As at the most of the Posts in Swan River Department they are short of Provisions they therefore have sent the most of their people to pass the remainder of the Winter with me, where we now have Buffaloe in abundance. Therefore our Family at present consists of upwards of seventy Souls, who require at least four hundred and fifty pounds of Meat per Day to feed them. Yesterday I accompanied Mr. Ferguson &c. as far as the Hudson's Bay House where we past the night with Mr. Miller, and in the morning we separated, Mr. F. to go to Swan River and I returned home.

February 19 [24?], Sunday. On the 8th Inst. two Men arrived from Montagne a la Basse, with a Packet of Letters informing me of a Coalition that took place last Autumn at Montreal between the North West & X. Y. Coy's—which Letters I have forwarded to Fort des Prairies.

On the 16th Inst. I left this in a Cariol [carriole] (drawn by a Horse) and went about two Days march into the Plain to where a number of our People have past the greater part of the Winter—and in my pleasant ride I saw thousands of Buffaloe.

March 4 [2], Saturday. People arrived from Fort des Prairies with Letters from that place the English River &Athabasca. On the first Inst. Swans past this [flying] to the northward.

March 19 [17], Sunday. Messrs. Ferguson & Angus McGillis &c. after having past several Days with us this morning set off to return to their respective homes, Swan River & Fort Dauphin.

March 20 [18], Monday. Came in a Band of Crees & Assiniboins who are upwards of one hundred in number, and as they brought a good many Furs and a considerable quantity of Provisions, they of course drank several Days, and while thus diverting themselves, one of the latter Tribe stabbed one belonging to the former. However the wound is not thought to be mortal, but the aggressor gave the wounded Indian a Horse and now to all appearance they are as great friends as they were before the quarrel.

[The printed text adds: "It is a common thing among all the Natives, for an offender to offer property in satisfaction for an injury; and when this is accepted by the injured party, contention between them entirely ceases. Even murder is, sometimes, in this way, atoned for; but not commonly. In ordinary cases, nothing but the death of the murderer, or of some of his near relatives, will satisfy the desire for revenge in an Indian, whose relative has been murdered."]

April 10, Wednesday. On the 24th Ult. I accompanied by one Man a Horse back sat off for Montagne a la Basse, and when we arrived there we were not a little surprised to find the Gates shut and about eighty Lodges of Crees & Assiniboins encamped about the Fort, who threatened to massacre all the White People who were in it, and those blood thirsty Savages had the boldness to throw Balls over the Palisades & tell our People to gather them up, as they might probably want them a few Days hence. I after having past several Days there sat off to return home but as I got out of the Fort

Gate, three rascally Indians stepped up towards me, one of whom laid hold of my Horses Bridle and stopped my Horse, in saying that he belonged to him and added that he would take him from me. However I told him that he had sold the Beast to Mr. Chaboillez, and he had given him to me, therefore he must go and speak to that Gentleman about the Horse as I had nothing to do with him, but the rascal would not let go of the Bridle, and when I saw that, I gave a pretty good blow with the butt end of my whip on his knuckles and then another to my Horse, which made him spring forward & leave the Indian behind, & so I continued my route. But the villain with one of his companions followed us nearly half of the Day, but after that we saw them no more. On my return I remained four Days at Riviere qui Appelle where I past my time very agreeably in the company of Messrs. John McDonald & Thomas McMurray (both for the X. Y. Company) and Andrew Poitras—but in leaving that place I had the River to cross, and at that late Season the Ice was bad, so much so that my Horse with me upon him fell through twice, and the last time I was very nigh going under the Ice, but kind Providence spared me once more. While at Montagne a la Basse Mr. Chaboillez got me to consent to leave the above mentioned place about the beginning of June next with Six or Seven Canadians and two or three of the Natives to go on a *Discovery,* and the first place at which we shall make a stop will be at the Mandelle [Mandan] Village on the Missisouri [Missouri] River, and from thence shall steer our course towards the Rocky Mountain, in company of a number of the Mandells [Mandans] who every Spring go up that way to meet Indians who come to traffic with them from the other side of the Mountain, and from the latter place we shall turn about and come home, where we hope to arrive in the month of November next. Mr. Chaboillez's motive for sending [me] there is in hopes that we shall discover a Country abounding with Beaver. [The following note is here inserted in the manuscript: "But my illness in the Spring prevented my undertaking the above excursion, therefore Mr. La Roque went in my stead, but went no farther than the Mandelle Village, so of course nothing was gained from the jaunt."][40]

[40]See *Journal of Larocque from the Assiniboine to the Yellowstone,* edited by L. J. Burpee, Ottawa, 1910.

April 18, Thursday. We are Packing up our Furs to be sent to the General Rendezvous—and the X. Y. People have already abandoned their Fort to go to Riviere qui Appelle. [The printed text adds: "I shall abandon this fort [Alexandria], and the Indians in this vicinity will go either into the region of Riviere qui Apelle [Fort Qu'Appelle] or up the Sisiscatchwin [Saskatchewan] River, near Fort des Prairies."]

Fort Alexandria to New Fort

May 5, Sunday. About three Leagues below Alexandria, which place we left and abandoned on the 28th Ult. and have all our property aboard two large Boats, but some of us are a Horse back. As it has not Rained since last Autumn the River is uncommonly low and is the cause why the people in the Boats make so poor progress—and as we have a Pit Saw with us I have ordered some of the People to go into the Woods and saw Boards to make another Boat, in order to lighten the others.

May 8, Wednesday. Riviere qui Appelle. On the 6th Mr. Goedike &c. & myself left our Boats a horseback and as the fire this Spring had past over the Plains we came through, it was with some difficulty that we could find grass for our Horses.

May 10, Friday. Sent Mr. Goedike to Swan River to transact business, as I am too unwell to undertake the jaunt myself.

May 15, Wednesday. Montagne a la Basse, where I am in company with Mr. La Roque &c. (whom I found at Riviere qui Appelle) arrived this afternoon.

May 20, Monday. This morning my Boats cast up and as I am still unwell shall in a few Days set off for the New Fort, where I hope to get some Medical assistance.

May 22, Wednesday. About twelve Miles below Montagne a la Basse which place I in a Boat left this morning, and am on my way to the General Rendezvous.

May 27, Monday. Riviere a la Souris, or Mouse River [Fort Assiniboine, also known as Fort La Souris]. Here are three Forts belonging to the North West X. Y. & Hudson's Bay Companies. Last evening Mr. Chaboillez invited the People of the other two Forts to a Dance & we had a real North West Ball, for when three fourths of the People were so much intoxicated as not to be able to walk strieght, the other fourth put an end to the Ball or rather Bawl! And this morning we were invited to breakfast at the Hudson's Bay House with a Mr. McKay & in the evening to a Ball, which however ended in a more decent manner than the one we had the preceding evening at our House—not that all were sober, but we had no fighting.

It is now upwards of fifty years since a French Missionary left this, who had resided here a number of years to instruct the Natives in the Christian Religion. He taught them some short Prayers, the whole of which some of them have not yet forgotten.

May 30, Thursday. In the morning I left Mouse River, and have along with me forty Men in five boats and Seven Canoes.

June 1, Saturday. A little below what was called the Pine Fort, and [it] is now twenty years since it was built and eleven that it has been abandoned. The River at present being so low (as we have not had a drop of Rain since last Autumn) and we having such a number of Crafts with us we drive the Sturgeon upon the Sand-banks where there is but little water, and there we kill any number we please, which are excellent eating.

June 12, Wednesday. Mr. Goedike has just returned from Swan River, and I hope we shall separate no more till we reach Head Quarters.

June 13, Thursday. Portage la Prairies, where the North West Co. have a missirable Fort, but the most beautiful situation I have seen in this part of the World. Opposite the Fort there is a Plain as level as a House floor, which is about Sixty Miles long & from one to ten broad. [The printed text adds: "To this place the Natives resort every spring, to take and dry sturgeon."]

June 15, Saturday. We are now encamped under a beautiful range of Oaks, (and the first that I have seen in this Country) which separate the River from an extensive Plain. Ever since we left Mouse River the soil on either side appears to be excellent. [The printed text notes that "the timber is very different from what it is" near the river's source: "We here find oak, elm, walnut, basswood, &c. and I am informed that there are grapes and plums in this vicinity."]

June 18, Tuesday. Not far from where we are encamped there is
a pretty large Camp of Sauteux, and among them I saw another of
my unfortunate Countrymen who was like the other (of whom I
have already made mention) taken from his Parents when quite a
Child, which is the way that many a fond Mother has lost her darling Child! [The printed text continues: "but this fellow is lost, beyond recovery, for he now speaks no other language, but that of the
Indians, among whom he resides, and he has adopted all their manners and customs; and it would now be as difficult to reconcile him
to the habits of civilized life, as it would be, were he a real Indian."]

June 19, Wednesday. The Forks or where the Upper [Assini-
boine] and Lower Red Rivers form a junction—and hereabouts the
Country appears to have a richer soil than at any other place I have
observed in this part of the World—and is covered with Oak, Basswood, Elm, Poplar and Burch &c. also are here Red Plumbs &
Grapes &c.

June 21, Friday. We are now encamped where the Red Rivers
run into Great Lake Ouinipick [Winnipeg]. It is now almost five
years since I saw this Lake, but that long span of time appears but
as a moment, yet when I reflect on my transactions since in this
Country, then it appears as though I had past the great part of my
Days here.

June 24, Monday. Bottom or entrance of Ouinipick [Winnipeg]
River, where we find a number of Gentlemen from their winter
quarters, who are like ourselves on their way out to the New Fort.

July 5, Friday. Rainy Lake—where we see many people the
same as ourselves bound for the New Fort. I also received Letters
from home, which afford me no small satisfaction as they inform
me they left all my friends below enjoyed good health and my
earnest prayers are that they may long continue to enjoy the same
blessing.

[A long passage is here interpolated in the printed text: "On the
margin of the waters, which connect this lake with the Great Winnipick Lake, the wild rice is found, of which I have spoken on a former occasion. This useful grain is produced in no other part of the
North West Country; though [Jonathan] Carver erroneously
states, that it is found every where. It grows in water, about two

feet deep, where there is a rich muddy bottom. It rises more than eight feet above the water; and, in appearance bears a considerable resemblance to oats. It is gathered about the latter end of September, in the following manner. The Natives pass in among it in canoes. Each canoe has in it two persons, one of whom is in each end, with a long hooked stick, in one hand, and a straight one in the other. With the hooked stick, he brings the heads of the grain over the canoe, and holds it there; while, with the other, he beats it out. When the canoe is thus sufficiently loaded, it is taken to the shore and emptied. This mode of gathering wild rice, is evidently more simple and convenient, than that which was practised in Carver's day. This grain is gathered in such quantities, in this region, that in ordinary seasons, the North West Company purchase, annually, from twelve to fifteen hundred bushels of it, from the Natives; and it constitutes a principal article of food, at the posts in this vicinity."]

July 6, Saturday. Rainy Lake and about ten Miles from the Fort, where we have been encamped the most of the Day to allow the People time to repair the Canoes.

July 8, Monday. Cross Lake [Lac la Croix]. Met several canoes this Season from Montreal, who are taking Goods to the Rainy Lake Fort, for the Athabasca People. It is in this Lake we leave the route to go to [i.e., that leads to] the old Grand Portage.

July 9, Tuesday. All this Day we have been crossing small Lakes and coming down what deserves the names of Brooks rather than Rivers. Met eight Canoes who are going with Goods to Rainy Lake.

July 12, Friday. The Plain Portage. In the fore part of the Day we met Mr. A. N. McLeod on his way to Athabasca, which place he left the beginning of June last. We put ashore and took breakfast with him and he has taken from me my friend Mr. Goedike, who had past nearly four years with me, and all that time we lived on the most friendly terms, therefore both of us were very loth to separate. He it is true had romantic Ideas, but I believe him to have a generous humane heart—and susceptible of the strictest ties of friendship. He has good natural parts, and has had a tolerable education, which he strives to improve by reading—but I can without boasting say that it was me who taught him to be fond of books (as

Mr. McLeod had done to me) and I am as willing to acknowledge that he assisted me greatly in learning me to read and speak the French Language, which was his Mother tongue, but received the most of his education in the English Language. He is not master of this, but knows enough of both for common business. He has an even temper and is fond of his Mother.

July 13, Saturday. Over took Swan River People & fell into what is called Nipigon River [presumably the present Dog River], which is about ten Rods broad, and will be making a few Portages (on account of Rapids) take us to the New Fort.

July 14, Sunday. Dogs Portage [on the present Kaministikwia River]. In the Morning we met Mr. David McKenzie &c. who are on their way to Athabasca and this afternoon Mr. Alexander Henry Jur. bound for the lower Red River.

July 15, Monday. The Mountain Portage [Kaministikwia River]—and where the North West Co. have a Store, to where they send Provisions from the New Fort as the [Kaministikwia] River is generally so shallow & full of Rapids, that those who are going into the Interior, cannot leave the Fort with full loads, therefore they take their Provisions here.

July 16, Tuesday. New Fort or as the Natives call it *Kâ-mi-nis-ti-qui-â* is built on the bank of a considerable River [the Kaministikwia] which runs into Lake Superior about 4 or 500 Rods below the Fort. Here the French had an Establishment previous to the Englishe's taking possession of Canada—and here we find a number of Gentlemen, some this Summer from Montreal and others from the different parts of this Country, and about fifteen hundred labouring Men—and the greater part of the latter are Canadians. [The printed text adds: "The vessel that runs on that lake [Superior], can come, with a part of her lading, quite up to the quay, before the fort.... The country, for some considerable distance round, is covered with heavy timber, consisting of a kind of red pine, poplar, aspin, birch, cedar, &c., but the soil does not appear to be of the first quality. Potatoes, pease, oats, &c., however, grow tolerably well here."]

July 17, Wednesday. This afternoon William McGillivray Esqr. (head Agent of the North West Coy.) &c. set off for Montreal.

July 22, Monday. Here I have past several days not unpleasantly in the company of a number of young Gentlemen, but who now begin to leave this for their Winter quarters, and tomorrow I shall follow their example by setting off for Fort des Prairies, and as two other young Gentlemen who I know to be sociable & agreeable companions, will be in the same Brigade, I therefore expect to have a pleasant passage to my winter quarters.

THE SASKATCHEWAN: 1805–1807

NEW FORT TO SOUTH BRANCH HOUSE

July 27, Saturday. On the 23rd Inst. Messrs. William Smith Angus Bethune & myself &c. left the New Fort, but nothing worthy remark occurred fill we reached this place—Dogs Portage—where we overtake Messrs. John McDonald (Garth) & John Duncan Campbell &c. the former bound for Fort des Prairies & the latter for English River—and in this company we past the greater part of the Day, while our People were bringing our Canoes & lading across the Portage, which is three Miles long.

August 2, Friday. French Portage. Today we met Mr. John McDonell from Athabasca and who is on his way to Canada.

August 7, Wednesday. Rainy Lake, where the North West Co. have a tolerable Fort and the X. Y. People had another before the coalition took place, but the Hudson's Bay Coy's People never came into this quarter.

August 18, Sunday. Bottom of Ouinipick [Winnipeg] River— and where I find a Letter left me by Mr. Goedike, which informs me he past this in good health the beginning of this Month and was on his way to Athabasca—therefore we cannot expect to meet again for years to come!

August 28, Wednesday. Foot of the Grand Rapid and where the Si-si-scach-win [Saskatchewan] River disimbogues into the north end of Ouinipick [Winnipeg] Lake, which is a noble River and about two hundred Fathoms broad—and the Lake two hundred & fifty or three hundred Miles long and at one place at least Sixty broad.[41] The above mentioned River just passes through the end of the Lake and then continues its course till it falls into Hudsons Bay at York Factory,[42] and where the Hudson's Bay People of Fort des Prairies & the English [Churchill] River, get their Goods and take their Returns.

[41]Lake Winnipeg is actually 240 miles long, and its greatest breadth is 55 miles.

[42]Harmon is referring to the Nelson River, which he considered to be simply a continuation of the Saskatchewan.

September 5 [3], Tuesday. Cumberland House, which Fort stands on the bank of a considerable Lake called by the Natives Sturgeon Lake [now Cumberland Lake], and where those Fish are taken plentifully. This place was first established thirty-three years ago by Mr. Joseph Frobisher[43]—and here is where the Fort des Prairies People, those of the English River & Athabasca take different routes. The former go up the Si-si-scach-win [Saskatchewan] & the latter up the English [Churchill] River. On the 30th Ult. we crossed Lac Bourbon [Cedar Lake] which is about forty Miles long—and where the North West Co. formerly had a Fort but which was abandoned in 1802. [The printed text includes a description of the region: "There are few mountains or hills to be seen, between this place and Lake Winipick. The country has a pretty heavy growth of timber, and the soil is rich. In the lakes and rivers of this region, excellent fish are taken, such as sturgeon, white-fish, cat-fish, pike, pickerel, &c. This country abounds in fowls, among which are swans, bustards, geese, and many kinds of ducks. Moose are found in considerable plenty; there are a few black bears, otters, muskrats and martins; and rarely, a beaver is found."]

September 21, Saturday. South Branch Fort and about one hundred Miles [actually about 70 miles] above the Fork or where it forms a junction with what is called the North Branch [the North Saskatchewan] and then assumes the name of Si-si-scach-win River. Both Branches take their rise in the Rocky Mountain, but at a distance of several hundred Miles one from the other. The South Branch passes thro' large Plains, but the other at least on the north side is a Woody Country. This Fort was put up last Summer and a couple of Stores built, but the Dwelling Houses we still have to make. Buffaloe I am informed are plentiful within a half a Days march of this. There are four Tribes of Indians who come to trade at this Establishment viz.—Crees, Assiniboins, Sauteux & Muskagoes, also a few of the Black feet Indians come now and then.

---

[43]The Frobisher brothers—Joseph and Thomas—were among the first English traders from Montreal to reach the valley of the Saskatchewan. Their post, built in 1773, was on Pine Island Lake, about ten miles east of the site of Cumberland House. The latter was built by Samuel Hearne for the Hudson's Bay Company in 1774. *See* W. S. Wallace, *The Pedlars from Quebec,* Toronto, 1954. In the entry dated Aug. 17, 1808, Harmon again refers to Joseph Frobisher's activities.

In coming up this River, we saw many places where Forts had stood, but some of which have been abandoned thirty years, and others of a later date, but there was one about Six Miles below this, which was abandoned fifteen years ago and on account of the Rapid Indians who in the Summer at a time when there were but few People either at the North West or Hudson's Bay Forts came in a Band of about one hundred & fifty a Horse back and killed all the Hudson's Bay People except one Man, and after taking out of the Fort all the property they could conveniently carry away with them, they sat fire to it and consumed it to ashes, and then they went to the North West Fort (which stood only a couple of hundred Rods from the other) expecting to serve that in the like manner. At the time there were only three Men & several Women & Children—a Monsieur Chatellain [Louis Chastellain] who had charge of the Fort at the time (and who retales me the circumstances) but he had providently shut the Fort Gates previous to the Indians approach and when they came nigh enough, the three Men who had placed themselves in the Block Houses & Bastions fired upon them, but the blood thirsty Savages soon returned the shot, which however had no effect, but the contest lasted until towards the evening when the assailants saw they were but second best, for they had lost several of their party whereas the People in the Fort had not received the least injury, therefore the Indians after dragging their Dead into the River made off with themselves, and were never seen thereafter. Yet Monsieur Chatellain &c. did not think it proper to remain there any longer—of course [in the course of] the Day following they embarked all their property aboard several Canoes and drifted down the River about two hundred Miles where they sat about building another Fort.[44]

Mr. William Smith & I along with two Interpreters & fifteen labouring Men &c. are to pass the ensuing Winter here, and at a few hundred paces from us the Hudson's Bay People have a Fort in charge of a Mr. Joseph Howse.

[44]The Indian attacks took place in the autumn of 1793. The Rapid Indians had suffered repeatedly at the hands of the Crees, who had more valuable furs to offer to the traders and as a result were much better supplied with fire-arms. The former therefore regarded the white men as being in league with their enemies. The attacks thus had two motives—to average themselves on the whites, and to seize arms and ammunition.

SOUTH BRANCH HOUSE

October 10, Thursday. This Day a Canadians Daughter (a Girl of about fourteen years of age) was offered me, and after mature consideration concerning the step I ought to take I finally concluded it would be best to accept of her, as it is customary for all the Gentlemen who come in this Country to remain any length of time to have a *fair* Partner, with whom they can pass away their time at least more sociably if not more agreeably than to live a lonely, solitary life, as they must do if single. In case we can live in harmony together, my intentions now are to keep her as long as I remain in this uncivilized part of the world, but when I return to my native land shall endeavour to place her into the hands of some good honest Man, with whom she can pass the remainder of her Days in this Country much more agreeably, than it would be possible for her to do, were she to be taken down into the civilized world, where she would be a stranger to the People, their manners, customs & Language. Her Mother is of the Tribe of the Snare Indians, whose Country lies about the Rocky Mountain. The Girl is said to be of a mild disposition & even tempered, which are qualities very necessary to make an agreeable Woman and an effectionate Partner.

October 12, Saturday. Messrs. Hamilton & Finan McDonald &c. arrived in two Canoes, the latter this year from Canada & the former from Cumberland House.

October 15, Tuesday. In the morning Mr. Hamilton &c. set off to return to Cumberland House where they are to pass the ensuing Winter.

October 20, Sunday. Mr. F. McDonald &c. set off a Horse back to go to Fort Vermilion, which is about Six Days march from this up the North Branch.

November 7, Thursday. The River last night froze over, but as yet we have little Snow.

December 25, Wednesday. This Day has been passed as all Christmas are in this abandoned part of the World, Drinking all Day by our Men and Dancing in the evening by all hands.

1806

January 10, Friday. Three Men arrived from the Upper Red River with Letters & I of course receive a number from my acquaintances in that quarter.

January 16, Thursday. Sent back the three Men to the Red River, by whom I answered those Letters I recd. from there.

January 18, Saturday. Sent People to Fort Vermilion with letters brought from the Red River & others of our writing.

March 13, Thursday. On the 10th Inst. Nine Men arrived from Fort Vermilion, and this morning we sent them off with Goods to return to the above mentioned place & by whom I wrote Messrs. J. McDonald & James Hughes.

March 15, Saturday. This evening the Northern Express arrived and I am sorry to learn that no letters come from Athabasca this Season, which failure is thought to be owing to the great depth of Snow they have in that quarter. [The printed text adds: "Buffaloes have been found in plenty within a few miles of the fort, during the whole winter."]

March 17, Monday. Sent the Northern Express to the Red River by which I wrote Messrs. H. McGillis & Msrs. Henry.

March 25, Tuesday. The Most of the Snow is dissolved and we have sent four Men about a Days march to make Sugar.

April 19, Saturday. The grater part of our Indians have gone to wage War upon the Rapid Indians, their inveterate enemies—with whom they often patch up a Peace, but is never of a long duration.

April 28, Monday. This afternoon the Ice in the River broke up. A few Days since a small War party of the Rapid Indians, came & killed several Assiniboins, who were encamped within fifteen Miles of our Fort. They also Scalped and stabbed an old Woman in several places, who notwithstanding is still alive and to all appearance will recover of her wounds.

May 7, Wednesday. Our Neighbours [the Hudson's Bay people], have abandoned their Fort and gone to take their Returns to York Factory.

June 2, Monday. Last evenings Messrs. Hughes & Alexander Stewart came here a Horse back from the North Branch (which passes within a dozen Miles of this) where they left their Canoes &

People to wait their return when they will continue their route to the New Fort—but Mr. Smith and I are to pass God willing the ensuring Summer at this place where we have three Interpreters four labouring Men, and a number of Women & Children—and as my Companion Mr. Smith is a sensible well informed and a sociable young man and about my age (he being only one Month older than me) I therefore hope to pass my time both pleasantly and profitably.

June 4, Wednesday. Sent off our People with our Returns in three Canoes & a Boat.

August 8, Friday. Six Assiniboins, arrived and inform us that about Eighty Lodges of Crees & Assiniboins with about as many of the Black feet Indians, were on their way to wage war on the Rapid Indians, their common enemy, but the two former Tribes fell out on the way and fought a Battle among themselves, in which twenty-five of the Black feet Indians and three of the Assiniboins fall, which put an end to their Wars for this Season. [The printed text states that the quarrel between the tribes was "respecting a horse, which they both claimed, and which neither would relinquish."]

August 28, Thursday. [Mistakenly dated June 28 in the manuscript.] The Hudson's Bay People are returned from their Factory, and if they have news of consequence from England they are determined to keep all to themselves for they give us none.

September 3, Wednesday. Two Men arrived from Cumberland House, who have brought me Letters from home, which announce the trule melancholy and grievous tidings, that my Dear & honoured Father is no more to be numbered among the living! but who after a short yet a severe illness of only a few Weeks met his dissolution with a becoming Christian resignation to the dispensations of a just God on the 25th of June 1805! What an inexpressible satisfaction it would have been to me (and no doubt to him also) to have seen & conversed together once more ere he bid eternal farewell to this World of trouble disappointments & Sin! "But Gods will be done & not as we would" and thanks be to God that I as well as the rest of his bereaved Children have in the loss of so worthy & kind a Parent the greatest and best of consolations—which is, that from the exemplary life he lead while in this probationary World, we have all reason to hope & expect that he has gone to another where he will be infinitely more happy than he possibly could have been in this. And it ought to be our constant endeavours to keep fresh in our memories his regular & Religious life while on Earth, which will influence us to strive to follow the good example he has set us, so that we may when our Maker sees fit to call us out of time into eternity meet with the like happy change of Worlds. Amen.

I have also received Letters from Messrs. A. N. McLeod & John McDonald (Garth) which inform me that I am to pass the ensuing Winter at Cumberland House & for which place I shall in the course of a few Days leave this.

CUMBERLAND HOUSE

September 11, Thursday. Cumberland House—where I arrived this afternoon and find Messrs. [James] Hughes & David Thompson &c. who will in a Day or two set off for Fort des Prairies.

September 17, Wednesday. Sent Monsieur Pérâs [Pierre Perra] along with four labouring Men and a small assortment of Goods to go and pass the Winter at Moose Lake, which place lies about two Days march from this, and where the Hudson's Bay People have a Fort as well as another within one hundred Rods of this. The latter is in charge of Messrs. [Peter] Fidler and [James] Sutherland.

[The printed text adds: "The Indians, who resort to this establishment, are Sauteux and Muscagoes. Moose and black bears are pretty abundant in this vicinity; and a few beavers are found. We subsist principally upon sturgeon and white fish, which we take out of the lake. Geese and bustards are numerous, in the fall and spring. The surrounding country is very low and level, so that, at some seasons, much of it is overflowed. This accounts for the periodical influx and reflux of the water, between this lake and the Sisiscatchwin [Saskatchewan] River, which are distant six miles."]

October 3, Friday. Hudson's Bay People in three Canoes are just arrived from York Factory with late news from England and among other things they inform us that the [Napoleonic] War on the Continent of Europe still continued to rage as much as ever.[45]

---

[45]The news doubtless included accounts of the three major military events of the last months of 1805: the capitulation of Ulm (October 19), the Battle of Trafalgar (October 21) and the Battle of Austerlitz (December 2).

October 25 [24], Friday. We now have about four inches of Snow and last night the greater part of this Lake froze over. I have sent People to the other side of the Lake to fish for Sturgeon, which as I am informed will weigh from ten to one hundred pounds. They also take out of this Lake several other kinds of Fish. [The printed text continues: "They are taken in spread nets, which is the manner in which we generally take all kinds of fish, in this country. Some kinds, however, such as trout, cat fish and pike, we at times take, by setting hooks and lines."]

December 20, Saturday. Three Men arrived with Letters from Fort des Prairies.

December 25, Thursday. As the greater part of our People are now absent from the Fort, I have in some measure been able to pass this Day somewhat like an accountable being and a Christian—that is in reading and in meditating on the birth &c. of our Saviour. In the morning I invited over Messrs. Fidler & Sutherland to breakfast with me.

1807

January 13, Tuesday. Monsieur Pérâs [Perra] has come to pay me a visit and was accompanied by his Neighbour, a Mr. [Alexander] Kennedy.

January 30, Friday. Two of the Hudson's Bay People arrived from Fort des Prairies and were so obliging as to bring me several Letters from Gentlemen in that quarter. [The printed version adds: "The greater part of the North West and Hudson Bay people, live on amicable terms; and when one can with propriety render a service to the other, it is done with cheerfulness."]

February 3 [1], Sunday. Sent People with Letters to Fort des Prairies.

April 6 [5], Sunday. The Ice in the Si-si-scach-win [Saskatchewan] River is broke up, and the great quantity of Snow that lately has been dissolved has caused that River to rise so high as to give another course to a small River of nearly Six Miles long, which generally takes its water *out* of this Lake, whereas it *now runs into it.*

May 23, Saturday. This Lake is free from Ice, and we have Planted Potatoes & sewed our Garden Seeds.

May 26, Tuesday. Monsieur Pérâs [Perra] &c. are arrived bag and baggage from Moon [Moose] Lake. Wild Geese are now plentiful hereabouts.

May 30, Saturday. Mr. John McDonald &c. in Seven Canoes are just arrived from Fort des Prairies, and are on their way out to the New Fort, and whom I shall accompany there.

CUMBERLAND HOUSE TO FORT WILLIAM

June 7, Sunday. Grand Rapid. On the 1st Inst. Mr. John McDonald myself and the People of Seven Canoes & one Boat left Cumberland House and arrived here on the 5th and where we have ever since been stopped by the Ice in Lake Ouinipick [Winnipeg], which is not yet broke up. Here we Spear any number of Sturgeon we please, as they are going up or down the Rapid.

June 8, Monday. Lake Ouinipick [Winnipeg]. Last night there arose a strong wind that broke up the Ice and drove it to the other end of the Lake, and we of course in the morning embarked aboard our Crafts and have sailed all Day.

June 14, Sunday. Bottom, or entrance of Ouinipick [Winnipeg] River where we find Messrs. [John] McDonell and Alexr. Henry &c. on their way out to the New Fort—also Mr. William McKay who past last winter at this place is still here.

June 16, Tuesday. White [Winnipeg] River. In the morning we left the Fort [at the mouth of the Winnipeg River], and this afternoon Mr. A. N. McLeod &c. from Athabasca over took and encamp with us—and with whom after so long a separation I was happy in passing an evening. He appears to be a worthy Man and has ever been a friend to me, therefore I cannot help esteeming him above any other person I know in this Savage Country.

June 24, Wednesday. Rainy Lake, where we see many others like ourselves hurrying out to the General Rendezvous.

July 4, Saturday. New Fort, where I once more find myself among Friends (according to the general acceptation of the word) and acquaintances. I also receive Letters from home, which thanks be to God bring me the best of news, as they inform me they left my friends enjoyed good health, and as successful in the affairs of this world as they had any reason to expect to be. But how much greater would be my satisfaction if I could instead of hearing from them, see and converse with them! Altho' the Seven Years for which I was under engagement to the North West Company are now expired, yet I cannot with the least degree of propriety gratify the earnest desire I have to go down this year, and when that so much wished for moment will arrive God only knows. It certainly is very hard and trying to the feelings of a person who has the least affection for his Relations, to be thus separated from them & for such a series of years! And in such a Savage Country where there is little to be learnt that we could wish to know. Yet after all since I am here I must try to make the best I can of it. However notwithstanding the many bad examples we see Daily, a person nevertheless *can* be as *virtuous* in this as in any other part of the World. It is true that if a person was to lead what may be said to be a truly *Religious* life *here*, he would I fear find but few associates, who would converse with him on the subject of Religion, but in what part of the world is it otherwise?

July 19, Sunday. This which formerly was called the New Fort, is now named Fort William, in honour of William McGillivray Esqr., on which occasion the Comerce made a present to their common labouring Men, of a considerable quantity of Spirits & Shrub &c. and also a similar present was made to the Natives who are encamped about the Fort.

July 20, Monday. Messrs. John McDonald, Peter Rocheblave, and John McGillivray &c. sat off for their respective Winter quarters, viz: Fort des Prairies, Athabasca & the English River.

July 24, Friday. As I am still unwell (yet without knowing what my complaint is) I shall pass the ensuing Winter with Doctor McLoughlin at Sturgeon Lake in the Department of Nipigon, which place lies almost North of this.

FORT WILLIAM TO STURGEON LAKE

July 25, Saturday. This afternoon I in company of three Canoes left Fort William, and came & encamped on an Island in Lake Superior, and am thus far on my way to Sturgeon Lake.

August 1, Saturday. Pointe a la Gourgaine.[46] In the morning Messrs. [John] Haldane, [James] Keith, [Charles] Chaboillez, [Dr. John] McLoughlin, Ranald & Dougall Cameron & Roderick McKenzie &c. over took and came on with us till about noon, when we put ashore, and as we are to take different Routes when we leave this, we therefore have passed the afternoon over a few Bottles of Wine, and some of us (as the Irishman says) got more than two sheets in the wind.

August 3, Monday. First long Portage in the Nipigon Road. Yesterday we separated with Messrs. Chaboillez and Leith [Keith], who are gone to Winter at the Pic & Michipicotton [Michipicoten], which places lie toward the Sault St. Mairies [Marie], and to Day we left Lake Superior.

August 7, Friday. Fort Duncan, which stands on the North side of Nipigon Lake, the latter being about one hundred and fifty Miles long and from one to twenty broad,[47] out of which are taken the most famous Trout of any place throughout the whole North West Country, some of which will weigh Sixty or Seventy pounds. [The printed text includes a description of the region: "The surrounding country is very rough; but where the ground is arable the soil appears to be good.—Moose and carriboo are found in this vicinity; and there are, also, a few black bears, beavers, otters, muskrats, martins, &c. Great numbers of white fish are taken out of the lake, particularly in the fall of the year. These are hung up by their tails, in the open air, and are preserved good, in a frozen state,

---

[46]Point à la Gourganne, on the western side of the entrance to Nipigon Strait from Lake Superior.

[47]Lake Nipigon is about 70 miles long and 50 miles wide.

during the winter. Most people prefer those that have been thus kept, to fish that are taken immediately out of the water."]

August 9, Sunday. In the morning we sent off three Canoes but in the after part of the Day, some of the people returned with the melancholy tidings that one of their Companions was drowned, in going up a small Rapid when the Canoe he was in upset, but all the others saved themselves by swimming ashore—also the most of the property they had on board was lost.

August 12 [13], Thursday. In the morning Mr. Haldane, the Doctor and myself &c. left Fort Duncan, where Mr. [Roderick] McKenzie will pass the ensuing Winter, and where we separated also with the Mr. Camerons, as there we took different routes—they Northward & we Westward.

August 24, Monday. Portage du Fort, Sturgeon Lake, where we arrived yesterday and this morning Mr. Haldane &c. left us to continue his route to Red Lake, but the Doctor & I with four labouring Men are to Winter at the other end of this [lake], and for which place we shall leave this tomorrow.

STURGEON LAKE FORT

September 1, Tuesday. Our People are putting up houses for us to pass the Winter in. Here we take White Fish pretty plentifully. This Lake may be about forty Miles long and from one to five broad. The Country after leaving Lake Superior lies low and pretty level. There are no Mountains to be seen & but few Hills. However there are a great number of small Lakes & Ponds, and Rivers & Brooks, and [this] has been a Beaver Country, but now those Animals are become scarce, for they have been continually hunted by the Natives for more than a hundred years.

October 3, Saturday. Sent People to the other end of the Lake to make a Fishery of White Fish, Pike & Carp &c. which when taken are hung up by their tails in the open air and in this way will keep good till the mild weather in the Spring—and they are the principal food of the People of this part of the World—yet there is no want of Moose & Cariboux hereabouts. The Indians who frequent this Post are Sauteux & Muscagoes. [The printed text adds: "In this country, which is at least seven hundred miles long and five or six hundred broad, more people have starved to death, than in all the rest of the Indian country. At this lake, several years since, eleven Canadians lost their lives for want of food. We experience at present, no difficulty in this respect; and I am of opinion that the distresses of our predecessors were, in a considerable measure, owing to the want of good management."]

November 9, Monday. Our People are returned from the Fishery & say that they have taken fourteen hundred, however with them & what Corn, Flour, Wild Rice and Meat we have, we hope not to want during the Winter. But we are in a solitary place, where we see no one except the Natives—but we must bring our minds to our situations, and then we can be contented even here. Fortunately for us we have a few good Books and in perusing them we shall pass the greater part of our time—and then again the Doctor (who is about my age) is an excellent Companion, good humoured & fond of conversation, which with the little I may have to say will serve to keep up our spirits, and even make the moments pass away agreeably and I hope I shall have cause to say profitably also. We now have about four inches of Snow, which will in all probability pass the Winter with us.

November 15, Sunday. Last night this Lake froze over.

December 4, Friday. We now take great numbers of excellent Trout with Hooks and Lines under the Ice. Early this morning the Woman who remains with me was brought to bed of a Boy, whom I name George Harmon.

December 28, Monday. Doctor McLoughlin accompanied by two Canadians & an Indian has gone to pay a visit to Mr. Haldane at Red Lake.

1808

January 14, Thursday. One of the Men who accompanied the Doctor has returned, with a Letter from him & another from Mr. Haldane.

February 19, Friday. The Doctor &c. are returned from their long jaunt, whose company I am happy to enjoy after having been for such a length of time alone as it were. I find that another year is past and gone which makes me thirty years of age! How short is the life of Man! Yesterday a child, today a Youth, tomorrow a Man and the next in the Grave or about to enter that gloomy Dwelling! In fact the time is so short that is allowed us to remain in this World, that it really is not worth our while troubling ourselves much about anything in it—and yet we are continually harassing and teasing ourselves in hopes of gaining Masses of Silver and Gold, when a very little reflection would teach us that it would not require much to serve our turn for the short time we can make use of it.

May 13, Friday. The Doctor with one Man in a small Canoe, has sat off for Fort William, where he will be wanted to attend on the sick, as soon as People arrive from their Winter quarters, for among such a number as resort there every Summer, there are always a few who want Medical assistance. However I believe this to be one of the most healthiest parts of the World—for here we are seldom troubled with Diseases or Distempers of any kind. The Doctor has not been able to learn (to his satisfaction) what my complaint is. *He* says it is more imaginary than any real Disease—but however that may be, the Medicins I have taken in the course of the last Winter, have been of much service to me (as I think). I am therefore encouraged to hope that ere long I shall regain my former state of good health. [The printed text continues: "The Indians of this place have subsisted during the greater part of the past winter, upon hares.— There is an old Sauteux woman here, who compels her own son to have criminal intercourse with her."]

May 24, Tuesday. As this place will not be kept [open] during the Summer, I therefore have sent our People with the Goods we have remaining on hand to the next Establishment—Lac Seul which place lies about four Days march from this.

STURGEON LAKE FORT TO FORT WILLIAM AND THENCE TO DUNVEGAN

June 9, Thursday. Portage du Fort—and where we shall wait the arrival of all the People of this Department, and then continue our route to Fort William. It is nine months and fifteen Days since we arrived here last Autumn, which shows that the *Winters* in this part of the Country are long, and I may with truth add *dreary also.*

June 22, Wednesday. Fort Duncan. The People for whom we were waiting at Portage du Fort arrived on the 12th & the Day following we all sat off for this place where we arrived this afternoon. *June 25, Saturday.* Yesterday we left Fort Duncan and have come and encamped on an Island in Lake Nipigon where we shall remain a few Days to fish for Trout which are plentiful and of an excellent quality.

July 7, Thursday. Yesterday morning, I arrived at Fort William where I had barely time to read Letters from home & answer them, prepare myself for a long journey, say to my friends how do you do, and bid them good by, and this afternoon embarked for Athabasca, in company of a Mr. John George McTavish, with whom I last Summer at Fort William became acquainted. Both of us are to remain at Athabasca at least three years, and our Salaries are one hundred pounds Halifax Currency per annum, besides being furnished with Cloathing and victuals &c. &c.

July 20, Wednesday. Rainy Lake—and where we find all the Athabasca People except one Brigade of Seven Canoes that are expected Daily.

July 23, Saturday. Ever since my arrival here we have been busily employed in preparing to leave this for our Winter quarters. As Mr. A. N. McLeod is desirous of visiting Canada this year, Mr. Donald McTavish will take his place in superintending the affairs of Athabasca.

July 26, Tuesday. Rainy Lake River. In the morning I left the Fort, and have with me a Mr. Archibald McGillivray. Our Brigade consists of ten Canoes & in each there are five Men.

July 29, Friday. Portage de L'Isle—In Ouinipick [Winnipeg] River. In the morning we met Mr. David Thompson &c. from the Columbia River (on the west side of the Rocky Mountain).

August 1, Monday. Lake Ouinipick [Winnipeg]. In the morning we arrived at the Fort [Bas de la Rivière], where we remained till twelve, and while there I wrote a few lines to my old friend Mr. Wm. Henry who is at the lower Red River, and from whom I also received a Letter informing me of his Fort's having been attacked this Summer by a considerable party of Sioux—but after they had received a couple of shots of Cannon from the Block-House, they ran off, and have not been heard of since. However as they were going away, they said that ere long they would come back and make a second trial on the Fort. They are a numerous Tribe of Indians, whom are scattered over a large tract of Country that lies between the Missisippi & Missisouri Rivers, and who I am informed are the greatest Rascals in this part of the World.

August 6, Saturday. Grand Rapid (North end of Lake Ouinipick [Winnipeg]). The wind has been high all Day, and in the after part of it one of our Canoes filled, but fortunately it was not far from an Island yet the People to save themselves were obliged to throw part of its lading overboard. Here we find Monsieur Périgné, who formerly was at Swan River for the North West Co., but lately has as he tells me been to Canada, and came up on his own account—that is, he intends hunting the Beaver himself, as well as carry on a small traffic, with the Natives—but I am apprehensive that the distance is too great from this to the Civilized part of the World, (and of course from a Market for him or any other without a considerable capital to enable them to carry on the trade on a larger scale) to make much profits. Severals [*sic*] have been known to make the trial, but all without one exception have failed.

August 12, Friday. Cumberland House. Nothing worthy remark has occurred to us since we left Grand Rapid.

August 13, Saturday. Entrance of Riviere Maligne or Bad River [the present Sturgeon-weir River] which runs into Sturgeon [now Namew] Lake.

August 14, Sunday. Beaver [now Amisk] Lake. We have passed the greater part of the Day, in coming up the above mentioned River, which is a continuation of Rapids from one end to the other, and much water in it. The country lies low, and the Timber much the same as the most of the other parts of the North West—small.

August 16, Tuesday. Pilican [Pelican] Lake, but have been most of the Day sailing over Lac Martin [now Mirond Lake].

August 17, Wednesday. Portage du Fort du Traite or Trading Portage, so named from a circumstance that happened here thirty-four years ago to Mr. Joseph Frobisher, who met here a considerable Band of the Natives whose Canoes were loaded with Furs which they were taking to York Factory (Hudson Bay) however the above mentioned Gentleman gave them Rum to drink and they soon were prevailed upon to traffic their Beaver, and Mr. Frobisher

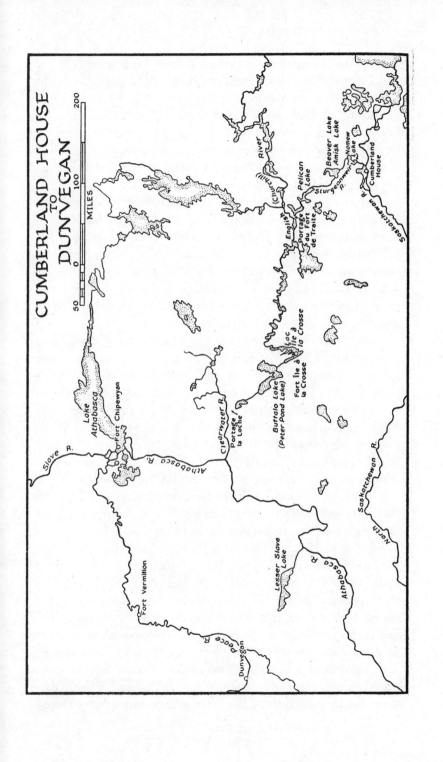

built a Fort, where they past that and several following Winters, which was at that time the most northern Post belonging either to the North West or Hudson's Bay Coy's.

August 18, Thursday. This afternoon we saw a Canadian who has past the summer with the Natives and the latter let us have a little Meat which we find very palatable after having lived on Salted Provisions ever since we left Fort William, as in-land we never eat any thing Salted—yet there is no want of Salt in this Country.

August 24 [23], Tuesday. Isle a la Cross Lake. Ever since we left Sturgeon Lake, we properly speaking have been in what is called the English [now the Churchill] River (so named in honour of Mr. J. Frobisher who is an English Man & the first White Person or rather trader that ever came up this way) which however passes through several Lakes—and in this River our way has been obstructed by thirty-six Portages—that is [places] where the Canoes & lading is carried on the Peoples back.

August 25, Thursday. Isle a la Cross Fort—and where we find Messrs. Donald McTavish & Robert Henry, the former Gentleman having past us on the 23rd Inst. and the latter past the Summer at this place. This Fort which is well built stands on the North side of the above mentioned Lake—and here they have an excellent Kitchen Garden, and out of the Lake they take the best of White Fish the whole year round and is the only place in this Country where those Fish are to [be] taken at all Seasons. The Indians who come to this Establishment are Chipiwyans and a few Crees.

August 27, Saturday. Buffaloe Lake [now Peter Pond Lake]. In the morning we left the Fort of Isle a la Cross—and this is only an arm or deep Bay of the last mentioned Lake.

August 30, Tuesday. Portage la Loche or Luch [Loach] Portage (so named from a neighbouring Lake where they take those Fish in abundance). The Portage is full twelve Miles over, and across which the People are obliged to carry both Canoe & Ladings—however the road is excellent, as it is over a level Country but thinly Timbered. [Portage la Loche, or Methy Portage, crosses the height of land that separates two of the great watersheds of the continent, and the printed text adds: "The streams, before we cross this portage, discharge themselves into Hudson's Bay at Churchill Factory; but afterward, the water, after passing through Athabasca,

Great Slave, and other lakes, enter the North Sea (i.e., the Arctic Ocean)."]

September 3, Saturday. North West end of Portage la Loche and where we find a small Band of Chipiwyans who assist our People in crossing our property. They also let us have Provisions, which comes in a good time, as what we had is getting low. Just as we arrive at this end of the Portage, we have from a high hill an extensive & beautiful prospect of the level Country that lies before us as well as of the different windings of a small River that we are to descend.

[For publication, Harmon's editor rewrote his modest description in more glowing terms: "About a mile from this end of the portage is a hill, which towers majestically, to the height of a thousand feet, above the plain below; and which commands a most extensive and delightful prospect. Two lofty and extensive ridges, enclose a valley, about three miles in width, which stretches, far as the eye can reach. The Little River, which is, also, by different persons, denominated Swan, Clear water, or Pelican River, winds, in a most delightful manner, along this charming valley. The majectick forests, which wave upon these ridges, the delightful verdure of the intervening lawn, and the beautiful stream, which wanders along through it, giving a pleasing variety to the scene, until these objects become blended with the horizon, form, on the whole, the most delightful, natural scenery, that I ever beheld."]

September 4, Sunday. In the morning we left the Portage, and are now in little Athabasca [the Clearwater] River which may be about twenty Rods wide.

September 6, Tuesday. Great Athabasca River. In the morning we past the place where little Athabasca & Red Deer Rivers form a junction, and then assumes the name of Great Athabasca River, and at several places along its banks is to be found Tar or Pitch plentifully. We also saw another place where there is Sulphur. [The printed text adds further details: "At about twenty miles from the Fork, several bituminous fountains are found, into which a pole twenty feet in length, may be plunged, without the least resistance. The bitumen, which is in a fluid state, is mixed with gum, or the resinous substance collected from the spruce fir, and is used for gumming canoes. When heated, it emits a smell, like that of sea coal."]

September 7, Wednesday. Fort Chipiwyan [Chipewyan], which stands on a Rocky Point on the West side or rather end of Athabasca Lake. This is the General Rendezvous of all Athabasca—that is, it is here where all the Outfits are made out for the different Posts in this Department, and where the most of those who have charge of those Posts come every fall to receive their Goods, from those who brought them from the Rainy Lake. A few Crees but a great number of Chipiwyans resort to this Establishment. This Lake I am told is large & extends down a considerable distance towards York Factory (Hudson Bay). At only a few Days march from this, there is several places where almost any quantity of excellent Salt could be taken and from whence the most of the North West is furnished with that necessary article. [The printed text adds: "The country around this place, is low and level, and, in the spring of the year, much of it is covered with water. A few moose are found, in this vicinity; but, the fish of the lake form the principal dependence for food, and they are abundant, and of an excellent quality.—Every fall and spring, bustards and geese are found in greater numbers, than in any other part of the North West."]

September 21, Wednesday. Cold raw wind. Ever since my arrival at this place, People from almost every corner of this extensive Department have been flocking in—one of whom is a Mr. Simon Fraser from New Caledonia (on the West side of the Rocky Mountain) who accompanied by Messrs. John Stuart and J. M. Quesnel and a Dozen of Canadians as well as two of the Natives, is just returned from a voyage to the Pacific Ocean, and for which place they early last Spring left New Caledonia, in two Canoes.[48] He says they met with some ill treatment from the Indians who live along the Sea-coast, but were hospitably received by all those they saw further up the Country, who he says are not scattered about here and there a Lodge as in the other parts of this Country, but live in villages and have Houses or Huts made of Wood. Mr. Stuart also

[48]This expedition was the first to descend the Fraser River. Fraser and Stuart left Fort George late in May, 1808, reached the mouth of the river on July 2, and arrived back at Fort George on August 6. The journey was a major feat of exploration, but its immediate result was a great disappointment to Fraser. The North West Company was seeking a route to the mouth of the Columbia, and Fraser had hoped that he was following that river.

says the Country they past through is far from being well stocked with Beaver or any other kind of Animals—of course the Natives live principally upon Fish.

September 22, Thursday. This afternoon Mr. Alexr. Roderick McLeod & I accompanied by a number of People in several Canoes, left Fort Chipiwyan and after coming a couple of Miles in Athabasca Lake we entered a small River which runs out of the above mentioned Lake.

September 23, Friday. Peace River, which is about thirty Rods broad and takes its rise on the West side of the Rocky Mountain, and I am also informed that about one hundred & fifty Miles from this it runs into the Great Slave Lake, through which it passes and then continues on till it disembogues [discharges] into the Pacific Ocean, perhaps no great distance from Kamshatkay Bay where the Russians have Settlements.[49]

October 2, Sunday. Fort Vermilion, which at present is in charge of a Mr. William Mackintosh, who past the Summer here. Great numbers of Beaver Indians bring their hunts to this Post, also a few Iroquois from Canada hunt hereabouts.

October 7, Friday. Encampment Island Fort. This place also is established for Beaver Indians, in short I am informed that is the only Tribe who live along this noble River. Until a short distance below this the whole Country appears to be covered with Timber, but now we begin to see small Plains, where I am informed there are Buffaloe, Moose, Red Deer & Cabri &c. [The printed text adds: "Great numbers of black bears are found, that feed on the berries, which are abundant on the hills, on both sides of the river."]

---

[49]Harmon's geography is here wildly inaccurate. The drainage basin of the Peace River is wholly east of the Rocky Mountains, and the Peace itself ends just north of Fort Chipewyan, where it joins the Slave River. The waters of the Peace ultimately reach the Arctic Ocean, not the Pacific, through the Slave River, Great Slave Lake and the Mackenzie River. The entry dated Oct. 10, 1809, shows that Harmon soon became better acquainted with the country.

DUNVEGAN

October 10, Monday. Dunvegan, which is a well built Fort and stands in a pleasant situation, with Plains on either side of the River. Here is where my friend Mr. A. N. McLeod used to Winter, while in Athabasca and here I find my former companion & friend Mr. Frederick Goedike &c. who past last Summer here—and about the Fort are encamped a number of Iroquois-Hunters[50] and Beaver Indians, who have been waiting our arrival. And at long last I have reached the place where I shall pass, God willing, the ensuing Winter, also Messrs. Donald McTavish, J. G. McTavish & Joseph McGillivray and thirty-two labouring Men, nine Women & several Children, which makes it differ much from the solitary place where I was last Winter. Here our principal food will be the Flesh of Buffaloe, Moose, Red Deer & Bears. We also have a tolerable Kitchen Garden, therefore we have what would make the most of People contented—that is those who only think of filling their greedy Bellies. As I have mentioned what we have to nourish our *bodies,* I must also add that we have a very good collection of Books to satisfy our *minds,* and if we are so disposed will make us grow wiser & consequently better. And to complete the whole the above mentioned Gentlemen are sociable & agreeable Companions—and now if I do not pass a pleasant & profitable winter it must be my fault. This evening I have past in agreeable chat with my friend Goedike of our transactions together in the Red River &c. &c.

October 14, Friday. This morning Mr. F. Goedike &c. set off for St. Johns [Fort St. John], which place lies about one hundred Miles up this River,[51] and where they are to pass the ensuing Winter.

November 12, Saturday. We now have about a foot of Snow.

---

[50]Iroquois Indians came to the West in some numbers to engage in the fur trade. They were disliked by the natives for reasons noted by Harmon in the entry dated Oct. 13, 1818, in which he reports the murder of an Iroquois.
[51]Changed to 120 miles in the printed text.

December 1, Thursday. Last evening Seven Men arrived, three from the Rocky Mountain Portage (which place lies about one hundred and eighty Miles up this River) and the other four from St. Johns, who brought letters of course from the Gentlemen of those places.

December 20, Tuesday. Last night this River froze over, and at nine OClock this morning the Thermometer was 40 Degrees below o or Cypher.

December 25, Sunday. Mr. A. N. McLeod &c. arrived from Encampment Island (their Winter quarters) and are come to pass the Holy Days with us.

December 26, Monday. Two Men arrived from Fort Chipiwyan with the Express.

December 29, Thursday. Messrs. Simon Fraser & Goedike &c. arrived, the former from the Rocky Mountain Portage & the latter from St. Johns.

1809

January 10, Tuesday. On the 6th Inst. Mr. McLeod &c. left us to return home and this morning Messrs. Fraser and Goedike &c. set off also for their respective abodes, but in their agreeable company the few Days they were here I past many an agreeable moment, espetially with the latter Gentleman my old friend and messmate for nearly three years, and we had (as may be supposed after so long a separation) much to say in relating the most material circumstances that had occurred to each other since our separation in 1805, as well as talk over many, many things that took place while we were together at Alexandria. And in our conversation we had (I imagine) much the same satisfaction and delight that two old Soldiers have when they meet after a long separation in relating what might have befallen them in a later campaigne. What is there in this changeable World to be preferred to a *real* Friend?

January 18, Wednesday. Sent the Express to Lesser Slave Lake, from whence it will be sent to Fort des Prairies &c.

March 1 [2], Thursday. Came in a Band of our Indians who last fall went a considerable distance to the Northward, where they say that they had such an extraordinary depth of Snow, as occasioned them to starve greatly, but hereabouts we at no time have more than two feet & a half.

March 20, Monday. The Snow is dissolving fast. Mr. A. N. McLeod &c. arrived with the melancholy news of the Death of Mr. Andrew McKenzie (natural Son of Sir Alexander McKenzie) who departed this life at Fort Vermilion on the 1st Inst. We are also informed that several Canadians have starved to death in the vicinity of Great Slave Lake some of whom ate their dead companions. They came up into this Country *free* [i.e., as independent traders], to hunt the Beaver, and being at so great a distance from any of our Establishments, they could get no assistance before it was too late for the most of them. [The printed text adds: "it is reported, that one man killed his wife and child, in order to supply himself with food, who, afterwards, himself starved to death.... It is not unfrequently the case, that, the surviving part of a band of the Natives, subsist upon the flesh of their dead companions, when compelled to do it for want of other food, sufficient to sustain life. I know a woman who, it is said ate of no less than fourteen of her friends and relations, during one winter."]

March 22, Wednesday. Sent People to look for Birch Rind or Bark to make Canoes, to take our Returns to the Rainy Lake, as those we bring in would not be good to take out.

April 6, Thursday. Mild. The People whom we sent for Bark are returned with one hundred & eighty Fathoms which will make nine Canoes, that will carry about three Tuns burthen each—and two Men will easily carry one of them on their Shoulders.

April 11, Tuesday. Bustards &c. begin to come from the South.

April 18, Tuesday. This morning the Ice in the River broke up.

April 27, Thursday. All of our Indians have come in with their Spring Hunts—and I am busy in writing my Friends in the United States of America.

May 7, [Sunday]. The Plains around us are on fire. Planted Nine Bushels of Potatoes & sewed the most of our Garden Seeds. For several Months last past I have been taking Medicins, which (thanks be to God) have restored me to my former state of good health.

May 10, [Wednesday]. Mr. F. Goedike &c. arrived with the Returns of St. Johns.

May 11 [Thursday]. Yesterday, Sent off eleven Canoes loaded

with the Returns of this place & St. Johns—and early this morning
Messrs. D. McTavish, J. G. McTavish, F. Goedike & Joseph
McGillivray &c. embarked aboard two *light* Canoes, bound for
Fort William—but I am (God willing) to pass the ensuing summer
at this place—and where thank God we have a number of excellent
Books. The Winter (notwithstand[ing] my illness) has been the
most agreeable of any that I have past in this Country—and I flatter myself that I learnt much, which knowledge this Summer I intend to strive to improve.

May 16 [Tuesday]. In the morning Messrs. Simon Fraser &
James McDougall &c. arrived in four Canoes—the former Gentle-
man from the Rocky Mountain Portage & the latter from New
Caledonia, which is (as already mentioned) on the West side of the
Rocky Mountain and lies four hundred & fifty or five hundred
Miles up this River.[52] The above mentioned People after having
past the most of the Day with me reembarked to continue their
route to the Rainy Lake.

June 2 [Friday]. The Seeds that we sewed in the Garden have
sprung up & grow remarkably well—and if we may judge of the
future from the present appearance of things, we shall be blessed
with Berries in abundance—such as Red-Rasp-Berries, Straw-
Berries, Poires and Cherries &c. &c. This River since the beginning
of May has risen twelve feet & still continues to rise, which is in
part owing to the late Rains we have had, but more so to the dissolving of the great quantity of Snow on the Rocky Mountain.

June 13, Tuesday. Came to the Fort an Indian who says that one
of their Chiefs is dead, and for whom they want a Chiefs
Cloathing, that he may be decently interred, as well as a little Rum
to drink at his burial—all which he takes back to his bereaved
Friends—for the deceased was a good Indian.

July 12 [Wednesday]. Mr. John Stuart &c. arrived from New
Caledonia, and are come here for Goods. Poires begin to ripen.

July 19 [Thursday]. Mr. Stuart &c. have left this to return to

[52]Harmon much exaggerates the distance. From Dunvegan to Fort
McLeod, as the crow flies, is about 185 miles, and to Stuart Lake, in the heart
of what was formerly New Caledonia, it is no more than 250 miles. The
winding courses of the rivers and trails followed by the fur-traders would
not add more than about another hundred miles to these distances.

New Caledonia—but the few Days he was here were by me past much to my satisfaction. We rambled about together in the adjacent Plains, and conversed as we walked, but now and then we would stop to eat a few Berries, which are plentiful everywhere. He I perceive has read much & reflected not a little—and how happy should I be to have such a Companion for the whole Summer! But such is the nature of this Country, that we meet but seldom and the time we can remain together is never long. We only have time to begin to form an acquaintance, when we must separate perhaps not to meet again for years to come! Baptiste La Fleur (my Interpreter) will accompany them as far as St. Johns, in hopes of getting some tidings of his Brother, who it is supposed has been killed by a rascally Indian, while on his way last Spring from the Rocky Mountain Portage to St. Johns.

July 29 [Sunday]. B. La Fleur, is returned from St. Johns without having been able to learn the least news of his poor Brother, or the two Indians who were to come down the River in the same Canoe as himself. Therefore we are apprehensive that all three were drowned in coming down the Rapids, as their Canoe was small and not very strongly built as it was made of the Bark of a Species of the Pine Tree.

July 21 [31?]. We have cut down our Barley, which is I think the finest I ever saw in any Country. In short the soil on the Points of land along this River is excellent.

The Mother of the Chief who died this Summer (and who is far advanced in years) remains in a small Lodge within a few Rods of our Fort, as many of the Natives of both sexes are wont to do, when they become old and infirm, of course not much able to walk as they would be obliged to do were they to remain with their Relations who live upon the chase, and are therefore under the necessity of travelling about almost constantly, and of course have it not in their power to take that care of their aged which is easy for us to do. The above mentioned old Lady almost every Day, towards the sitting of the Sun, goes to the place where her Deceased Son used generally to encamp whenever he came to the Fort, and there she cries and sings a mournful kind of a Song the words or rather the sense of which when translated into English run thus:—"My Dear Son come to me! Why do you leave me my Son!"—which she repeats over and over again for hours together in the most plaintive and melancholy tone imaginable.

It is customary among the Beaver Indian Women, that whenever they loose a nigh Relation to cut off a joint of one of their fingers, and in consequence of so barbarous a custom, we often see some of their aged Women who want the two first joints of each finger on both hands—but the Men content themselves by cutting their Hair close to their heads and in scraching [scratching] or cutting their faces and arms in a most shocking and cruel manner. The Beaver Indians are a peaceable and quiet People and perhaps the most honest of any on the face of the earth. A Thief among them is but seldom to be met with, and when a person is known to be of that description, he is by the others looked upon in much the same light as a Robber in the Civilized part of the World. The greater part of them are now cloathed with European goods & have fire arms instead of Bows and Arrows. Formerly they were cloathed with Buffaloe Skins &c. and cut their Wood with sharp Stones, and made use of the Bones of Animals in lieu of Knives, the same as the other Savages throughout the whole Continent of America before they became acquainted with civilized Peoples.

September 1 [Friday]. On the 29th Ult. Several People arrived in a Canoe from Fort Chipiwyan, and delivered me letters from Gentlemen in that quarter—and today they set off to return from whence they came, and have taken along with them five thousand pounds weight of Provisions, for those who are on their way from the Rainy Lake. Fowls begin to leave the North to return to the Southward.

October 6 [Friday]. As the weather begins to be cold we have taken our vegetables out of the Ground, which have been very productive.

October 7 [Saturday]. Mr. A. N. McLeod &c.[53] in three Canoes past this and are gone to the Rocky Mountain Portage and New Caledonia. They delivered me letters from home as well as others from people in this Country all which brought news of the most pleasing nature as they informed me that my friends were well & doing well. What a great satisfaction it is in any Country, but more

[53]Corrected in the printed text to A. R. McLeod.

particularly so in this, situated as we are here, to receive Letters from people whom we esteem and for whom we have an affection, and who [we] may presume wish us well! They never fail of being the best cordial to cheer up our too often drooping spirits. How often have I thanked the Inventer of *Letters,* which enables us to keep up as it were a conversation (while at such an immense distance) with those whom I hold dear above anything in this fleeting and vexatious World.

October 10 [Tuesday]. In the morning cast up Messrs. D. McTavish, J. Clarke & J. McGillivray, &c. Mr. J. Clarke is this Summer from McKenzie's River, which place lies beyond Great Slave Lake.

October 11 [Wednesday]. Seven Canoes arrived loaded with Goods for this place & St. Johns.

October 20 [Friday]. Mr. Archibald McGillivray arrived from St. Johns where he past last Summer, but as Mr. Clarke has gone to superintend the affairs of that place Mr. McGillivray will Winter here—but as he has a very uneven and unhappy temper I do not expect to have much satisfaction in *his* company.

1810

January 6 [Saturday]. Sharp cold weather. Messrs. A. N. McLeod [A. R. McLeod] and J. Clarke have been here to pass the Holy Days with us, but this morning they sat off for their respective homes, Rocky Mountain Portage and St. Johns [Fort St. John], and along with them we sent three Men with letters to the Gentlemen who are at New Caledonia.

February 15 [Thursday]. My Woman brought to bed of two Boys who appear to have been prematurely born, and it is believed that they cannot long survive!

February 22 [Thursday]. In the morning expired one of those Children that were born on the 15th Inst.!

February 25 [Sunday]. Last night the Brother of the Deceased Child died also! And to Day they were both buried in the same Coffin. May they be happy where they are thus early gone! Perhaps they have been snached [snatched] so soon out of this World of sin and misery to prevent their feeling the troubles and vexation which they must have experienced had they been allowed to reach the age of manhood—and however I may regret their early dissolution, I must also know it was an act of the all wise and just God who has deprived me of my Children, and Who alone knows what is for the best. [In the printed version, Harmon's editor has revised this passage to read as follows: "He who gave them life, has taken it away. He had an undoubted right so to do; and though his ways are to us, inscrutable, he has the best reasons for whatever he does. It becomes us, therefore, humbly to acquiesce in this afflictive dispensation."]

February 26 [Monday]. Mr. John Stuart &c. arrived from New Caledonia—the former to transact business with Mr. McTavish.

April 12 [Thursday]. Mr. Archibald McGillivray [has] gone to pass the ensuing Summer at St. Johns [Fort St. John].

May 3 [Thursday]. The Ice in the River broke up.

May 12 [Saturday]. Sent People to take three Horses in a Boat to Fort Chipiwyan.

May 15 [Tuesday]. Early in the morning Messrs. D. McTavish & J. McGillivray &c. sat off for Fort William—and this afternoon Mr. Clarke &c. in five Canoes past this on their way to the Rainy Lake—and I shall, God willing, pass the Summer at this place, which indeed is pleasantly situated, and here we have very good Horses, which we can when so inclined mount and make short excursions into the adjacent Plains, where there are Buffaloe, Moose, Deer & Bears &c. (Black and Grey) and as to Books I am very well supplied, therefore I hope & expect to pass the Summer without experiencing much what the French call *ennui.*

May 22 [Tuesday]. Messrs. John Stuart & Ferris (Hugh Faries &c. past this in four Canoes with the Returns of New Caledonia & Rocky Mountain Portage—and are like many others on their way to the Rainy Lake.

June 23 [Saturday]. Last night the weather was so cold as to freeze the tops of our Potatoes &c. and this morning as several Deer were crossing the River from the opposite side, one of our People jumped into a Canoe pursued them & killed one.

August 27 [Monday]. Mortimore arrived from Fort Chipiwyan with Letters from Gentlemen in that quarter & two from McKenzie's River.

September 2 [Sunday]. In the morning our People perceived a

Black Bear nigh the Fort, which they pursued & were so fortunate as to kill. Grizzly, Brown & Black Bears are plentiful here abouts—the former often pursue the Natives, and when they can reach them will tear them to pieces—but the latter kinds will at the sight of a Human being run off—unless they are females that have Cubs with them, then in that case if they are pursued too closely will turn about and try [to] defend their young ones.

September 13 [Thursday]. Two Men arrived from New Caledonia with the disagreeable news that Salmon this season do not come up the Rivers in that quarter the same as usual, and as it is Salmon that form the principal food both for the Natives as well as the White People who are there it is apprehended that all will be obliged to abandon the plan [place] to go in search of others that have been more favoured by fortune or Providence.

October 3 [Wednesday]. We have taken our Potatoes out of the ground and find that the nine Bushels planted the 10th of May, have produced upwards of two hundred & fifty. [The printed text reduces the yield to one hundred and fifty bushels and adds: "The other vegetables in our garden have yielded an increase, much in the same proportion.... I am of opinion, that wheat, rye, barley, oats, pease, &c. would grow well in the plains around us."]

October 6 [Saturday]. Mr. John Stuart &c. in four Canoes have arrived from Fort Chipiwyan, and have on board Goods for the Establishment at the Rocky Mountain Portage and New Caledonia. The above mentioned Gentleman delivered me a Packet of Letters from home, as well as a number of others from Gentlemen in this Country, one of the latter was from D. McTavish, John McGillivray & Simon Fraser Esq. (all Partners of the North West Co.) desiring me to go and superintend the affairs of New Caledonia—or if I think proper to accompany Mr. Stuart there (who is well acquainted with that part of the Country having already passed several years there) and be second in command for the ensuing Winter; but in the Spring (as I shall then it is to be supposed have learnt the ways of the Country) assume the whole management myself—but knowing as I do the great advantage a person who is well acquainted with any part of this Savage Country has over an entire stranger (as I am to the above mentioned place) induces me to prefer accompanying Mr. Stuart rather than go alone—

especially after having got such unfavourable news as has lately come from there.

DUNVEGAN TO STUART'S LAKE

October 10 [Wednesday. St. Johns [Fort St. John]. On the 7th Mr. Stuart & myself &c. left Dunvegan and this evening we arrived here, but all the way up we had bad weather—both Snow and Rain, which makes it very unpleasant travelling in such Crafts as we make use of in this Country—Canoes. Here I find my old messmate Mr. Archd. McGillivray &c.

October 11 [Thursday]. In the fore part of the Day our people were busily employed in preparing Provisions to take us to New Caledonia—but this afternoon Mr. Stuart &c. in three Canoes set off for Rocky Mountain Portage, while I having a little business to attend to shall pass the night with Mr. McGillivray, but tomorrow morning follow those who left this to Day.

October 15 [Monday]. Rocky Mountain Portage, Fort. Here we find about eight Inches of Snow on the ground. Mr. A. N. McLeod [A. R. McLeod is meant] has the management of this Post, and here Mr. Stuart &c. arrived yesterday & I this morning, since when we have been busy in delivering the goods for this place, and in separating the remainder among our People to be taken on their backs to the other end of the Portage, which is twelve Miles over. However we leave our Canoes here & take others at the other end of Carrying place. From Great Slave Lake to this place there are few Rapids and only one fall, but at several places the current is very strong, and yesterday in the afternoon we were coming up one of the latter places—and of course stemed [stemmed] the current but slowly. I therefore debarked alone to walk along the beach but after having come some distance I arrived at a place I could not pass without making a considerable turn in the Woods—therefore I left the River side and after I had walked a Mile or two fell upon a good foot path, which I imagined would take me straight to the Fort, but after I had followed it several Miles, I perceived it had been beaten by wild animals, and I though [thought] leading me a contrary way from the one I ought to take, but as I was loth to follow it back I struck off in another direction, hoping soon to fall upon the River

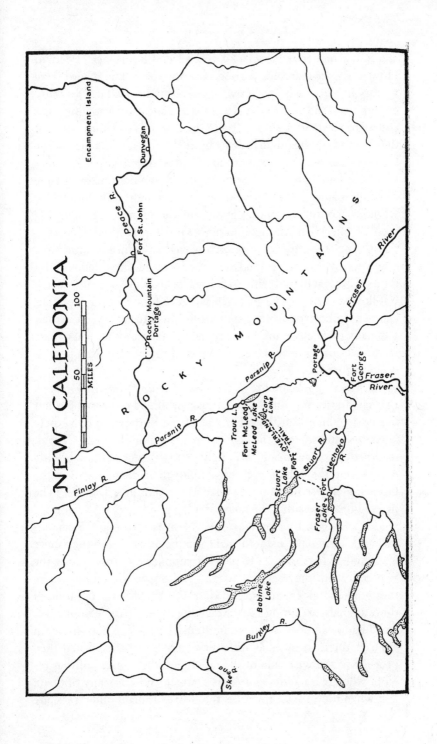

but much higher than where I had several hours before left it. However after marching a good pace for some time where there was about eight inches of Snow, I at last found myself in a Swampy country, and the Sun on the eve of sitting, and I not knowing what course to steer. Soon after in these thick woods it became so dark that I could not distinguish any object above ten yards distance— however as I had nothing with me to strike fire, and without that sociable element it would be cold (besides I should run great risque of being torn to pieces by wild Beasts) I thought it best upon the whole to continue walking about till the light of the morning would come when I thought possibly I might perceive the Banks of the River as they are very high. However by chance or rather as I ought to say guided by kind and all-protecting Providence about nine OClock at night I with great joy reached the River side, which I followed down some distance where I found our People encamped about a roaring fire, and happy was I to see myself in their company once more and little inclined to take another walk alone in the Woods. During the greater part of my ramble Rain poured down in torrents.

October 17 [Wednesday]. Northwest end of Rocky Mountain Portage. In the morning Messrs. Stuart, McLeod & Myself &c. left the Fort (which is at the other end of the Portage) to come here where we find some of the People repairing four old *crazy* Canoes, in which no one would willingly embark who values his life much—but the others are still employed in bringing over the Goods. Here we begin to see lofty Mountains at a distance. [The printed text states that the men carrying goods across the portage were "assisted...by some of the Natives, who are Sicannies (Sekani). They have just returned from the other side of the Rocky Mountain, where they go to pass the summer months. During the winter season, they remain on this side of the Mountain, where they find buffaloes, moose and deer. On the other side, none of these animals, excepting a few straggling ones, are to be found.

["The Sicannies are a quiet, inoffensive people, whose situation exposes them to peculiar difficulties and distresses. When they proceed to the west side of the mountain, the Natives of that region, who are Tâcullies and Atenâs, attack and kill many of them; and when they are on this side, the Beaver Indians and Crees, are continually making war upon them. Being thus surrounded by enemies, against whom they are too feeble successfully to contend, they frequently suffer much from want of food; for when on the west side, they dare not, at all times, visit those places where fish are in plenty, and when on the east side, they are frequently afraid to visit those parts, where animals abound. They are compelled, therefore, oftentimes to subsist upon the roots, which they find in the mountains, and which barely enable them to sustain life; and their emaciated bodies frequently bear witness, to the scantiness of their fare."]

October 19 [Friday]. Yesterday, Mr. McLeod (who is a good honest generous soul) returned to his Fort, and this afternoon we embarked aboard our Canoes to continue our route and have [come] about ten Miles.

October 21 [Sunday]. One of our Canoes being so leaky that we were under the necessity of taking out its lading & put it into the other three, and the other sent back to the Portage by two of our people.

October 22 [Monday]. Snowed & Rained by turns all Day. Over take a Band of Indians, who a few Days since left the Fort to go and hunt the Beaver on the other side of the Mountain. They call themselves Sicannies [Sekani] but it is supposed that formerly they belonged and were a part of the Beaver Indian Tribe—who on some quarrel separated themselves from their Countrymen by leaving their lands to come higher up the River & who are now as I am informed a pretty numerous Clan or Tribe. We now find ourselves in the heart of the Rocky Mountain, whose summits on either side of the River appear nearly to reach the Sky, and are by far the most lofty Mountains that I have ever seen in this or any other Country.

October 24 [Wednesday]. Although the Current has been uncommonly strong ever since we left the Rocky Mountain Portage, yet until to Day we have met with no place where we were under the necessity of unloading our Canoes in order to stem the Current. This afternoon we past Finlay's [River] or the North Branch, which appears to be about the same magnitude as the one we follow. Those two Rivers [which unite at Finlay Forks to form the Peace River] as I am informed take their rises in quite different directions from this. The source of the South west Branch [the Parsnip River] (the one we are to go up) is in the Rocky Mountains nearly two hundred Miles from where we now are, but the other runs out of a very large lake (by the Natives called Bears Lake)[54] and may be about one hundred and fifty Miles from where they form a junction, till when they both pass along the foot of the Mountain, as if in search of a place to make their passage through.

November 1 [Thursday]. McLeods Lake [Fort McLeod][55] and where we find Mr. J. M. Quesnel and Dallaire—the latter past the summer here but the former has just arrived from Stuart's Lake. After leaving the Rocky Mountain Portage we have not seen a Plain or any place where the Country was not covered with thick Timber, but since we left Finlay's Branch the Country on the west side appears to lie low and level. In coming here we always followed Peace River [meaning the Peace River proper and then its south branch, the Parsnip River] until [within] about fifteen Miles of this when we left that to come up a small River [the Pack River] which is not more than five or Six Rods broad, which runs through a small Lake [Tudyah Lake] a little below this. The Indians who frequent this Establishment are also Sicannies [Sekani], and belong to the same Tribe as those who take their Hunts to the Rocky Mountain Portage. Their dialect differs little from that spoken by the Beaver Indians—but they appear to be a wretched starving People, and as I am told are often drove to the necessity of living upon Roots, as there are few large Animals in this part of the Country, and the depth of Snow is too great in the Winter (for they generally have from four to Six feet) for them to kill many Beaver in that Season, neither can they at that time of the year take many Fish. Yet they would not willingly leave this part of the Country to go anywhere else—which is natural, for almost every person is

[54]This huge lake, shown as Great Bear Lake on Harmon's own map, did not exist. The Finlay River originates in the relatively small Thutade Lake. The river was first explored by Samuel Black, of the Hudson's Bay Company in 1824. His journal was published in 1955 by the Hudson's Bay Record Society.

[55]Fort McLeod, established by Simon Fraser and John Stuart in 1805, is the oldest continuously occupied settlement west of the Rocky Mountains in Canada. It was named in honour of Archibald Norman McLeod, Harmon's friend and superior officer at Alexandria in 1800-1.

partial to the part of the World that gave him birth, even allowing it to be ever so difficult to procure a livelyhood there. [The printed text adds: "Small white fish and trout are here taken; but those who reside here subsist, during the greater part of the year, on dried salmon, which are brought in the winter, on sledges, drawn by dogs, from Stuart's Lake."]

November 2 [Friday]. We have past the Day in examining the property we brought here, and in giving ou loads to our People to take on their backs to Stuarts Lake over land, as the distance is too great to go there by water (espetially at this late Season) for to go there in a Canoe would take twelve or fifteen Days, whereas through the Woods a person can easily reach there the Sixth Day after leaving this with a load of fifty or Sixty pounds weight on his back.

STUART'S LAKE

November 8 [Thursday]. Stuart's Lake, where Mr. Quesnel myself and thirteen labouring Men arrived this afternoon, having left McLeods Lake on the third, where Mr. Stuart intends passing the ensuing Winter. Our road here has been over an uneven Country, generally covered with thick Timber—however we past several small Lakes, but saw one about Six Miles long [Carp Lake]. This Fort stands in a very pleasant place at the East end of what is now called Stuart's Lake, and is as I am informed about one hundred Miles long[56] and from three to fifteen broad. Within about two hundred Rods of the Fort a considerable River runs out of the Lake, where the Natives who call themselves *Tâ cul lies* have a Village or rather a few small Huts made of wood and where they remain during the Salmon time—that is while they are taking and drying those Fish, but this Season very few came up this River [the Stuart River].

November 11 [Sunday]. Mr. Quesnel accompanied by ten common Men with a small assortment of Goods have gone to reestablish Frasers Lake, which place lies about fifty Miles from this,[57] and where we understand that the Natives this fall dried a considerable quantity of Salmon. I have also sent People to the other side of this Lake in hopes they may take a few White Fish, notwithstanding the Season for them is nearly past.

November 14, Wednesday. The Lake opposite the Fort is frozen over, and Mr. Stuart &c. arrived from McLeods Lake.

November 17, Saturday. We now have about eight inches of Snow on the Ground.

---

[56]As usual, Harmon exaggerates; its length is about 50 miles. Stuart Lake was named by Simon Fraser in honour of John Stuart. The name of the post on the lake was changed to Fort St. James in 1822.

[57]The distance is about 30 miles. The lake was named after Simon Fraser, who built the first post there in 1806. Later the establishment was known as Fort Fraser, and the modern community carries that name.

November 18, Sunday. Mr. Stuart &c. are gone to Frasers Lake and whom I accompanied to the other side of this, where I saw all the Indians of this Village & who may amount to about ninety Souls—and a ragged set of People they appear to be, and who as I am informed speak much the same dialect as the Sicannies [Sekani]—who no doubt formerly were one and the same Tribe.

November 24 [23], Monday. The Corpse of a Woman of this place who died on the 20th Inst. was burnt this afternoon as it is the custom among the *Tâ cullies* or Carriers always to burn their Dead and then gather up the Ashes, which they put into a kind of Box, that is placed under a Shed erected for that purpose—but while the Corpse was burning the Natives made a terrible Savage noise, by crying and a kind of Singing.

December 3, Monday. Several Days since Mr. Stuart &c. returned from Frasers Lake, and tells me that while he was there they purchased five thousand Salmon, and it was though [thought] that Mr. Quesnel would be able to procure a few more there and at a neighbouring Village which will be a sufficiency for all of our People for the Winter. Mr. Stuart is returned to McLeods Lake.

December 29, Saturday. Frasers Lake. On the 25th Mr. Stuart arrived at Stuart's Lake and the Day following we both accompanied by nine of our Men sat off for this place where we arrived this afternoon and find Mr. Quesnel &c. The road to this place is over a rough Country covered with thick Timber, but [we] saw several small lakes. This Fort stands at the East end of what is now called Frasers Lake (from the Gentleman of that name [Simon Fraser] who first made an Establishment here) and about a Mile from this there runs a considerable River out of the Lake [the Nechako River], where the Natives have a Village, and is where they take and dry Salmon. This Lake may be about eighty Miles in circumference.

1811

January 1, Tuesday. This being the first Day of the year our People have past it as is customary for them—Drinking & fighting. Some of the principal Indians of the place desired us to allow them to remain at the Fort to see our People drink, but as soon as they began to be intoxicated and quarrel among themselves, the Natives were apprehensive that something unpleasant might befall them also, therefore they hid themselves under beds & elsewhere, and said they thought the White People had become mad. But those who were in the fore part of the Day the most Beastly, became in the afternoon to be the quietest, they therefore observed that their senses had returned to them again, at which change they appeared to be not a little surprised.

January 4, Friday. Severe cold weather. Messrs. Stuart and Quesnel &c. are gone to *Stillâ* (which place lies about fifteen Miles from this at the other end of this Lake) to trade Salmon &c.

January 10 [15], Tuesday. Messrs. Stuart & Quesnel are returned from *Stillâ* and say they have purchased the quantity of Salmon required for the Season.

January 18, Friday. Messrs. Stuart and Quesnel have set off for their respective homes, the former to McLeods & the latter to Stuarts Lakes, but I shall remain here [Frasers Lake] till the beginning of April.

January 27, Sunday. The Natives have burnt the Corpse of one of their Chiefs who died the beginning of this Month. One of his Nieces shortly after his death, painted her face Vermilion and in other respect arrayed herself in the gayest manner possible, which conduct her Mother observed, and upbraided her for such unbecoming behaviour so soon after the dissolution of her Uncle, by telling her that she ought rather to paint or daub her face with black and cut off her hair, but those reproaches she took so much to heart that soon after she went into the Woods (no great distance from the Village) where she hung herself to the limb of a Tree, but fortunately for her, soon after people past that way, and saw her in that sad condition when they ran and took her down, but senseless, however shortly after she recovered, and is now to all appearance as well as ever, but I presume little inclined to tie the Cord a second time about her neck. Instances of *Women's* hanging themselves often occurs in this Country, among all the different Tribes with whom I have been acquainted, but it is seldom that any of the *Men* attempt suicide.

January 30, Wednesday. Night before last an Indian came a [and] cut a hole in one of the windows (as they are of Parchment) of my Room which is not more than two feet from the foot of my bed, where I there lay but asleep, and took from off the Table several articles of clothing—however the next morning two other Indians brought me back part of the stollen property, and told me who the thief was and where I could find him. Soon after I accompanied by my Interpreter, went and found the young Rascal in a Hut made under the Ground, along with about a dozen of others who are as great Thieves as him himself. However I told him that as he was still young I hoped it was the first time he had ever stollen and that if he returned the property he had taken away I would for once forgive him, but that if he was for the future to be guilty of any misbehaviour towards us that he might depend upon being severely punished—and I then returned to our House (for as yet we have not Palisades about them) and soon after two Indians brought me the remainder of the stollen property—and to whom I gave a little ammunition, as a recompense for having declared the Thief. Almost all the Carriers are much given to pilfering, but there are few among them who dare steal from us.

February 15, Friday. Yesterday and today we have found the cold more intense than at any other time this Season.

March 9, Saturday. Three Men arrived from Peace River with Letters from that quarter.

March 18, Monday. My Interpreter (Baptiste Bouché) has taken to Wife the Daughter of one of the Carrier Chiefs & she is the first Woman of that Tribe kept by any of the White People.

April 5, Friday. Stuarts Lake. In the morning I abandoned Frasers Lake and this evening arrived here with part of my People & the remainder will cast up tomorrow.

April 15, Monday. Fine pleasant weather—and to all appearance we shall have an early Spring. Swans and Ducks (of several kinds) have past the Winter with us, but it is only now that Bustards begin to come about.

April 21, Sunday. A few Days ago I sent the most of our People to McLeods Lake to prepare for the voyage to Rainy Lake—and tomorrow I shall accompanied by Mr. Quesnel &c. set off for the above mentioned place and take along with me my Son George, in order to send him to my friends who are in the United States, that he may be in time instructed in the Christian Religion. From this to Montreal Mr. J. M. Quesnel will have the care of him.

April 24, Wednesday. McLeods Lake, and where we find Mr. Stuart &c. busy in preparing for the voyage to the Rainy Lake, however the Spring does not appear to be so far advanced here as it did at Stuarts Lake.

May 8, Wednesday. People arrived from Stuarts Lake and inform me that my Woman on the 25th Ult. was brought to bed of a Daughter—whom I name Polly Harmon. As the Ice in the River begins to be bad, it is expected that a few Days hence the navigation will be open, when Messrs. Stuart & Quesnel &c. will embark with the Returns for the Rainy Lake. Dallaire remains here and tomorrow I shall set off for Stuarts Lake where God willing I shall pass the ensuing Summer—but all my most serious thoughts are taken up on reflecting on the separation which is so soon to take place with me and my beloved Son—who a few months hence will be at such an immense distance from his affectionate Father! And it is very probable I shall never see him again in this World! What can be more trying to the feelings of an affectionate Parent than thus to be separated from so young and so tender a Darling Child? There is no consideration that could induce me to send him down (especially while so young) but the thoughts that he soon will be in the arms of my kind Relations who will have it more in their power to bring him up in the paths of virtue in the civilized part of the World, than it would be possible for me to do in this Savage Country—and as I do what I flatter myself will in the end be to his advantage, so I also earnestly pray our Gracious God to protect him while in this world of trouble and sin & bless him in the next. Amen.

May 12 [Sunday]. Stuarts Lake, where I this afternoon arrived, after having past four [of] the most disagreeable Days I ever experienced, owing greatly to my late separation with my darling Son, and in part to the uncommon bad Roads, as we have the most of the way three feet of Snow, which owing to the mild weather became very soft and of course made it very fatiguing walking, but I am happy to see myself at last at a place where I can get a little repose after such an unpleasant jaunt.

May 14, Tuesday. All hands busily employed in clearing away the rubbish from a piece of Ground for a Garden.

May 21, Tuesday. This afternoon the Ice in this Lake broke up—and Musquetoes [mosquitoes] begin to come about and troublesome fellows they are.

May 22, Wednesday. Planted our Potatoes & sewed Barley & Turnip Seeds &c. [The printed text adds that these seeds were "the first that we ever sowed, on this west side of the mountain."] We now take out of the Lake Trout pretty plentifully with Hooks & Lines but are none of the best. [The printed version continues: "It is, perhaps, a little remarkable, that pike or pickerel have never been found in any of the lakes and rivers, on the west side of the Rocky Mountain."]

May 31, Friday. Sent two of my People to put up the body of a House at McLeods Lake, when done they will return to this place and complete this, for which I this Spring got Boards sawed.

June 11, Tuesday. Three Indians arrived from *Sy-cus* (a Village lying about four Days march down this River) who say there is an extraordinary powerful Being on his way here from the Sea, and when he arrives will transform me into a Stone, and do many other wonderful and miraculous deeds—and all those reports the Natives are so simple and credulous as to believe—yet they think that I or any one who can read and write is able by looking into our Books to take the life from any one we please let the distance be ever so great between him and us. And they as fully believe that we can make it fair or foul weather at pleasure, therefore whenever they are desirous of going any considerable distance from this Village they previous to their departure will come to ask us to allow or make it fair weather during their jaunt, and for which service they will promise a recompense. But I have often told them it is that Being alone who made the Sun, Moon, Stars, and this World and every thing that is in it Who has power or influence over the wind & weather as well as of the lives of His Creatures &c. and yet none of them appear to believe me.

June 16, Sunday. Our Indians who about the middle of April (as I am informed they are wont to do every year about that Season) left their Village to go and live upon fish that they take out of the small Lakes no great distance from this now begin to come in as they say the season has arrived that they cannot take fish at those places. Therefore they are going to other Lakes to fish. The Nets they make use of are made of the inner Bark of the Willow Tree or

Nettles which answer full as well for fishing as those we have made of Twine or Thread. A number of Indians arrived from the other end of this Lake in Six Canoes and among them were two the Father and Son belonging to a Tribue who call themselves *Nâte-ote-tains* [Nataotens],[58] and are the first of that nation ever saw here. But they say they are a numerous Tribe who are scattered over a large tract of Country almost west of this, and that it is not more than eight or ten Days march to their first Village. They also inform us of a large River that passes through their Country, and no great distance from there it disembogues [discharges] into the Pacific Ocean. They likewise say that every Autumn a number of White People come up that River in Barges to traffic with the Indians who live along its banks but I could not learn from them of what Nation those white people belong. However I imagine they are my Countrymen [Americans] who came round Cape Horn to make Coasting-trades—for I cannot learn that they attempt to make Establishments.

July 2, Tuesday. Yesterday five Sicannies [Sekani] from McLeods Lake came here and who form a small War party. Their Chief or head Man desired me to allow them to go wherever they thought proper upon which demand I asked them what course they wished to steer and what they intended to do. He said that when they left their lands their intentions were to go and take a Scalp or two from the Indians of Frasers Lake. I then desired him to tell me whether he thought we supplied them with Guns & Ammunition &c. to destroy their fellow creatures or to enable them to hunt the Beaver, and that if they were in the fall to bring in a hundred Scalps, they would not get a pint of Rum nor a Pipe of Tobacco for them whereas if they brought Beaver they would get their necessaries. After they had reflected for a few moments on what I had said to them, they told me they would follow my advice by returning to hunt the Beaver.

July 6, Saturday. One of my Men has returned from McLeods Lake and says there are Indians lurking about that place, who as is supposed are watching a favourable opportunity to attack the Fort.

[58]The Nataotens, a Babine tribe, lived in the region around Lake Babine. The river referred to in the succeeding sentences would be the Skeena and its tributary, the Bulkley.

July 29, Monday. The Poires begin to ripen. I am just returned from McLeods Lake, where I went to see what was going forward there—but could get no tidings of those Indians who had been lurking about the Fort.

August 2, Friday. Five Salmon is all the Provisions we have in the Fort & we are no less than ten persons neither can we at this Season take fish out of this Lake, and what will be come of us unless the Salmon begin soon to make their appearance in the River. However we cannot believe that we shall be allowed to starve.

August 10, Saturday. Sent all of our People Men, Women & Children to gather Berries at *Pinchy* (a Village about twelve Miles from this) where as I am informed there is a small Lake out of which the Natives take a small Fish that very much resembles Salmon both in shape and taste but are not more than six inches long, yet very palatable but were they so or not people in our condition will find them not bad.

August 22, Thursday. One of the Natives has taken a Salmon therefore it is to be hoped that in a few Days they will be plentiful—and were it not for the Salmon that come up these Rivers every year more or less, the natives would be truly miserable, as they have little else that they can depend upon for subsistance.

September 2, Monday. We now have Salmon in abundance which the Natives take in the following manner:—They make a Dam across the River and at certain places leave spaces, where they put a kind of long Basket Net, which generally is about fifteen feet in circumferrence & fifteen or twenty in length, one end of which is made like a wire Mouse Trap, & into that the Salmon enter, but when once in cannot go out, till the Basket is taken ashore, when they open a Door made for that purpose & turn them out, and in one of those Baskets they often will take four or five hundred Salmon that will weigh from five to seven pounds each—but the Natives often Spear them as they come up the River, however this way is attended with much more labour for a person must be accustomed, to Spear two or three hundred in a Day. Just as they are taken out of the water they are good eating, but when cured as these Indians are wont to do by drying them in the Sun, they are not at all palatable, but the wretched Natives when they have a plenty of them appear to be contended & even happy, while they (both Men & Women) pass the greater part of their time at play [i.e., gambling], and often loose the last rag of clothes about them without even complaining—nay they are even proud of having lost every thing!

September 12, Thursday. We now begin to take a larger kind of Salmon, which will weigh from thirty to seventy pounds. As soon as the Salmon come into this Lake they go up the small Rivers & Brooks that fall into it where they soon die, and are at some places in such great numbers that they cause for a considerable distance around a terrible stench—but the Natives often even in that condition gather them up to eat & even appear to like them better than good Salmon.

September 17, Tuesday. Between nine and ten OClock this forenoon, the Sun was eclipsed for nearly a half an hour, at which circumstance the Natives were much alarmed for they looked upon it as a bad omen or as a foreboding of some evil that would shortly befall them—therefore they began crying and made a terrible Savage noise but their Priest or Magician took handfulls of Swans Down and threw or rather blew it up towards the Sun and implored that luminary to accept the offering to put upon his Sons head, but to spare the Indians for they suppose the Sun has Children, and they like the Carriers are fond of putting Swansdown on their heads when they dance. But when I had informed them of the real cause of the darkness they appeared to be pleased and said the way I accounted for it appeared reasonable, but were much surprised and astonished that I should have a knowledge (as they expressed themselves) of such hidden things.

September 23, Monday. Bustards begin to come from the Northward. In the fore part of the Day I gave a tolerable *decent* beating to the Chief of this Village—but he is the first Indian that I ever lifted my hand to strike although this is the eleventh year that I have been in this Savage Country! But few I believe can with truth say so much.

[The printed text includes a lengthy description of this event, which involved the famous Carrier chief whose name is usually spelled *Kwah:* "The following circumstances attended this transaction. The name of the Indian, who was chastised, was Quâs. He had a friend, who was a worthless fellow, to whom he wished me to advance goods on credit, which I declined doing for two reasons. The first was, that I did not believe that the Indian would ever pay me for them. The other was, that Quâs wished to make the Indians believe, that he had a great deal of influence over us, which would be prejudicial to our interest, if he should effect it. He tried every method, which he could devise, to persuade me to advance the goods, but to no purpose; for I perceived what was his object. He then told me, that he saw no other difference between me and himself, but this only: 'you,' said he, 'know how to read and write; but I do not. Do not I manage my affairs as well, as you do yours? You keep your fort in order, and make your slaves,' meaning my men, 'obey you. You send a great way off for goods, and you are rich and want for nothing. But do not I manage my affairs as well as you do yours? When did you ever hear that Quâs was in danger of starving? When it is the proper season to hunt the beaver, I kill them; and of their flesh I make feasts for my relations. I, often, feast all the Indians of my village; and, sometimes, invite people from afar off, to come and partake of the fruits of my hunts. I know the season when fish spawn, and, then send my women, with the nets which they have made, to take them. I never want for any thing, and my family is always well clothed.' In this manner the fellow proceeded, for a considerable time.

["I told him that what he had said, concerning himself and his family, was true; yet, I added, 'I am master of my own property, and shall dispose of it as I please,' 'Well,' said he, 'have you ever been to war?' 'No,' replied I, 'nor do I desire to take the life of any of my fellow creatures.' 'I have been to war,' continued he, 'and have brought home many of the scalps of my enemies.' I was now strongly tempted to beat him, as his object manifestly was, to intimidate me. But I wished to avoid a quarrel, which might be evil in its consequences; and especially to evince to the Indians, who were spectators of what passed between us, that I was disposed to live in peace with them.—Quâs proceeded to try me another way. He asked me if I would trust him with a small piece of cloth, to make him a breech cloth? This I consented to do, and went into the store, to measure it off. He followed me together with my interpreter, and ten or twelve other Indians. I took up a piece of cloth, and asked him, if he would have it from that? He answered, no. I then made a similar inquiry, respecting another piece, to which he made a similar reply. This persuaded me, that his only object was to provoke me to quarrel with him. I, therefore, threw down the cloth, and told him, if he would not have that, he should have this, (meaning a square yard stick which I had in my hand) with which I gave him a smart blow over the head, which cut it, considerably. I then sprang over the counter, and pelted him, for about five minutes, during which time, he continually called to his companions, all of whom had knives in their hands, to come and take me off. But, they replied that they could not, because there were two other white people in the room, who would prevent them. It was happy for us that these Indians stood in such fear of us; for there were only four white men, at this time in the fort, and they could easily have murdered us.—As Quâs and his company left us, he told me that he would see me again tomorrow, when the sun should be nearly in the south, meaning between ten and twelve o'clock."]

October 7, Monday. [In the printed text the entry for this date begins as follows: "The next day after I chastised the Indian, as above described, he sent one of his wives to request me, either to come and see him, or to send him some medicine. I, therefore, sent him some salve, with which to dress the wound in his head.—A few days after, he became so well as to be able to hunt; and he killed and brought home a number of beavers, with which he yesterday made a feast. He sent an invitation to me to attend this feast; and I concluded that it would be necessary for me to go, or he might think that I was afraid of him. I, accordingly, put a brace of pistols in my pocket, and hung a sword by my side, and directed my interpreter to arm himself in a similar manner, and to accompany me." In the original journal, Harmon simply describes the feast itself.] Yesterday I was invited to a Feast by the Chief to whom I a few Days before had given a beating, and another from *Pinchy* [the Indian village about twelve miles away]—and after we were all seated in a large Hut, the first thing presented was a whole boiled Beaver, which one of the Chiefs held in both hands standing, while I ate what I thought proper, then he passed on and done the same to my Interpreter, but when he had ate what he chose the Chief gave to eat in the same manner to all the Indians who were seated in the circle. After him followed the other Chief with the whole of a Beaver and done the same as the first and in this manner they continued to make the round till a part of each Beaver had been eaten that was intended for the entertainment. But now the Women came in with large Dishfulls of Berries, and of them every one ate what he liked and then the Men & Women joined in singing a few Songs—the airs of which were not altogether unpleasant to the ears of Civilized People, but as soon as their Songs were over, each person retired with a Dish full of Berries that had been placed before him. Before the Chief began to go round with his Beaver, he stood up in the middle of the Hut and in an audable voice made an harangue, in which he did not forget to make mention of the late beating he had got from me—and said that if it had been given him by any other but me, he most assuredly would either have lost his own life or taken that of the others—but now he said he considered himself as my *Wife*, for added he that was the way he served his Women (and of whom he has no less than four) when they misbehaved—and that he thanked me for what I had done to him for he said I had given him sense—but he told the Indians that if he heard of any of them laughing at him for having got a beating he should repent of his untimely mirth—and a Braver Indian than he is I do not know of ever having seen. [The printed text describes Harmon's response to the Chief's speech: "To this I replied, that, in a remote country, I had left my friends and relations, who wanted for none of the good things of this world, and had come a great distance, with such articles as the Indians greatly needed, and which I would exchange for their furs, with which I could purchase more; and in this way, I could always supply their necessities; that I considered the Indians as my children, and that I must chastise them when they behaved ill, because it was for their good. 'You all know,' said I, 'that I treat good Indians well, and that I strive to live in peace with you.'— 'Yes,' replied the father-in-law to the chief, 'Big Knife [the name given by the Indians to Harmon] speaks the truth. My son had no sense, and vexed him, and therefore deserved the beating which he has received.'"]

October 12, Saturday. For the three last Days it has constantly Snowed & fell nearly two feet.

October 21, Monday. We now have 25,000 Salmon in our Store which will be a sufficiency for all hands till next. Autumn—four per Day is what is allowed for a Man. Sent People to fish for White Fish.

October 31, Thursday. Two Men arrived from McLeods Lake and delivered me several Letters—one of which from Mr. James McDougall who accompanied our people from Rainy Lake—and who informs me that the Canoes were stopped by the Ice on the 12th Inst. about three Days march below McLeods Lake and where they of course still are as well as the property they had on board.

November 16, Saturday. Our Fishermen are returned to the Fort and inform me that they have taken 7000 White Fish in the Nine Nets of Sixty Fathoms long each.

November 17, Sunday. Clear and cold. Last night the Lake opposite the Fort froze over, but the most of the Snow that was on the ground is now dissolved.

December 13, Friday. On the 20th Ult. I with twenty of our People set off to go and bring the Goods to the Fort that remained last October along the way—and while at McLeods Lake I sent two Men with Letters to Peace River. Mr. McDougall &c. come here to pass the Holy-Days with us. [The printed text continues: "Our goods were drawn on sledges by dogs. Each pair of dogs drew a load of from two hundred, to two hundred and fifty pounds, besides provisions for themselves and their driver, which would make the whole load about three hundred pounds. I have seen many dogs, two of which would draw on a sledge, five hundred pounds, twenty miles, in five hours. For a short distance, two of our stoutest dogs will draw more than a thousand pounds weight. In short, there is no animal, with which I am acquainted, that would be able to render half the service that our dogs do, in this country, where the snow is very deep in the winter season. They sink but little into it, in following a person on snow shoes."]

1812

January 1, Wednesday. This being the first Day of the year, Mr. McDougall & I Dined with all of our People in the Hall, and after our repast was over I invited several of the Sicanny [Sekani] and Carrier Chiefs & most respectable Men among them, to come and partake of what we had remaining—and I must acknowledge that I was surprised to see them behave with so much decency & even propriety as they did in drinking off a Flaggon or two of Rum, and after their repast was over they smoaked their Pipes and conversed rationally on the great difference there is between the manners & customs of Civilized People and those of Savages. [The printed text adds: "They readily conceded, that ours are superior to theirs."]

January 7, Tuesday. On the 4th Inst. I accompanied by several of our People sat off for Tachy a Village towards the other end of this [Stuarts] Lake, and where we saw a number of Indians who appear to be extremely indolent, and are of course wretchedly cloathed and not better fed. From where we went up a considerable River [probably the upper Stuart River] about half a Days march, where we came to another Village whose Inhabitants appear to be mostly Sicannies [Sekani], and who appear to be more industrious than the last mentioned People and therefore better cloathed and fed.

January 13, Monday. On the 9th Inst. A sicanny died at this place and today his Corpse was burnt in the following manner:— The Corpse was placed on a pile of dry wood with its face upwards, which was painted and bare, but the body was covered with a Robe made of Beaver Skins, his Gun, Powder Horn as well as such trinkets as he possessed when alive were placed by his side—but just before they set fire to the pile of wood, one of his Brothers asked him if he would ever come among them again (for they suppose that the Deceased can if they chuse come back upon the face of the Earth but in other bodies—therefore they must believe in the immortality of the Soul since they suppose that *that* part never dies, but is progressively changing its situation ie: leaving one body to enter into that of another). The Deceased had two Wives, who were placed one at the head and the other at the foot of the Corpse and there they remained till nearly all of the hair of their heads were consumed by the flames when they rolled on the ground almost senseless, but as soon as they had a little recovered their strength, they stood up and began to slap the breast of the Corpse with the palms of their hands one after the other and that disgusting Savage ceremony was continued till the Corpse was nearly consumed— but they were often interrupted by faintings, occasioned by the great heat of the fire. However if they did not arise soon the relations of the Deceased would take them up by the hair of their heads and push them into the flames and thus oblige them to continued striking upon the Corpse—and when it was entirely consumed the Women gathered up the Ashes into a Box, which is put under a Shed erected for that purpose in the centre of the Village.

[The printed text concludes quite differently: "When the body was nearly burned to ashes, the wives of the deceased gathered up these ashes, and the remaining pieces of bones, which they put into bags. These bags they will be compelled to carry upon their backs, and to lay by their sides, when they lie down at night, for about two years. The relations of the deceased will then make a feast, and enclose these bones and ashes in a box, and deposit them under a shed, erected for that purpose, in the centre of the village. Until this time, the widows are kept in a kind of slavery, and are required to daub their faces over with some black substance, and to appear clothed with rags, and frequently to go without any clothing, excepting round their waists. But, at the time of this feast, they are set at liberty from these disagreeable restraints."]

January 20 [30]. Thursday. On the 17th Inst. I accompanied by Mr. McDougall & twelve of our People and also two Carriers, sat off for the *Nâte-ote-tains* [Nataotens] Lands and Tribe who never had any intercourse with White People & after searching hard Seven Days generally upon Lakes we arrived at their first Village whose inhabitants were not a little surprised and alarmed to see People among them of so different a complexion from themselves. As their Village stands on the border of a long Lake they perceived us at a considerable distance & came out to meet us (Men & Women) armed some with Bows & Arrow & others with Axes or Clubs &c. However they did not attempt to do us the least injury, but they made many savage gestures, as if in defyance. But after we told them we had not come to war upon them, but to bring them such articles as they stood in need of, in exchange for their Furs we ever after were treated with much respect and great hospitality. The Day following we proceeded further on and during our jaunt saw four others of their Villages and at all of which we were well received for at the second we found the two Indians who last Summer came to our Fort therefore they were not much surprised to see us among them, for I had promised the two that I would in the course of this Winter pay them a visit to see their Country &c. and they now gave us some account of the White People who came up the large River as they had done before when at the Fort last Summer and to convince us that what they had said was true they showed us many articles, which they barter from their Neighbours the *Atenâs* who purchase them directly from the white people which were Guns, Cloth, Blankets, Axes and cast Iron Pots &c. At the five Villages we visited we might have seen two thousand Souls, who are well made and appeared healthy, but they like the Carriers subsist principally on Salmon & other small Fish. Their cloathing was much the same as that of the Carriers. They let me have vessels curiously and ingeniously wrought of the smaller Roots of a Species of the Pine Tree, and are made into different shapes and sizes, some like that of an open Kettle, which serves to put water &c. in—and they also let me have a Blanket or Rug which was manufactured by the *Atenâs*, of the wool of the Sheep that are numerous on the Mountains in their Country. They told us that we saw but a small part of the *Nâte-ote-tains* for added they 'we are a numerous Tribe." They have a dialect peculiar to themselves, yet the most of them speak the tongue spoken by the Carriers. [The printed text adds: "The country, which we travelled over, in this route, is generally level. Few mountains are to be seen. A heavy growth of timber evinces, that the soil is good.—We saw no large animals, excepting the cariboo; but we were informed, that black bears, and other kinds of the larger animals, exist in considerable numbers, in that region."]

February 4, Tuesday. Mr. McDougall and Family &c. have set off to return to McLeods Lake, but while he was here I past my time pleasantly in his agreeable company, for he wishes to please & therefore does please.

February 9, Sunday. Three Men arrived from Peace River with Letters from Gentlemen in the different parts of the Country and two from my friends below, which bring me truly melancholy news. They inform me that my poor Brother Joseph is no more! but was carried off by the Consumption, after having for several years been troubled with that lingering complaint! However I am happy to find they can add that from the exemplary life he lead for a considerable time before he met his dissolution, they have all reason to hope and believe his change of Worlds has been a happy one to him—he having left a world of trouble & sin for that where blessed Spirits go! And such a belief surely is the greatest consolation that he possibly could have left his bereaved Friends who lament his premature end. How fast my dear Relations are called to their eternal home! Which are grievous events that ought to serve to remind the survivors that we also must soon (and who knows how soon) follow them to the silent and gloomy abode! And therefore it becomes necessary to set about in earnest to prepare ourselves with the assistance of Gods holy Spirit to meet that awful event on which our eternal welfare must depend! Happy are those who are wise in time!

February 23, Sunday. I am just returned from a jaunt of eight Days to Frasers Lake and Stillâ, but nothing worthy remark occurred to us during our trip. Wherever we went the Natives as usual appeared pleased to see us consequently we ever met with kind receptions. [The printed text notes that Stillâ lay "about twenty miles beyond" Frasers Lake.]

February 26 [28], Friday. Sent two men to Peace River with Letters to Gentlemen in that part of the World.

March 26, Thursday. I am just returned from paying Mr. McDougall a visit at McLeods Lake. While [during] my stay with him there fell about a foot of Snow which of course made our Roads bad.

April 6, Monday. Six Indians arrived from Frasers Lake and delivered me a Letter wrote by Mr. David Thompson, dated August 28th, 1811, *Ilk-koy-ope* Falls [Kettle Falls] Columbia River—which informs me that he accompanied by Seven Canadians last Spring descended the above mentioned River to where it empties itself into the Pacific Ocean, and where they arrived on the 16th of July and found a number of people building a large Fort for the American Company or rather Astor & Co. [meaning the Pacific Fur Company][59] and that Mr. Alexander McKay &c. (one of the Partners but formerly for the North West Co.) had gone to the Northward, in the vessel [the *Tonquin*] that brought them out, on a

[59]Fort Astoria, at the mouth of the Columbia River. The forts and trading interests of the Pacific Fur Company were purchased in the fall of 1813 by the North West Company, and the post was then renamed Fort George. Harmon refers to the purchase in the entry dated Feb. 4, 1814.

coasting-trade.[60] Mr. Thompson Writes that after having remained Seven Days with the American People he set off to return to his Establishments which are nigh the source of the Columbia River and from whence he wrote the above mentioned letter, and delivered it to an Indian to bring it to the next Tribe, that they might forward it to the next and so on till it reached this place, which manner of conveyance accounts for the great length of time it has been on its way, for the distance is not so great but the People might come from there in a Months time at most.

May 11, Monday. This morning I returned from McLeods Lake where I had been to send off our People who are to go to the Rainy Lake and while I was there one of our men (Pierre Lambert) in crossing a small Lake on a Sledge fell through the Ice & was drowned before any of his companions who were not far off could reach the place where he was, to give him the necessary assistance. The Day following his Corpse was brought and buried nigh the Fort. On my way home I had exceeding bad roads as is usually the case at this Season for we had about three feet of Snow on the Ground and such Mild weather as made it become very soft and to make bad worse about ten Miles from this I left my Guides to come on ahead but had not come far before I got out of my way (there being no path) yet I might have returned back upon my tracks but that I was loth to do (for I never like to do a thing twice over) so I wandered about the remainder of the Day, and as the night came on I found myself in a thick wood, however I struck up a fire ad smoaked my Pipe, but had nothing to eat. I past the night in reflecting on my unpleasant condition for any person must I think pass disagreeable moments, when he does not know where he is or what course to steer to reach his home for I had now passed several places where there was no snow therefore I could not follow my tracks back however this morning I rose early and I left my fire, but without knowing what direction to take, and to make things worse it was cloudy & rained hard, but before I had gone far I perceived a Hill at no great distance, which I with not a little difficulty ascended, (as there I had more than three feet of Snow) but from its

[60]The *Tonquin* never returned from her trading cruise. In June 1811—ten months before Harmon received Thompson's letter—she was seized by the Indians in Clayoquot Sound, Vancouver Island, and all her crew were killed.

summit fortunately for me I could see this Lake, for which place I took my course and several hours after with much joy reached the Fort where I returned sincere thanks to kind Providence for having directed my steps to where I find my home and Family. [In the printed text, Harmon explains how he followed the correct direction after sighting the lake from the hilltop: "Having ascertained the course which I must take, I descended into the valley, and took the following method to keep in the direction of the fort. I at first marked a tree; and from that, singled out one forward of me, to which I proceeded; and by means of these two fixed upon another, in a straight line ahead; and continued the same operation, for several hours, until, with great joy, I reached the fort."]

May 21, Thursday. Last night an East wind arose and drove the remainder of the Ice to the other end of the Lake—a great part of which had been some Days free of Ice.

June 3, Wednesday. A Indian from McLeods Lake arrived with letters from Peace River that inform me of the death of Mr. Richard Campbell, who after only a few Days illness departed this life at Dunvegan on the 14th of March last, and his premature end is much lamented by all who knew him as he was a young Gentleman who bore a good Character.

June 23, Tuesday. The Natives this morning took a Sturgeon that might weight about two hundred pounds, but there are many in the Lake much larger, but the Natives had no method for taking them, neither are the Nets we have sufficiently strong to hold them.

August 15, Saturday. Salmon begin to come up this River. [The printed text adds: "As soon as one is caught, the Natives always make a feast, to express their joy at the arrival of these fish. The person, who first sees a salmon in the river exclaims, Tâ-loe nas-lay! Tâ-loe nas-lay! in English, Salmon have arrived! Salmon have arrived! and the exclamation is caught with joy, and uttered with animation, by every person in the village."]

September 2, Wednesday. Mr. McDougall &c. who arrived on the 25 Ult. this morning set off to return home. How agreeable and satisfactory it is now an [and] then to pass a few Days with a friend! Few know except those who are situated as we are, in this lonely out of the way part of the World.

October 25, Sunday. Early this morning nine Men arrived from the Rainy Lake and say two others will be here tomorrow. By them I received a number of Letters from People in this Country but not one from home!

October 26, Monday. The two men who remained along the way are arrived and delivered me several letters from home which give me more satisfaction than I know well how to express—as they inform me they left *all* my Relations blessed with good health—and that my beloved Son George had arrived *safe* among them—which are blessings I [am] full [fully] conscious within myself that I cannot be sufficiently thankful [for], unless our merciful God is graciously pleased to change my heart of Stone and give me a heart of Flesh.

November 6, Friday. We now have about Six Inches of Snow. On the 27th Ult. I sat off for McLeods Lake where I arrived the 29th and found Mr. John Stuart &c. who had cast up the Day before from Fort Chipewyan and are thus far on their way to the Columbia River down which they will descend to the Pacific Ocean in company with J. G. McTavish &c. who are to pass the ensuing Winter near the source of the above mentioned River. At the Sea it is expected they will meet Donald McTavish Esqr. &c. who last October were to sail from England round Cape Horn to the entrance of the Columbia River. This afternoon Mr. Stuart and myself &c. arrived here, where both of us shall God willing pass the ensuing winter and have with us twenty-one labouring Men & five Women &c.

December 20, Sunday. Mr. McDougall &c. arrived from McLeods Lake and are come to pass the Holy Days with us.

1813

January 23, Saturday. On the 29th Ult. Mr. Stuart and myself with the most of our People set off to go and purchase Furs & Salmon at Frasers Lake and *Stillâ*—as at this place last fall the natives did not take one fourth part of the quantity of Salmon required for us for the Season. However at the two above mentioned places we procured the quantity wanted and this afternoon returned to this place and glad to be where we can be more quiet than among Indians—although we cannot complain of them much for they behaved themselves remarkably well. [This last remark is at variance with the account given in the printed text: "While at Frazer's Lake, Mr. Stuart, our interpreter and myself, came near being massacred by the Indians of that place, on account of the interpreter's wife, who is a native of that village. Eighty or ninety of the Indians armed themselves, some with guns, some with bows and arrows, and others with axes and clubs, for the purpose of attacking us. By mild measures, however, which I have generally found to be the best, in the management of the Indians, we succeeded in appeasing their anger, so that we suffered no injury; and we finally separated, to appearance, as good friends, as if nothing unpleasant had occurred. Those who are acquainted with the disposition of the Indians, and who are a little respected by them, may, by humouring their feelings, generally, controul them, almost as they please."]

STUART'S LAKE TO DUNVEGAN AND RETURN

February 12, Friday. McLeods Lake [Fort McLeod], and am thus far on my way to Peace River & have along with me five Canadians and a Carrier [Indian]. I shall God willing go as far as Dunvegan to transact business with Mr. John McGillivray.

February 21, Sunday. Rocky Mountain Portage, where we arrived this afternoon. As the Mountains along the River on both sides are very high for about three Days march there generally is a strong wind passing either up or down the current, and at this Season renders it extreme cold and disagreeable travelling and on the 18th we were in the heart of those Mountains and had such a strong head wind that my upper lip became frozen even without my perceiving it at the time, but it is now much swollen and very painful, that together with a severe cold I caught (as well as all those who are with me) the second night after leaving Stuarts Lake renders me almost incapable of speaking loud enough to make myself understood. Here we find only two Canadians, as Mr. A. R. McLeod who has the superintendence of this Post is now absent to his Hunters Lodge, which is at a distance of five Days march from this, as there are few or no Animals hereabouts, which is owing as I imagine to the great depth of Snow that always falls in this quarter it being so nigh the Mountains. The people who are here told us that last fall their Hunters had such difficulty in finding Animals of any kind that they actually went five Days without eating!

February 25, Thursday. St. Johns [Fort St. John], having left the Rocky Mountain Portage on the 22nd we reached this yesterday where we found Mr. A. McGillivray &c. who informs me that they do not want for the Staff of life as Moose, Deer & Buffaloe are tolerably plentiful hereabouts. My frozen lip and cold now trouble me more than when I left the Rocky Mountain Portage and was it not absolutely necessary that I should proceed farther down the River, I most assuredly should not leave my Bed.

March 1, Monday. Dunvegan, where I have at length reached and where I past the years 1809 & 10—and to visit a place where I had remained so long, causes many a pleasing reflection to arise in my mind—such as the many agreeable hours I past in pleasing conversation with the Gentlemen who were then here &c. Here I find Mr. Collin [Colin] Campbell in charge of the Fort during the absence of Mr. John McGillivray, who is on a visit to Lesser Slave Lake. My lip is not so painful as it was and I am getting the better of my cold.

March 14, Sunday. I past my time agreeably enough either in conversing with Mr. Campbell or in reading till the 10th when I was agreeably apprized of the arrival of Mr. McGillivray &c. who appeared as pleased to find me here as I was to see him return home, since when we have conversed together and I find him to be an agreeable Companion, free, open, appears to be sincere and I have every reason to believe him to be an honest upright Man and a true Christian, which are qualities that make him one of the most worthy Characters we have in this Country. But as I now have got through the business that brought me here, I therefore shall tomorrow set off to return to New Caledonia. Here I received the news of Mackana [Mackinac, or Michilimackinac] & Niaga's [Fort Niagara] having surrendered to the British forces, but not before many valuable lives had been lost on both sides—which makes me with sorrow reflect on the many calamities that must befal numbers of my deluded Countrymen for having plunged themselves as it were into such a ruinous and as I think unnecessary a War.[61] May God protect &

[61]The War of 1812–14 between Great Britain and the United States broke out in June, 1812, Michilimackinac surrendered to a Canadian force on

preserve the guiltless, and cause a speedy opening of the Eyes of my Countrymen in general that they may see & know what is for the real interest and welbeing of America. But Buonaparte has too many of *his* diabolical Emmissaries there, who have no Countries good or welfare at heart—all their pleasure is to keep different nations in continual broils and misunderstandings, so that they (the French) while others are fighting for the Bone of contention and when either party become considerably weakened they are in hopes of being able to step up and carry it off with impunity! May God frustrate their wicked designs and cause the blast that they so long have been preparing for others to fall at least on their own guilty heads.

March 17, Wednesday. St. Johns [Fort St. John]. Having bid adieu to Dunvegan on the 15th and all of us thanks be to God enjoying tolerable health, we arrived here this evening, where we shall take Provisions to bring us to McLeods Lake.

March 21, Sunday. Rocky Mountain Portage, where we arrived this evening and I am happy in finding Mr. McLeod at home he has a good heart, and always in high spirits.

March 23, Tuesday. West end of the Rocky Mountain Portage. Yesterday was past much to my mind in the company of my friend Mr. McLeod at his Fort, but [I] sent off my people ahead to beat the road this far, and this morning I left the Fort myself in company of Mr. McLeod, who has come here to pass the night with us, but tomorrow morning we must separate he to return home and we to continue our route. How pleasing and satisfactory it is after a long separation to pass away a few hours in the company of those whom we esteem and regard!

March 31, Wednesday. McLeods Lake [Fort McLeod], where we arrived this morning & find my friend McDougall & Family enjoying good health. He informs me that nothing remarkable has occurred in this quarter during my absence.

April 4, Sunday. Stuarts Lake, and am pleased to find myself once more at home (home is home, let it be ever so homely!) but sorry and grieved to learn that my friend Stuart as well as several of our People are very unwel.

July 17. Harmon is mistaken in his reference to Niagara; the second American fort that fell to the British at this time was Detroit, which surrendered on August 16.

SECOND SOJOURN AT STUART'S LAKE

April 12, Monday. I am just returned with Mr. Stuart &c. from Frasers Lake [Fort Fraser], where nothing occurred worthy remark.

May 1, Saturday. As we have all reason to think it cannot be long before the Ice breaks up in the Rivers, to enable our People to set off for the Rainy Lake, we therefore have sent the last of them to McLeods Lake where they will embark with the Returns and by whom we forward Letters to People in this Country as well as to our Friends in the Civilized part of the World.

May 13, Thursday. Fine weather. In the fore part of the Day Mr. Stuart Six Canadians and two of the Natives embarked aboard two Canoes, and took with him a small assortment of Goods (as pocket money) and Provisions for a Month and a half, in order to go and join Mr. J. G. McTavish &c. at some place on the Columbia River, and there with them proceed down to the Sea—and should Mr. Stuart be so fortunate as to discover a water communication between this and the Columbia, we shall for the future get our yearly supply of Goods from that quarter, and send our Returns out that way, which will be shipped there directly for the China Market in Vessels which the Concern intends building on that Coast—but while those deep-laid plans are putting in execution, I in a more humble sphere it is true, but full as sure of succeeding in my undertakings shall attend to the little affairs of New Caledonia! and pass the Summer at this place. Perhaps there is no Country in the World, where people have business to attend to in order to gain their livelyhood, who have so much time to themselves as we in this Savage Country—for few of us here are employed more & many much less than one fifth of our time in transacting the business of the Concern—therefore we have at least four fifths at our disposal, and if we do not employ those leisure moments in improving our understandings it must be our fault—as there are few Posts where they are not tolerably well supplyed with Books but it is true they are not all of the best kind, however there is something to be learnt to our advantage out of every Book when read with due attention—and I often think that were I deprived of the few I have I should experience many an unpleasant & solitary hour, for even with their aid I but too often feel moments of deep melancholy especially when I begin to reflect on the great length of time I have been absent from my native land, and thus *cruelly* separated from all I hold very dear in this World. However those gloomy moments thank God are never of a long duration, neither do they occur often, for when I take time to reflect seriously on my situation, I am contented and satisfyed with the lot Providence has assigned me in this World of trouble and disappointments hoping always that I may with the aid of God's Holy Spirit so conduct myself while here below, that my Soul when it leaves this vile body may be prepared to enter that blessed abode prepared for the righteous only. Amen.

May 27, Thursday. Three Indians arrived from the Forks below [probably meaning Fort George, at the junction of the Nechako and Fraser rivers] which place lies about three Days march down the River who delivered me a Letter from Mr. Stuart & several others from Gentlemen at the Columbia River.

June 12, Saturday. A Sicanny [Sekani] just arrived who says that a little this side of McLeods Lake as he was encamping with his Family an Indian of the same Tribe rushed out of a Wood, fired and killed his Wife, whose Corpse he immediately burnt and then with his Son and two Daughters set off for this place. All Savages who have had a relation killed are never quiet till they have revenged the death by killing the murderer or some of his nigh relations—and that spirit of revenge has been the cause of the above mentioned Old Woman's having lost her life and I presume justly too. It is true she had never killed any one with her own hands but she last Summer prevailed on her Husband to go and kill the Cousin of her Murderer without any further provocation than because her Son had lately been drowned whose blood now has fallen on her own wicked head. The Indians in this quarter suppose that when any one looses his Life, it was occasioned by some of his fellow creatures—and of course strive to revenge their deaths, and is the reason why they commit so many murders.

June 20, Sunday. Yesterday an Indian of this place killed another who was here on a visit from the other end of this Lake as he was embarking in his Canoe to return home. The former stepped up and gave the latter five stabs with a Lance or hand Dag [dagger], and ripped up his belly in such a shocking manner that his entrails immediately fell upon the ground, and soon after he of course expired, and the Murderer ran off. However the Chief of the village wrapped the Corpse in the Moose Skin and sent it to its relations— but the people of this place being apprehensive that the Relations of the murdered [man] will come to war upon them, therefore tomorrow they will set off to go some distance down this River, where they will pass the greater part of the Summer—that is till Peace & quietness is reestablished between the People of the two Villages. The cause as is supposed why the murder was committed was on account of the Murderer's being jealous of his Wife (who is known to be a worthless Woman) and he suspected that the Deceased had unlawful connexions with her. All Carriers are remarkably jealous of their Wives, but to their Daughters while single they will allow every liberty!

August 12, Thursday. Salmon again begin to make their appearance in this River, which we are happy to learn for we have not Provisions in the Fort for but a very few Days, and the Natives for some time past have starved greatly. How thankful therefore ought we to be to the every bountiful Providence that watches over and supplys us with every necessary of life! Surely in so Benevolent a God we ought willingly to put our trust—and accept with grateful hearts the innumerable favours which He constantly is bestowing upon us, the least of which we by no means cannot pretend to have merited.

September 1, Wednesday. Mr. McDougall who a few Days since arrived from McLeods Lake has now gone to accompany all the People of the Fort to Pinchy who are gone there to gather Berries and I am left entirely alone, not a soul in the Fort except myself. I therefore have a favourable opportunity of turning my thoughts inwards and examine my past life—but in so doing I am struck with astonishment and grieved to find it has been so different from that of a true Christian! And those reflections bring on a remorse of conscience, and as I connive I have had a more wicked life than the most of my fellow creatures, I therefore consider it both proper and necessary that I shall henceforward *Fast & Pray* the first Day of every Month—that is to eat nothing in the morning and to pass the whole Day in prayer, reading the Bible or some other good Book and in meditation—and thus shall keep *that* fresh in my memory for which I must (on the appointed Day) render an account to my

Creator—and I pray God that through His infinite goodness, that this way of living for the future may in some manner serve to blot out my past Sins (or rather He will forgive my trespasses thro' the merits of our Blessed Redeemer) which I know to be without number—as well as be a means (with the aid of His Holy Spirit without which I am conscious I can do nothing) of keeping me in the path of virtue & holiness, and thus become prepared for the World of bliss when my Gracious Maker sees fit to call my immortal part from hence. By setting apart certain fixed Days for the purpose of examining myself & with sincerity confessing & heartily repenting of my Sins, I shall not put off the necessary task from one time to another, and by so doing should run the risque of omitting to do it at all. I also have composed two Prayers and by repeating them Daily with a sincere heart, I hope and trust that our benevolent God will vouchsafe to grant the humble requests therein mentioned.

A MORNING PRAYER.

Most Gracious God, Accept the thanks which I now presume to offer Thee, for the refreshing repose I have received this Night, as well as for thy infinite goodness in sparing me to see the light of another morning, also teach me I beseech Thee so to conduct myself throughout this Day and ever after, that I may thereby be imboldened to persevere in offering up my earnest prayers for a continuation of Thy all-powerful aid and assistance, of which I am conscious of standing so much in need to guard me against the snares and in keeping me from falling into the temptations of this World of Sin. Grant this O God, for Christ's sake, Amen.

AN EVENING PRAYER.

Most Great and Merciful God, cause I intreat Thee my polluted heart to be so changed that I may with sincerity and truth be thankful for thy innumerable past favours likewise forgive me my past trespasses and listen to my earnest prayers for a continuation of thy kind protection from the evil machinations of the wicked and keep me from falling into temptations and Sin. Also vouchsafe to grant me Thy Holy Spirit to cause me to have a willing heart to follow and live up to Thy Holy Commands that when you seest fit to call my immortal Soul to leave its present clayey tenement it will through Thy infinite though unmerited goodness & mercies and the kind intercession of our Blessed Mediator be found fit to enter that World of Bliss prepared for the Righteous only:—and to Thee and thy worthy Son our Lord Jesus Christ be all Honour and Praise and Glory world without end, Amen.

[In retrospect, Harmon evidently regarded this day as the date of his conversion, for the heavily revised account in the printed text includes the following: "Until this day, I have always doubted whether such a Saviour as the scriptures describe, ever really existed, and appeared on earth!... As I was praying to-day, on a sudden, the faith, respecting which I was so solicitous, was, I trust, graciously granted to me. My views of the Saviour, underwent a total change. I was enabled, not only to believe in his existence, but to apprehend his superlative excellency; and now he appears to be in truth, what the scriptures describe him to be, the chiefest among ten thousand, and one altogether lovely. May the grace of God enable me to follow his heavenly example through life, that I may dwell with him in glory, forever!"]

September 25, Saturday. An Indian arrived from below and delivered me three Letters from Mr. Stuart, the last of which was wrote at O-ki-na-gun [Okanagan] Lake and as he writes but a short distance from the Columbia River. A few Days previous to their arrival at the Lake they past a Fort [Kamloops, on the Thompson River] which was built last Autumn by Messrs. [Joseph] La Roque & McDonell for the North West Co. but was abandoned by them in the Spring. Mr. Stuart also writes that he had met with every kindness and assistance from the natives he saw along the way. He after descending eight Days down this River was obliged to leave his Canoes and take his property on Horses back to the above mentioned Lake [Okanagan], a distance of more than one hundred and fifty miles, but from there he writes they can go by water to the Sea,[62] by making a few short Portages, which place he expected to reach in the course of twelve or fifteen Days at the farthest—but he has other Canoes to make before he can proceed any farther on his voyage.

[62]Stuart's route is not clear. He was searching for a practicable travel route for fur and supply brigades between New Caledonia and the Columbia River. In later years the brigades bound for the coast left the Fraser River near Alexandria and proceeded overland to Kamloops. Thence they

October 1, Friday. A Prayer for the first Day of every Month. Most Beneficient God, I implore Thee to cause my deluded eyes to be opened that I may have a true sense of my present vileness in having transgressed Thy Holy Laws, and as I set this Day a part for fasting and prayer, and in meditating on my past transactions, enlighten my understanding that I may be enabled to make just reflections on my present condition, and also aid me I beseech Thee and teach me so to conduct myself henceforward that my life may be as free from sin as is consistent with my depraved nature—and as I am conscious that from the sinful life I have hitherto lead, there is nothing I can do in my own behalf, so without Thou vouchestsafe to grant thy free Grace and pardonest my transgressions through the all-sufficient merits of our Blessed Redeemer I unavoidably must though justly perish—but cause I intreat Thee so great a change to take place in my polluted heart towards Thee and all that which is Holy and good, that I may thereby be encouraged to hope I shall not be eternally cast off, but shall have my Sins forgiven me through the merits alone and for they worthy Son our Lord Jesus Christ's sake, Amen.

October 4 [14], Thursday. This afternoon we had a narrow escape from fire, occasioned by sparks flying through a chink in one of our Chimneys to the Roof of the House which is covered with bark and as dry as tinder, and unfortunately at the time we had a strong wind so that the whole Fort must in a few minutes have been consumed to ashes, had not kind Providence (Who is ever watchful over our lives & property) caused me at that critical moment to be inclined to go out of doors when I perceived a considerable part of the Roof in a blaze. However I called out to our people to bring water and shortly after the fire was extinguished, without its doing any material damage. But such a glaring instance of an interposing Providence in our behalf while in such imminent danger ought to call forth our warmest gratitude to the Author of all good.

November 7, Sunday. This afternoon Mr. Joseph La Roque &c. arrived from the Columbia River, who are this Summer at the Pacific Ocean along with Mr. J. G. McTavish &c. but on their way

---

followed the Okanagan Valley and the Okanagan River southward to the Columbia.

up the River they met Mr. Stuart and his party. Soon after Mr. LaRoque & two of Mr. Stuart's Men set off to come to this place, by the round about way of Lesser Slave Lake, and then to Dunvegan, from whence they were accompanied by our People who have been this Summer to the Rainy Lake—by whom I received a number of Letters from People in this Country, but only one from my friends in the States, which however gives me that real satisfaction I never fail to experience when I hear of the welfare of my Relations.

December 14 [12], Sunday. On the 1st Inst. I sat off for McLeods Lake [Fort McLeod], where I found several Letters from my Brothers, which announced the most grievous and truly heart-rending tidings—that my beloved Son George was no more to be numbered among the living! He who was enjoying good health the second of March was on the 18th of the same Month a lifeless Corpse! For some time I could not bring myself to credit what I read, yet I had no reason to doubt of the sad news being but too true! This stroke of Providence was so sudden and so great that I could hardly bear up under it with a becoming resignation to the dispensations of an ever just God! All my love and affections were placed on my darling Boy! and I had flattered myself with the pleasing hope and expectations that he would be the solace and comfort of my latter Days! But alas! delusive hope! he is no more! On what a weak foundation do we build our happyness in this World of disappointments and sorrow! Yesterday I thought myself one of the happyest of Men living; but now am the most miserable! What is there now this side the Grave worth placing my affections upon? My promising Son is no more! for whom alone I wished to live or should have been willing to die! Perhaps I placed too much of my love and affections on my departed Child, which was due only to my Creator—then I hope with Gods assistance I shall learn and become sensible of this all-important truth, that there is nothing in this changeable and fleeting World worth placing our affections upon, but ought to know that our hearts and souls belong wholly to our Gracious Maker, as well as believe that whenever we are chastised it is not without a sufficient cause—and should the dear object of our love be taken from us we may rest assured that all ultimately must be for the best, however grievous it may now be to us to bear up under. May the change my darling Son has so early made, be a happy one to *him*, and a seasonable warning to *me* to prepare myself with Gods aid (without which I am conscious I can do nothing) to meet that awful event which according to the course of nature must soon take place. Amen.

On my return from McLeods Lake I was accompanied by Mr. McDougall & Family, who are come over to mourn with me & my departed Son's Mother the loss of our Darling Child!

December 24, Friday. On the 20th Inst. Messrs. McDougall & LaRoque &c. accompanied me to the other end of this Lake, each of us in a Cariol [carriole] drawn by three Dogs and as the road was fine (upon smooth Ice) we had a pleasant excursion.

1814

January 22, Saturday. On the 4th Inst. Mr. McDougall & Family left this to return home and were accompanied by two Men who are gone to Peace River with Letters. Also on the same Day Mr. LaRoque and myself accompanied by fourteen of our People set off for Frasers Lake [Fort Fraser] where the former remained till the 9th when I sent him along with the two Canadians & as many of the Natives with Letters to the Columbia River. And I after having traded what Furs we could and purchased the quantity of Salmon we wanted Sat off on my return home where I arrived this morning.

February 4, Friday. This evening Mr. Donald McLennen &c. arrived from the Columbia Dept. with a Packet of Letters one of which is from Mr. John Stuart informing me that last Autumn [on October 16, 1813] the North West Co. purchased from the Pacific Fur Co. what Furs they had traded as well as all the Goods they had remaining on hand, and the People who were for that Company next Summer are to have a passage in the North West Co. Canoes to Montreal, unless they choose to remain in this Country for those who bought them out. And the young Gentleman who brought the Packet of Letters is one of those who thinks he had better remain a while longer in the Indian Country, which is the means of my having a companion till next Autumn at least.

February 10, Thursday. We now have about four feet of Snow on the ground, which is however a greater depth than generally falls here. Sent People to Peace River with the Letters from the Columbia as well as a few of my own.

March 12, Saturday. People arrived from Peace River with Letters from Gentlemen in that quarter and three from Fort William viz:—Messrs. A. N. McLeod, James Grant & F. Geodike.

April 1, Friday. Mr. McLennen & myself &c. are just returned from paying Mr. McDougall a visit and the two Days we remained with him were past much to our satisfaction in his agreeable company. And during our stay there, the two Men I had sent to Peace River returned with a number of Letters, some of which Mr. John McGillivray desires me to forward this Spring by Mr. McLennen &c. to the Columbia Dept. and therefore I shall again be left alone, however from long custom I have learnt how to pass away my time tolerable agreeably even when alone—yet I find it hard (though requisite) to be separated so soon from my young friend, who appears to be an amiable person, and with whom I flattered myself with the pleasing expectation of passing many an agreeable hour in the course of the ensuring Summer, but here again I am disappointed, and I begin to think there is little certainty of any thing in this World except disappointments and Death.

April 11, Monday. The Roof of the House (where I was sitting today all alone busily employed in writing my friends below and on whom all my thoughts and attention was taken up) became on fire and was in a blaze before it was perceived. However by the assistance of our People it was extinguished before it had done much injury, but how thankful ought we to be that such a circumstance did not happen in the night time when the whole Fort no doubt would have been consumed to ashes! How often we are made to acknowledge the mercies of a Gracious God! Almost hourly if our hearts were right we should see sufficient cause to return kind Providence our most sincere and grateful thanks for the favours which are constantly bestowed upon us.

April 17, Sunday. As this River appears to be free of Ice, I therefore have sent Mr. McLennen accompanied by two of our People in a small Canoe with Letters to the Columbia Department—and is the cause why I am deprived of an agreeable Companion for the ensuing Summer. Happy are those who have a Friend with whom they can converse!

April 22, Friday. As the time is drawing nigh when we may expect the Rivers will be free of Ice, I have sent off the last of the People who are going out with my Letters and accounts of the Post &c.—and shall myself, God willing, pass another Summer at this place where we are in all ten Souls. As it is only at this season of the year when we could leave this Country—so it is then that we have the most ardent desire of paying a visit to our native land and our hearts *yearn* to see and converse with our Friends. At other seasons we may wish it, but know at the same time of its being impossible and therefore must become reconciled to wait the return of another revolving Spring, when all those finer feelings of true affection again seize our very souls and if possible lay hold on them with an increased force. So the longer our absence the greater is our anxiety of beholding those who are by custom as well as by nature so dear to us.

May 7, Saturday. Fine weather and every thing far advanced for the Season. This Lake is free of Ice and the most of the frost is out of the Ground, Swans, Bustards, and Ducks are plentiful in the Rivers and small Lakes and during the last ten Days an incredible number of Cranes past this on their way to the Northward, but none of them stopped hereabouts. Three Indians have come from Frasers Lake for a piece of an Indians Garment of that place, which they say was cut off by an Indian of this Village, and they firmly believe that by virtue of that piece of garment the Indian who has it in [his] possession is able to cause the other to die whenever he pleases—which shews them to be a very credulous and superstitious People.

August 5, Friday. Salmon begin to come up this River.

August 29, Monday. Mr. McDougall & Family &c. came here on the 2nd Inst. but this morning set off to return home [to Fort McLeod]. The most of our time while my friend was here was passed in reading to each other or in agreeable conversation while walking by ourselves along the Beach, when now and then we would stop to eat a few Berries which are plentiful along the water side. There are I believe few Countries where Friendship is so rightly valued as in this where we meet so seldom.

September 20, Tuesday. We have but few Salmon here this year indeed it is only every other Season that they do come plentifully up this River, but what the cause is that they are more plentiful one year than another I am not able to determine. In the morning I sent off an Indian to Peace River with Letters, and he is to go as far as Dunvegan, which is a distance of at least five hundred Miles.[63]

September 25, Sunday. I connive it a rational and reasonable service and becoming dependant creatures as we are, as well as a duty we owe our Benevolent Creator, Who also is, the Bestower of every blessing we enjoy—to return Him our sincere and grateful thanks for every such favour, the least of which we cannot pretend to have merited, but especially for His Fatherly care in Daily providing for us food and raiment without which we could not exist. The above reflections have made me think it both proper and requisite to compose Prayers of thanks, in order that they shall be repeated with sincerity at the close or finishing of every Meal, hoping and trusting that our Benevolent God will continue to favour us with His Blessings.

A PRAYER OF THANKS.

Most Bountiful God, Merciful Father, vouchsafe to accept the thanks which I now presume to offer Thee, for the comfortable and refreshing repast with which Thou has graciously favoured me as well as for all Thy blessings bestowed on me through Jesus Christ our Lord, Amen.

or thus.

Most Bountiful God, Father of all mercy cause us we beseech Thee to have grateful hearts for the favours which Thou art constantly bestowing upon us, but particularly for Thy Fatherly care in providing for us Food and Raiment, as well as for the state of good health with which we are favoured (to enable us to enjoy Thy infinite though unmerited Blessings) which grant through Jesus Christ our Lord, Amen.

GRACE, OR BLESSING TO BE ASKED BEFORE MAKING A MEAL.

Merciful God, Sanctify we beseech Thee the refreshment which Thy ever bountiful Providence has laid before us, and cause it to strengthen our hearts and add cheerfulness to our spirits, that we

[63]As already noted, the distance by the route followed by the fur-traders probably did not much exceed 350 miles.

may with more earnestness and sincerity of heart strive to serve Thee better which grant for Christs sake, Amen.

September 20 [30], Friday. But few Salmon this Season have come up this River. However we hope and trust that kind Providence has sent them more plentiful to some of our Neighbouring Villages, where we shall be enabled to purchase what may be necessary (with the White Fish we hope to take) for our consumption during the ensuing Winter but let my condition be ever so deplorable I am resolved to place all my hopes & dependance on that Being who depends on none.

October 18, Tuesday. This afternoon I was agreeable surprised at the arrival of Mr. Joseph La Roque and ten common Men in two Canoes, laden with Goods from the mouth of the Columbia River (Fort George) [Astoria] which place they left the latter end of August last.[64] The Vessels from England [the *Isaac Todd* and *Columbia*] having arrived there in the Months of March & April—one of which sat sail again in the latter end of July for China (Canton) laden with Furs.[65] Mr. Laroque also brought the melancholy news of Messrs. D[onald] McTavish, Alexr. Henry and five Sailors having been drowned on the 22nd of May last in going in a Boat from Fort George to the *Isaac Todd,* which Vessel lay anchored at no great distance from the Fort. The former Gentleman was a Person with whom I past two winters at Dunvegan (Peace River) and for whom I had much esteem and regard, as I had every reason to believe him my friend, and as such I shall long lament the calamitous catastrophe that hurried him out of time into eternity! A sudden Death above all others appears to me the most shocking! What can

[64]this was a major event in the history of the fur trade, for Harmon here records the first occasion upon which the trading-posts in what is now the interior of British Columbia received their supplies from a depot (Fort George) on the Pacific Coast, to which goods had been brought by sea from England. Hitherto everything had been carried overland for thousands of miles from Montreal, by way of Fort William and Rainy Lake.

[65]Harmon's dates are not accurate. The *Isaac Todd* arrived at Fort George (Astoria) from England on April 23, 1814; the *Columbia* followed on June 29. The *Isaac Todd,* the first vessel to carry furs gathered by the North West Company to China for sale there, sailed for the Orient on September 26. Meanwhile, on August 26, the *Columbia* had set out on an extensive trading voyage to the Northwest Coast that took her to the Queen Charlotte Islands and Sitka. Later she followed the *Isaac Todd* to China.

be more awful than for a person who is in good health and therefore has every reason to expect that he may live for years to come, but who the next instant is summoned to appear before his Creator and his Judge! Then as we know we are liable at *any* time to be called out of this World how much does it become us always to be prepared to meet the awful event happen when it will!

October 23, Sunday. Sent Mr. La Roque and the People who came up with him with an assortment of Goods to reestablish Frasers Lake [Fort Fraser].

October 29, Saturday. People arrived from the Rainy Lake, and delivered me several Letters from home, which bring me the melancholy tidings that another instance of mortality has taken place in our Family! My Brother Reuben writes that his beloved and amiable Wife departed this life a year ago last June, and left him a Son & Daughter, to bewail her premature dissolution! Unhappy Brother! Unfortunate Children! How soon you have been taught to grieve! May the God of mercy protect you while in this World of sorrows and disappointments and by His free and Sovereign Grace prepare you to enter a better when he sees fit to call you from this. But still we have cause to be thankful to the Author of all good for having blessed the rest of the numerous Family with good health.

I have also received a Letter from Mr. John Stuart who is arrived at McLeods Lake, informing me it is requisite that I should leave this place to go and superintend the affairs at Frasers Lake, and send Mr. La Roque with several of the People who are there to this place that they may return to the Columbia Department from whence they came & where they are more wanted than here. Therefore tomorrow I shall with my Family &c. set off for Frasers Lake.

FRASER'S LAKE

November 2 [3], Thursday. Frasers Lake, where we arrived this afternoon, and found Mr. La Roque & People busy in trading Furs & Salmon & in building Houses. With the above mentioned Gentleman I have past the evening much to my satisfaction and am happy in finding that he from being a thoughtless licentious person, appears now quite the reverse. Its evident that of late he has reflected and meditated much on his former behaviour and loose manner of talking, and therefore is determined with the aid of Gods Holy Spirit on a thorough reformation. May he have the fortitude to persevere in so laudable and necessary resolution.

November 3 [4], Friday. It was with a reluctant hand and a heavy heart that I this morning bid adieu to Mr. La Roque, who has gone to Stuarts Lake and who I cannot at the soonest expect to see again till another long year is past and gone. Disagreeable Country! where as soon as friends meet they must begin to prepare for another long separation!

The People who remain here with me are going on with the Buildings while I am bartering with the Natives, and as long as we are thus employed we shall not much feel what the French call *ennui.*

November 14, Monday. I have just returned from Stuarts Lake where I went to pay a visit to my old friend Mr. Stuart who I was happy to find enjoying good health and after so long a separation it may be supposed that we past a few Days in agreeable conversation, in relating what had occurred to each other since our separation in the Spring of 1813.

December 20, Tuesday. Messrs. Stuart and McDougall &c. arrived from Stuarts Lake, and are come to go with me to *Stillâ,* in order to purchase Salmon, as the Indians of this Village do not appear to have a sufficiency for themselves and us, owing to the scarcity of Salmon at several of our neighbouring Villages, whose inhabitants flock to this place in hopes that their Countrymen will find [feed] them during the Winter.

1815

January 7, Saturday. On the 29th Ult. I accompanied my two Friends to Stuarts Lake where we past the Holy Days together and I am willing to acknowledge that I experienced a greater degree of satisfaction, from their conversation than I had for a long time before enjoyed, but how could it be otherwise since we are real Friends? Each related how he had past his youthful Days and even up to the present hour—and we all thought that our lives had been very different from what we then wished they had been—but I hope and believe that all of us parted fully determined on a thorough reformation. May none of us want fortitude and constancy to persevere in so good a resolution.

February 3, Friday. All the last Month it was the coldest weather by far that I have experienced in New Caledonia.

On the 11th Ult. I accompanied by Six of our People & two of the Natives set off to go to the Nus-koo-tain's [Nazkotens'] lands, which is along Frasers River (and the same Mr. Stuart followed some distance in going to the Columbia River) who are People who never had any intercourse with white People and we reached their first Village on the 19th but as they were starving and we had expended the Provisions we took from this we of course past only one night with them but continued our route down the River (every day passing a small village or two) until the 22nd when we met People from the Columbia with Letters informing me among other things that the North West Co. last Autumn sent a second Vessel [the *Columbia*] to Canton. Frasers River may be about three hundred feet broad & a pretty strong current. We were treated with hospitality by the Natives who also are Carriers and live principally upon Salmon the same as there hereabouts.[66] In going to the above mentioned River we were nine Days & the Country we past through lies pretty uneavin [uneven] however we past several Lakes from one to ten Miles long, and where the Natives remain the greater part of the Summer, and live upon White Fish and Carp, but towards the latter end of August they go to the River side to take & Dry Salmon for the ensuing Winter.

February 9, Thursday. Mild for the Season. On the 5th Inst. I went to Stuarts Lake, and about an hour after my arrival there Messrs. Stuart & McDougall &c. cast up from a jaunt of thirteen Days to the Nâle-ale-tain's Lands[67]—and those Gentlemens Companies I enjoyed till the 8th when Mr. McDougall sat off to return to McLeods Lake and I with then Men & my Family for this place [Fort Fraser], where I hope to remain quiet the rest of the Winter.

February 12, Sunday. As Salmon are getting to be scarce among

---

[66]On this journey Harmon probably descended the Fraser as far as the mouth of the Blackwater River—perhaps as far as the Quesnel River, where the town of Quesnel now stands.

[67]The identity of this tribe is uncertain.

the Indians of this Village, they are preparing to go and try to subsist on the small Fish they hope to take out of the neighbouring Lakes.

February 21, Tuesday. Severe cold weather, and thus far this has been much the coldest Weather I have experienced in this part of the Country, for it is generally mild here in comparison to the most of the other parts of the [north]. This afternoon I was agreeably surprised at the arrival of Mr. Stuart & Family &c. who are come on a visit.

February 27, Monday. Mr. Stuart &c. has left us to return home, but during the few Days hc was here I had as is ever the case when we meet much satisfaction in conversing together and I flatter myself that both of us shall reap much benefit from the friendly meeting. Religion was the subject on which we discoursed most, for we found it to be the most interesting and pleasing—and indeed what ought to interest us more than that which so much concerns our Eternal welfare? I am fully persuaded that were we to think or reflect more frequently and converse oftener on eternity, that we should live very different lives from what we now do. There are moments when I almost envy those who are in the civilized World the satisfaction they may experience from conversing with those who are both able and will to instruct, and of course strengthen their Faith in the true Religion. It is true we have in this Country some Books which treat upon Religion, but it appears to me that instruction generally has a more lasting and consequently a better effect on the most of people than what we read in Books, and there are (I fear) but few People in this part of the World who are able to give much light on the subject of Religion, and if there were we meet too seldom to reap much benefit from their conversation.

April 6, Thursday. Beautiful weather. On the 30th Ult. I accompanied by my Family &c. went to pay Mr. Stuart a visit, and I took along with me for my Friends perusal all the Letters I had wrote to my Friends below & People in this Country—and I had the satisfaction of reading those he had wrote to his Friends in the different parts of the World, which is a circumstance that sufficiently proves us to be Friends indeed—and I hope and trust that that friendship will be as lasting as our lives.

About ten Days since an Indian of this place lost his Wife after a lingering illness of several Months and during my absence from this, the disconsolate Husband hung himself on a Tree. For several Days previous to the fatal act he had appeared much more cast down than Indians generally are when they loose their Partners, which uncommon behaviour was observed by one of his Neighbours who told him to cheer up his spirits and not be so sorrowful, for he added that what had befallen him already had happened to many. But the widower's reply was that he would do as he thought proper, and he had not yet forgot what his deceased Wife told him but a little before her death, which he said was to accompany her. Not long after the Indian was missing, but when found was hanging to a Tree no great distance from the Village. A few Days after both of their Corpses were burnt on the same pile! Many People who are not well acquainted with Savages will not believe that their affections can be so deeply rooted as to make them commit suicide. But they are much mistakened, for such melancholy circumstances happen but too often in every part of the Indian Country.

April 24, Monday. The Snow is leaving us fast—and we begin to have a good many Fowls. In the morning People arrived with Letters from Peace River.

April 26, Wednesday. Sent my Letters for my Friends below and elsewhere to Stuarts Lake, which place they will leave on the first proximo. And I shall pass the ensuing Summer here, God Willing, where we are but five People, but from the manner I intend to divide my time, that is in reading meditation and exercise, such as walking about the adjacent Country I hope not to find many hours hang heavy on my hands. Indians it is true we see numbers Daily but they to those who have been long among them are but poor company.

May 10, Wednesday. We have surrounded a piece of Ground with Palisades for a Garden—in which we have planted a few Potatoes & Sowed Onion, Carrot, Beet, Parsnip, Seeds, as well as a little Barley, and also planted a little Indian Corn, but the latter I do not expect will come to perfection, as the nights here are too cool and the Summers too short to admit of it, for there is not a Month in the year but it freezes yet in the Day time it is warm, and we even have a few Days in the course of the Summer of sultry weather. The soil at many places in New Caledonia is tolerable good.

May 30, Tuesday. I am just returned from paying Mr. Stuart a visit, who passes the Summer at Stuarts Lake, and on the Mountain that we cross to go there we still found at least two feet of Snow.

June 16, Friday. Soon after the Natives left their Village last February to go to the small Lakes to Fish, no less than four of them met with dissolution, however their Corpses were kept by their Relations till now when they are bringing them to the Village to be burnt, yet there is little remaining of them but their bones. The Carriers often in the Winter Season will keep their Dead in their Huts for five or six months before they will allow them to be burnt, as they say that after they are consumed by fire, they shall never see them more. [The printed text reads: "At this season, the coldness of the weather enables them to keep the bodies, without their becoming offensive; and they are unwilling that the lifeless remains of the objects of their affection, should be removed forever from their sight, until it becomes a matter of necessity."]

June 18, Sunday. This afternoon eight of the Nâte-ote-tains [Nataotens] came to pay a visit to the Indians of this Village and where they at first met with a friendly reception, and soon after began to play [gamble] (as is ever the custom with the Indians of this part of the Country when People of different Villages meet) and everything for some time went on well, that is till the strangers began to be winners, then they began to dispute, but did not come to blows, as the property gained was returned to its former owners— which however caused a coolness between the two Tribes. Soon after the Strangers got up to return home, but as they were embarking in their Canoes, a worthless young fellow fired upon them and killed one, and the others of course made off with themselves as fast as they could, (as they had more than five to one) but at the same time threatening that they would soon return with a large Band of their Relations to revenge the death of their Companions. Treachery I believe is in the hearts of most Savages, which makes it necessary for those who are among them always to be upon their guard.

July 24, Monday. Berries of various kinds now begin to ripen & of which delicious food we soon shall have in abundance, and are blessings for which it becomes us to be grateful, by returning our hearty thanks to the Bestower of every blessing we do enjoy. Indeed we ought to be thankful for all the favours that we are continually receiving from the Fatherly hands of the ever bountiful

Providence. But in my opinion there are few we should prize more highly than the having a warm and disinterested Friend, who is both willing and able to rectify and put us right when we err [or] go astray from the paths of virtue—and who will through unseasonable apprehension of displeasing, attempt to hide the truth from us, although for the moment it may be disagreeable to be known, but who will as opportunities offer either by Letter or word of mouth, advise with, and endeavour to make us *see* our follies, or faults and consequently will in all likelihood make us strive to amend. Such a desirable Person I find in my nighest Neighbour Mr. Stuart, who has for some time past been in the habit of writing me frequently, long entertaining & instructive Letters which are a never failing cordial to cheer up my too often dejected spirits (which in part is owing to the solitary place at which I now reside, but more frequently brought on by contemplating on my past life of folly and sin) and as his justly esteemed Letters afford me so much real satisfaction, I in my turn strive to write him such as may prove not altogether uninteresting or unamusing and thus we keep up a friendly intercourse, from which I hope and trust that both of us may reap some advantage. And as it begun through the mutual esteem and regard we had for each other so I flatter myself it will end in the strictest ties of unalterable Friendship. There also is another Person, Mr. James McDougall, in this Department, who is equally dear to me, but he residing at a much greater distance from where I am, renders it impossible to write each other so often as either of us could wish. However when we meet we endeavour to make up in conversation for our long separation.

August 4, Friday. It is true that we may learn from the Holy Bible what our duty is towards God & Man yet perhaps it may be requisite for the most of People if not for all, to have some additional established rules, and by observing them they may serve to regulate their conduct, and thus cause their lives to be more exemplary and freer from sin while passing through this probationary. World.

The above reflection made me connive it proper to form the following Resolves and by the all-powerful aid of Gods Holy Spirit I hope to be enabled to live up to them.

RESOLVED.

That neither the scoffings nor the derideings of the thoughtless and wicked shall for a moment have any other affect on my conduct than to make me strive the more earnestly to lead a life of a sincere Christian.

RESOLVED.

To be in the company of the wicked as seldom as possible, and when among such People to endeavour to persuade them as far as may be consistent with propriety the folly & sin of having ungodly lives.

RESOLVED.

That no temptation however great shall in the least influence me to do an unbecoming or unworthy action.

RESOLVED.

To assist the poor and needy as far as may be consistent with my means: (hoping that avarice may never hinder me from judging right in such cases).

RESOLVED.

Never to let a Day pass over my head (while at home or when convenient abroad) without reading a portion of the Holy Bible and pass a half an hour or more in contemplating on what I have read:—and that the whole Day of every Sabbath (when not in my power to go and hear a Preacher) shall be spent in prayer, reading the Bible, a Sermon or some other religious Book, and in meditating on my present and future state.

RESOLVED.

To offer up Daily prayers to the Throne of all Grace for a right temper and disposition of mind ever to be constant and diligent in strictly observing the precepts contained in the above Resolutions. And I also pray that these humble endeavours (with the blessing of God) may greatly influence me to keep me in the path of holiness so that I may from Day to Day become better prepared to enter the World of Bliss, when my Gracious Maker and Redeemer sees fit to call my immortal part from hence, Amen.

August 7, Monday. At half past Seven a.m. we had an Earthquake, which lasted about twenty seconds. I was at the time sitting in a Chair in the House and the agitation of the Earth put the House and consequently me in much the same motion as when in a Canoe and rolled about by considerable swells. The Natives say that a similar shaking of the Earth happens almost yearly at this place.

August 13, Sunday. Salmon begin to come up this River which causes the natives as well as ourselves to put on joyful countenances for both them and us were almost destitute of Provisions of any kind. Kind Providence will not allow us to want although little deserving its favours.

September 6, Wednesday. On the 29th Ult. Messrs. Stuart and McDougall &c. arrived, and the former Gentleman remained with us till the first Inst. when he sat off to return home, and the latter also left us this morning. They informed me that nothing remarkable had occurred this Summer in their part of the Country. Our meeting as usual and the few Days we were together were past agreeably, but when we separated we had heavy hearts to think that a number of Months must do doubt pass away ere we meet again, and what seems to render that long space of time more tedious is to know that we must as it were be alone, that is neither of us have any one with whom he can converse on such subjects as our thoughts are generally employed upon. Thus situated there is no way of passing our time like rational and reasonable beings but by reading and meditation, hoping thereby to gain knowledge that will enable us to serve God better.

September 30, Saturday. On the 25th Inst. I accompanied by my Interpreter & an Indian who served as Guide sat off for Stuarts Lake, to pay a visit to my friend who I was happy to find & leave enjoying good health and in tolerable high spirits, and after having past two Days with him in pleasing conversation I sat off to return home, where I find all my people enjoyed the same state of good health as when I left them—and the Natives busily employed in taking and drying Salmon for the ensuing Winter.

October 2, Monday. Within a few days last past we have taken three Sturgeon in our Nets, one of which measured ten feet three Inches long and four feet one Inch round his middle and might weigh about four hundred pounds. All we have taken were remarkably fat and the best flavoured of any I ever ate in any Country.

Several nights previous to my departure for Stuarts Lake I had a remarkable Dream, which I thought very different from any I had ever made:—I dreamed that I was seated on the back of an enormous Animal, and with me was seated a young Lady cloathed in white who as I thought resembled the Godess Minerva as she is generally painted or represented in Books. The Animal appeared to carry us with great speed up and down the Country, and on either side of our way were an innumerable number of evil disposed beings, who as I imagined resembled Devils, and were constant in making the most frightful noises, which gave me such terror that I could not help expressing my fear to the young Lady of falling into their hands, which were I to do I thought they would instantly tare me to pieces. But she told me that if I paid no attention to them there was no danger of my falling off, and she added it was not in their power to do me the least injury as long as I remained where I then was—which gave me great consolation. Although I never had much faith and paid little attention to what past in my head or heart while asleep yet the above dream being so different from any I ever had before, I could not help thinking but it might have been given me as an instructive lesson or seasonable admonition. And after relating it to my friend Stuart I was surprised that he was of the same opinion (which however confirmed me in my own) and he gave the very same Interpretation of it as I previously had done, and was as follows:—the huge Animal (to whom it was not the power of either Men or Devils to do the smallest harm or to those who confided in his protection) was as we thought a striking and lively typifycation of our Blessed Saviour and his saving Gospel (that is to those who believe in it) and the young Lady cloathed in white was a propitious spirit or as it were my good *Genius,* who kindly tryed to strengthen my *faith,* by revealing to me so great a truth, and those Beings who were along the way were no other than bad Men, who are every where to be meet with, striving as much as in them lies by their wicked discourses to those who will listen to them to make them as bad as themselves. But as my good genius observed concerning those who remained firm on the back of the Animal no injury could happen to them, so to those who stick fast to and live up to what is laid down in the Gospel of our Blessed Redeemer there is nothing in this World or the Next that can do them any material injury. My sincere wish is that I may profit by the above Dream, and agreeable to the interpretation that my friend and I have given to it I think I ought.

October 13, Friday. This afternoon the Natives sent for me to go and see one of their young Women who is very sick at their Village, and I merely to please them went but could not expect to render her the least service with such Medicins as we have here. But after I had seen her I thought she was so far gone that it would not be proper in me to give her any thing, as I told them that were she to die shortly after taking any of our Medicins, they would say (as they are ever wont to do in such cases) that I was the cause of her death, however they told me they would not, for they said that they then considered her as a corpse, and therefore I could do her no injury, but might mitigate her pain and perhaps cause her to recover. Therefore I gave her a little Turtington. [This is referred to in the printed text as "a simple medicine, which I supposed could do her neither good nor harm...." A note has here been inserted in the manuscript that reads: "Several Days after however she died, but the Indians said it was owing to my Medicins that she did not meet her dissolution the very night she took it."] I also understood that her relations had said that a certain Indian with his magic had been the cause of her illness, and would at last take the breath of life from her. I took this opportunity to repeat again what I had often told them before—that no human being had the powers that they imagined were possessed by their Magicians of being able by magic to take the life of any one. But I told them that God who made every created thing had alone the power of causing their dissolutions whenever *He* thought proper. Hereupon one of their Chiefs who thought himself more knowing than the others said that it was the God who remained at the Sea, who was taking her life from her. But I told them that god was in Heaven above but had so penetrating an eye that He could see every thing that gook place on the face of the Earth. They said it might be so but they could not connive by what means I came to have knowledge of those things—which I endeavoured to explain to them.

November 1, Wednesday. This afternoon three of our Men arrived from the Rainy Lake & say they left the others at McLeod & Stuarts Lakes. They also delivered me several Letters from People in this Country, but not one from home. However they inform me that other Canoes are to come here late in the fall, who it is to be hoped will have some for me. But they bring the pleasing news that Peace has taken place between Great Britain and America.[68] May they long injoy the good effects arising from it.

November 16, Thursday. We now have about three Inches of Snow on the Ground.

December 21, Thursday. In the fore part of the Day I was much gratifyed at the arrived of Messrs. Stuart & McDougall &c. and to-morrow we shall all go to *Stillâ* to purchase Furs & Salmon.

December 24, Sunday. All hands returned from *Stillâ*, and find that we now have a sufficiency of Salmon for the Season.

December 27, Wednesday. All of us except two of our People who remain here to take care of the Fort, are preparing to go & pass New years at Stuarts Lake, and during the few Days we have been together I have past the time agreeable in the company of my two Friends.

1816

January 7, Sunday. This afternoon I returned from Stuarts Lake where I remained Six Days but the concourse of People being too great to allow us to indulge ourselves much in such conversation as we could have wished.

January 12, Friday. Mr. McDougall &c. arrived from Stuarts Lake, and are come to accompany me down Frasers River where I went last Winter.

February 1, Thursday. On the 15th Ult. Mr. McDougall & my-self accompanied by eight of our People and two of the Natives set off for Frasers River & this morning we returned from thence, but did not meet People from the Columbia as was expected, however in respect to every thing else we were uncommonly fortunate but what I prized the highest was the having with me an agreeable Companion, with whom I could converse along the way, and therefore make the long evenings after being encamped to pass away pleasantly.

[68]The War of 1812–14 ended officially with the signing of the Treaty of Ghent in December, 1814, but means of communication were slow, and it was several months before all military operations ceased.

March 17, Sunday. Owing to the late arrival at Fort Chipawyan of the People who went to the Rainy Lake, two Canoes Could not as was expected come to this place late in the Fall—and is the cause why I did not receive my Letters from home until today. I want words to express my grief at the truly melancholy tidings they bring. My respected Mother very much indisposed, owing in part to her advanced age but more to the loss of her Children who are leaving her almost Daily! Two of her beloved Sons, my affectionate Brothers, Stephen & Reuben lay at the point of Death of the Consumption! Spare them merciful God, till I can behold them once more in this World, and then if it is Thy Divine will, separate us till we meet in the next, never more to part. But there are still many, many Blessings with which our numerous Family are favoured, which ought to call forth our warmest thanks of gratitude to the Bestower of all good. This World is not our home, therefore we ought not to expect any great degre of happiness here, where we were pleased to prepare ourselves (with Gods aid) for a better, and where neither trouble nor sorrow can ever reach us. God grant that when we leave this World we may be prepared to enter that Blessed abode.

April 15, Monday. My desire to return to my native Country in hopes of seeing my aged Mother and my expiring Brothers ere they meet their dissolutions never was so great as at the present moment, and yet I cannot think of doing it this Season as it is thought absolutely necessary that I shall pass this ensuing Summer at this place. However a few Days hence I shall write my Friends below— and knowing as I do that there is little except disappointments & Death certain in this World of Disappointments and sorrows, I therefore am resolved to forward to them, by my Friend Mr. John Stuart, a copy of this Journal, in order that they (in case I never have the inexpressible pleasure and gratification of seeing them myself) may know the satisfaction I presume it will prove to be to them of knowing how their long absent Relative has been employed both as to Body & Mind while in this Savage Country.

HARMON'S JOURNAL:

APRIL 1816–AUGUST 1819

(From the first edition of the printed text, published in 1820.)

April 24, Wednesday. I have just returned from Stuart's Lake. While there, I agree with Mr. George McDougall to remain in this country two years or more, as clerk to the North West company. He came out the last summer from Canada, with Lord Selkirk's party, without having obligated himself to continue with them, for any definite time. After they arrived at Fort Vermilion on Peace River, he was treated by his superiour, Mr. John Clarke, in so unbecoming a manner, that he left them, and had come into this quarter to visit his brother, Mr. James McDougall, before he should return to Canada, which he designed to do the ensuing summer.

July 20, Saturday. Strawberries begin to ripen, and we have the prospect of an abundance of them, as well as of other kinds of fruit. I now pass a short time every day, very pleasantly, teaching my little daughter Polly to read and spell words in the English language, in which she makes good progress, though she knows not the meaning of one of them. In conversing with my children, I use entirely the Cree, Indian language; with their mother I more frequently employ the French. Her native tongue, however, is more familiar to her, which is the reason why our children have been taught to speak that, in preference to the French language.

September 9, Tuesday. Salmon begin to come up this river.

October 3, Thursday. We have taken our vegetables out of the ground. We have forty-one bushels of potatoes, the produce of one bushel planted last spring. Our turnips, barley, &c. have produced well.

November 23, Saturday. By our people who returned this afternoon from the Rainy Lake, I have received letters, which announce the afflictive intelligence, that two of my brothers, of whose decline I had before been informed, are gone into eternity. The happy days that I had fondly hoped that I should pass in their society on earth, I shall never enjoy. Such is the uncertainty of all earthly expectations. But the Judge of all the earth has done right.—My departed brothers gave evidence, to those around them, that they died in the faith and hope and peace of the gospel. They are gone, I trust, to a world where sin and suffering cannot follow them.

When the cold hand of death shall have been laid upon a few more of my relatives, there will be nothing remaining on the earth to console me for their loss. Nothing revives my drooping spirits in view of the departure of my friends, one after another, from year to year, into eternity, like the hope that, through rich grace, I may be at length permitted to join their society, in a world of perfect purity and of uninterrupted and everlasting joy.

We rarely prize our blessings in a suitable manner, until we learn their value by being deprived of them. I feel the force of this truth, in regard to my deceased brothers. To one of them in a particular manner, I am deeply indebted; and I have never been fully sensible of his worth, until now. During the whole period of my residence in this country, he has written to me annually, long affectionate, and instructive letters. For a number of years past, religion was the great subject of them. He was tenderly concerned for my spiritual welfare; and doubtless learned from my letters, that I was lingering on the gloomy confines of infidelity, and little disposed to heed, as I ought to have done, his friendly admonition. So far from being discouraged by this circumstance, it only rendered him more vigorous and persevering in his efforts; and his letters stand chief among the means, which have been blessed, as I would hope, to my conversion from the love and practice of sin, to the fear and service of God. These letters have also been of use to the few friends, to whom I have shown them. It would have given me great pleasure to have acknowledged, in person, the obligation which I am under to him; but it becomes not me to dictate to infinite wisdom.

I have, also, received letters from gentlemen in different parts of this country, which inform me of the many disasters that befel the people whom Lord Selkirk sent the year before, from Scotland, the Orkney Islands, and Canada, some of whom were destined to form a colony on the Red River, and others to traffic with the Natives, in different parts of the Indian country. They consisted at first, as I am informed, of two or three hundred men, together with a few women and children. Those, who went to establish themselves on the Red River, at a short distance from its entrance into the great

Winnipick [Winnipeg] Lake, began, soon after their arrival, to behave in a hostile manner towards the people of the North West
Company, who have establishments in that quarter. Of some of our
forts, they actually took possession, and carried away the property
which they found in them; and, in some instances, they set fire to
the forts, and reduced them to ashes. They also took Duncan
Cameron Esq. a partner of the North West Company, and another
gentleman, who is a clerk, whom they carried, in the spring, to
Hudson's Bay, with the intention, as they stated, of taking them to
England.—In the course of the winter, as the Express of the North
West Company was passing that way, destined to the Soult St.
Maries, they took possession of that also, perused the letters and
other papers which had been sealed up, and finally carried them to
York Factory, at Hudson's Bay.

All this unmerited treatment, at length so provoked the people
of the North West Company, that they proceeded to retake their
own forts, which had not been burned, as well as some property
belonging to those disturbers of the peace.

In June, a number of the Brulés [usually referred to as Métis],
that is, people whose fathers were white men, and whose mothers
were Indian women, proceeded from the upper part of Red River,
toward the place of its entrance into the Lake, in order to guard
some property there belonging to the North West Company. On
their way, they were obliged to pass, for about two miles, over an
open plain, directly behind Lord Selkirk's establishment. As soon
as they were observed, his people came out in a body, and fired
upon them, twice. This was unexpected by the Brulés; neither were
they prepared for such an encounter, as many of them had neither
gun nor ammunition. Perceiving however, that they must defend
themselves or be cut off, those who had arms returned the fire; and
the contest continued, until twenty-two of the noble Earl's people
fell, and some others were wounded.—This unhappy affair broke
up the colony. Some of the people went to Hudson's Bay; but the
greater number returned to Canada.

Those of Lord Selkirk's people [here meaning traders and other
employees of the Hudson's Bay Company] who came to the
English River and Athabasca, suffered greatly for the want of provisions. Out of nearly one hundred who came to Athabasca, twelve

actually lost their lives by starvation; and all the others must have shared the same unhappy fate, had not the people of the North West Company supplied them with provisions. In short, Lord Selkirk lost the last year, in fight and by starvation, sixty-eight of his men! and still, with the phrenzy of a madman, he is resolved on pursuing his wild projects.[69]

December 4, Wednesday. There is now about a foot and an half of snow on the ground.

I have sent fifteen men, with each a sledge drawn by two dogs and loaded with salmon, to McLeod's Lake, for the subsistence of the people who are to pass the winter there, and for the additional number who will be there in the spring, to make up the Furs into packs. Salmon are our chief subsistence here; and they are taken only in the waters which are discharged into the Pacific Ocean. The outlet of McLeod's Lake enters Peace River, whose waters, are finally discharged into the North Sea [Arctic Ocean].

1817

January 2, Thursday. I have just returned from a neighbouring village, where my interpreter gave one of the natives a decent drubbing, for having stolen from us. Soon after, the Indian who had been beaten, with a number of his relations, flew to arms, and surrounded our camp; but they proceeded at first no farther than to gesticulate in a threatening manner. This I permitted them, for a short time, to do, when I ordered my men to load their guns; though I was determined that they should not fire, unless it became a matter of necessity. I then told the Natives that we were prepared to defend ourselves, and, if they intended to fire upon us, to begin; or otherwise, to walk off, and lay aside their arms, which if they would not do, we should fire upon them. They concluded to retire,

[69]Harmon here touches upon two episodes in the bitter rivalry between the Hudson's Bay Company (at this time controlled by the Earl of Selkirk) and the North West Company. The famous "massacre of Seven Oaks," in which Governor Semple and nineteen of the Red River settlers were killed, took place on June 19, 1816. For an account of the whole episode, and of the efforts of the Hudson's Bay Company to establish trading-posts in Athabasca, which the North West Company regarded as its own preserve, *see* A. S. Morton, *A History of the Canadian West to 1870–71*, London, 1939.

and shortly after came back without their arms, and began to trade, as if nothing had happened.

February 10, Monday. This evening the mother of my children, was delivered of a daughter, whom I name Sally Harmon.

February 19, Wednesday. I am this day thirty-nine years of age. When I reflect on the events of my past life, and recollect, especially, in how many instances a merciful God has snatched me from the very jaws of death, when it would undoubtedly have delivered me over to everlasting destruction, I am grieved and ashamed, in view of the ingratitude with which I have requited such infinite kindness. My past life now appears to me to have been a continual course of sins, committed against a merciful Creator, Benefactor and Redeemer. I have even denied the Lord that bought me, and that because I could see no need of that atonement for sin, which is the only thing that has stood between me and hopeless perdition! If I have indeed been rescued from such a wretched condition, if I have been effectually convinced of my sinfulness, and have been led, in the exercise of faith, to apply unto the Lord Jesus Christ for pardon and for sanctification, surely, it can be attributed to nothing but the grace of God. Much of my life has been spent in the service of sin; the little that remains, ought to be sacredly devoted to God and the Redeemer. May the Holy Spirit enable me to live in the time to come, as a disciple of the blessed Saviour.

THIRD SOJOURN AT STUART'S LAKE

September 1, Monday. Stuart's Lake. On the 8th of May last, I left New Caledonia, and went as far as Fort Chipewyan, on the Athabasca Lake. This afternoon, I returned to this place. While I was at that lake, the Indians who were encamped about the fort, to the number of about one hundred, rose up in arms against us, on account of a quarrel between one of their people and one of our men. We did not, however, come to blows; and, after a parley, the Indians were persuaded to lay down their arms.—Those Chipeways are a savage people; and they have as I believe, killed more white men, than any other tribe in the North West country. A few years since, they burned one of our forts, and killed every person belonging to it.

On the 21st of June, I left Athabasca Lake, at which period, there was still ice floating about in it. In coming up Peace River, we saw many of the buffaloe and red deer, and killed as many of them as we wanted for our own consumption. Black bears, also, were in plenty; and of them, we killed eleven. One day as I was walking along the beach alone without a gun, a black bear, that had cubs, pursued me for nearly a mile. Happily for me, I could outrun her; and I therefore escaped from her terrible paws.

A little below the Rocky Mountain Portage, along the side of the river, there is a kind of marsh where earth, of a beautiful yellow colour is found, which when burned, becomes a pretty lively red. The natives use it as paint, for which it answers tolerably well. We, also, use it to paint our forts and houses.

October 4, Saturday. This evening, an Indian arrived from Frazer's Lake, bringing the disagreeable intelligence, that yesterday in the afternoon, our fort there was consumed by fire. We have reason to be thankful, however, that most of the property which was in it, was saved.

October 16, Thursday. We have taken our vegetables out of the ground. In consequence of the very dry summer, they yielded but poorly. There were months, during which not a drop of rain fell.—Fruit of all kinds has been uncommonly abundant this season.

1818

February 18, Wednesday. I have just returned from a jaunt of twenty-three days, to a place down Frazer's River. While there, the Natives had concerted a plan to massacre us all; but I discovered it, and kept my people on their guard. The Indians, perceiving this, dared not attempt to execute their bloody and unprovoked purpose.

May 2, Saturday. Expecting that the ice in Peace River will soon break up, I have sent off the last of our people who are going to the Rainy lake; and by them I have forwarded, as usual, my accounts of the place, and letters to my friends below. I look forward, with pleasing anticipation, to the return of another spring, when I hope, if my life is spared, I shall myself leave this country on a visit to the civilized world.

September 3, Thursday. Last night, there fell about four inches of snow, which is earlier than I have ever before seen it fall, in this part of the country. On the 6th ult. salmon began to come up this river; but they are not very numerous.

In the month of June, we took out of this lake twenty-one sturgeon, that were from eight to twelve feet in length. One of them measured twelve feet two inches, from its extreme points, four feet eleven inches round the middle; and would weight from five hundred and fifty, to six hundred pounds. All the sturgeon that we have caught, on this side of the mountain, are far superior in flavour, to any I ever saw in any other part of the world.

A few days since, we cut down and threshed our barley. The five quarts, which I sowed on the first of May, have yielded as many bushels. One acre of ground, producing in the same proportion that this has done, would yield eighty-four bushels. This is sufficient proof that the soil, in many places in this quarter, is favourable to agriculture. It will probably be long, however, before it will exhibit the fruits of cultivation. The Indians, though they often suffer for the want of food, are too lazy to cultivate the ground. I have frequently tried to prevail on some of them to hoe and prepare a piece of ground, promising them that I would give them potatoes and turnips, with which to plant it; but I have not succeeded. Having been from their infancy trained up to privation, the fear of want is a much less powerful stimulus to excite them to industry, than it is to those who have always been accustomed to the comforts of civilized life.

October 13, Tuesday. We have several inches of snow on the ground.

For several years past, Iroquois from Canada, have been in the habit of coming into different parts of the North West country, to hunt the beaver, &c. The Natives of the country, consider them as intruders. As they are mere rovers, they do not feel the same interest, as those who permanently reside here, in keeping the stock of animals good, and therefore they make great havock among the game, destroying alike the animals which are young and old. A number of Iroquois have passed several summers on this side of the mountain, which circumstance they knew to be displeasing to the Indians here, who have often threatened to kill them, if they persisted in destroying the animals on their lands. These menaces were disregarded. A month since, an Iroquois, with his wife and two children, were all killed, while asleep, by two Carriers of this village, which melancholy event, I hope, will prevent any of the Iroquois from coming into this region again.

November 7, Saturday. We have now about a foot of snow on the ground.—To-day our people returned from the Rainy Lake, and say that, on account of the large quantities of ice that was drifting in Peace River, they were obliged to leave the greater part of the goods, which they had on board of the canoes, but a short distance this side of the Rocky Mountain Portage. We shall be obliged, therefore, to bring these goods on sledges, drawn by dogs from that place, which is distant from this, about two hundred and eighty miles.

1819

February 28, Sunday. Mr. George McDougall has arrived here from Frazer's Lake, to remain, as I am going to McLeod's Lake, to prepare for a departure for Head Quarters; and my intention is, during the next summer, to visit my native land. I design, also, to take my family with me, and leave them there, that they may be educated in a civilized and christian manner. The mother of my children will accompany me; and, if she shall be satisfied to remain in that part of the world, I design to maker her regularly my wife by a formal marriage. It will be seen by this remark, that my intentions have materially changed, since the time that I first took her to live with me; and as my conduct in this respect is different from that which has generally been pursued by the gentlemen of the North West Company, it will be proper to state some of the reasons which have governed my decision, in regard to this weighty affair. It has been made with the most serious deliberation; and I hope, under a solemn sense of my accountability to God.

Having lived with this woman as my wife, though we were never formally contracted to each other, during life, and having children by her, I consider that I am under a moral obligation not to dissolve the connexion, if she is willing to continue it. The union which has been formed between us, in the providence of God, has not only been cemented by a long and mutual performance of kind offices, but, also, by a more sacred consideration. Ever since my own mind was turned effectually to the subject of religion, I have taken pains to instruct her in the great doctrines and duties of christianity. My exertions have not been in vain. Through the merciful agency of the Holy Spirit, I trust that she has become a partaker with me, in the consolations and hopes of the gospel. I consider it to be my duty to taker her to a christian land, where she may enjoy Divine ordinances, grow in grace, and ripe for glory.—We have wept together over the early departure of several children, and especially, over the death of a beloved son. We have children still living, who are equally dear to us both. How could I spend my days in the civilized world, and leave my beloved children in the wilderness? The thought has in it the bitterness of death. How could I tear them from a mother's love, and leave her to mourn over their absence, to the day of her death? Possessing only the common feelings of humanity, how could I think of her, in such circumstances, without anguish? On the whole, I consider the course which I design to pursue, as the only one which religion and humanity would justify.

Mr. McDougall informs me, that, not long since, an Indian died at Frazer's Lake, and left behind him a widow, who had been in similar circumstances before, by the loss of a former husband. A day or two before the corpse was to be burned, she told the relations of her late husband, that she was resolved not to undergo a second slavery. She therefore left the tent, secretly, in the evening, and hung herself from a tree.

Among the Carriers, widows are slaves to the relations of their deceased husbands, for the term of two or three years from the commencement of their widowhood, during which, they are generally treated in a cruel manner. Their heads are shaved, and it belongs to them to do all the drudgery, about the tent. They are frequently beaten with a club or an axe, or some such weapon.

STUART'S LAKE TO FORT WILLIAM

May 8, Saturday. McLeod's Lake. I arrived here about two months since. Yesterday, the most of our people embarked with the returns of this place, in three canoes; and a few hours hence, I shall, with my family, proceed in another, which will be pushed on by six Canadians.

It is now eight years and an half, since I came to the west side of the Rocky Mountain. My life, which has often been in jeopardy, is still preserved; my family have generally enjoyed, in a high degree, the comforts, which this part of the world affords; and, especially, they have been extensively blessed with health of body, and contentment of mind. Our worldly affairs have prospered, to as great an extent as we could reasonably expect. For all these blessings, it becomes us to return unfeigned thanks, to the great Giver of every good gift.

May 14, Friday. Rocky Mountain Portage. All the way to this place, we have drifted down, amidst great quantities of ice, by which, at five different places, the river was completely blocked up, so that we were obliged to tarry, until the water rose so high, as to remove these barriers. This is the reason why we have been so long in coming to this place. Had the river been high, and yet clear of ice, the current is so strong, that we might have reached here in two days.

August 18, Wednesday. Fort William. I have at length arrived at head quarters. In coming from New Caledonia to this place, which is a distance of at least three thousand miles, nothing uncommon has occurred. A few days hence, I shall leave this place, to proceed to Canada. As I have already described the country between this, and Montreal, I shall here conclude my Journal.

CHARACTER OF THE CANADIAN VOYAGERS

[This note appears in the manuscript version of the journal
after the entry dated November 16, 1815.]

They like their ancestors (the French) are ficle [fickle] & changeable as the wind, and of a gay and lively disposition, consequently
not subject to be often cast down or in lowness of spirits, which
unpleasant disposition of mind if ever they do experience has with
them but a momentary duration, for they are too volitile ever to admit any thing either good or bad to lay hold on their hearts or affections—and although they make Gods of their bellies, yet when
necessity obliges them, even when destitute of every kind of nour-
ishment, they will endure all the fatigue and misery of hard labour
& cold weather &c. for several Days following without much complaining. And at such times after being encamped at night about a
rousing fire they are even gay and appear to enjoy themselves as
well as people of other Nations when in much better conditions.
They are great talkers but in the utmost sense of the word thoughtless—make many resolutions which are as soon broke as formed—
never think to provide themselves to Day with what they may
want for the morrow, but allow each Day to provide for itself—and
they like Sailors seldom lay up any part of their earnings to serve
them in the decline of life, and they also resemble them in being
shocking blasphemers. At every trifling circumstance that may in
the least cross them, they fall into a rage of passion, but are as easily
appeased when vexed, neither will they for any length of time bear
a grudge to the person from whom they may have connived to have
received an injury. They are not brave, however when they think
there is little or no danger then they will as they say *faire L'Homme*
that is make the Man—and while before a person they are as bare-
faced flatterers, as they are base detracters when behind his back.
They are People of not much veracity, and appear to have as little
sense of what true honour is, as they actually have of real honesty.
Therefore there is little dependence to be placed on what they say
and they are much given to pilfering and will even steal when
favourable opportunities offer. A secret they cannot keep and

gratitude is a virtue that seldom or never enters into their hearts but they are extremely polite and obliging and I may add even generous, in short (they like other People) are a compound of what is good & bad but the latter qualities far out balance those of the former. They also are *obedient* but by no means *faithful* Servants. However by flattering their vanities (of which they have not a little) they may be made to go through fire and water. That is they may be prevailed on to undertake to do almost any good or bad action providing their *lives* thereby are not endangered. Although there is not one in a hundred of them who have the least education yet they (at least after having been a few years in this Country) are more knowing or have a better knowledge of the World & human nature, than the lower class of People in most other Countries. But as they leave Canada young and have but a slight knowledge of the *principles* of the Religion which their Parents profess to follow, so ere they have been many years in this uncivilized part of the World they do not appear to observe the Sabbaths or any manner of worship but little more than the Savages themselves.

About the Scholars

Dr. Jennifer S. H. Brown

Dr. Jennifer S. H. Brown is Professor of History at the University of Winnipeg. She holds a Canada Research Chair in Aboriginal Peoples in an Urban and Regional Context and is the director of the Centre for Rupert's Land Studies, University of Winnipeg.

Dr. Brown received her education at Brown and Harvard universities, culminating in her Ph.D. from the University of Chicago in 1976. She has written extensively on native history, the fur trade, and the Metis. Specifically, she has addressed fur-trade "country" marriages, fur-trade families, and their resulting inter-relationships and cross-cultural legacies.

Strangers in Blood: Fur Trade Families in Indian Country, one of her many books, studies the families of the officer class of the Hudson's Bay and North West companies before and after their merger in 1821. It has particular relevance in the context of Harmon and his fur-trade family. Among other publications, she co-edited *Reading Beyond Words: Contexts for Native History* and *The New Peoples: Being and Becoming Metis in North America.*

Dr. W. Kaye Lamb

William Kaye Lamb was born and brought up in British Columbia, and thus it was most fitting that he should have researched and edited one of the earliest British Columbian documents. He was Provincial Librarian and Archivist of British Columbia (1934–40), Librarian of the University of British Columbia (1940–48), then Dominion Archivist (1948–68). After founding the National Library of Canada, he was its Librarian (1953–67).

Dr. Lamb graduated from the University of British Columbia with first class honours in history. He spent three years on scholarship in Paris and returned to Vancouver to complete his M.A. in history. He was granted a Ph.D. from the London School of Economics in 1933.

In 1960, three years after the publication of *Sixteen Years in the Indian Country: The Journal of Daniel Williams Harmon*, Lamb published the first complete, annotated edition of the letters and journals of Simon Fraser. Interestingly, Fraser was not only the founder of Fort St. James and a fellow partner in the North West Company, but also Harmon's Bennington-born contemporary. As a historian, archivist, and librarian, Dr. Lamb was a prolific writer and was the founder in 1936 of the *British Columbia Historical Quarterly*, which he edited for ten years.

Index

New Fort. *See* Fort William
New Grand Portage, 16
New North West Company. *See*
   XY Company
Nipigon Department, Harmon in,
   xviii, 90–95
Nipigon River (Dog River?), 79
North West Company, and festi-
   vals observed at posts,
   Christmas Day, 41, 52, 58, 84,
   88, 104; New Year's Day, 30, 42,
   120–21, 131–32, 165; St.
   Andrew's Day, 28; hunters at
   trading-posts, xxv, 29, 31, 37,
   39, 42, 43, 47–48, 56, 58, 59, 72,
   139–40; ledger showing personnel accounts, xix, xx, xxxiv; relations with Hudson's Bay
   Company, xxiv, xxv, 88, 169–70;
   with XY Company, 57; with
   Pacific Fur Company, 135, 149;
   trading vessels on Great Lakes,
   9, 10, 12, 79; on Pacific Ocean
   and coast, 142, 153, 156;
   expands west of Rockies, 116,
   119, winter express, 31, 53, 85,
   104

Oak trees, 76, 77
Oats, 79, 111
Okanagan Lake, 146
Okanagan River, 147
O'Meara, Walter, xvi, xxxiv
Onions, 158
Orkney Islands, Hudson's Bay
   men from, 29, 168
Ottawa River, 4–7
Otters, 45, 82, 91

Pacific Coast, trade on and routes
   to, 125; Lewis and Clark, 71;
   Simon Fraser, 100; Pacific Fur
   Company, 135, 149; North West
   Company, 142, 146, 153, 156
Pacific Fur Company, 135, 149

Pack River, 116
Pangman, Joseph, 3, 6–7, 10
Parker, Gerrard & Ogilvy, 12
Parsnip River, 116
Parsnips, 158
Partridges, 45
Payet, —, 41, 42
Peace River, 101, 112–15, 116,
   139–41, 172, 174
Pease, 79, 111
Pelican Lake, 96
Pelican River. *See* Clearwater
   River
Pelicans, 20
Pemmican, 18, 38, 39, 67
Perigné, —, 24, 25, 96
Perra, Pierre, 87, 88, 89
Peter Pond Lake, 98
Pheasants, 25, 45
Pickerel, 82, 124
Pigeons, 5, 18, 45
Pike, 82, 88, 92, 124
Pinchy, Indian village, 126, 129, 144
Pine Fort, 76
Pine trees, 17, 24, 26, 79, 107
Pitch springs, 99
Plain Portage, 78; Meadow
   Portage so called, 22
Plums, 18, 76, 77
Point à la Gourganne, 91
Pointe aux Pins, 10
Pointe Claire, 3
Poitras, Andrew, 70, 74
Poplar trees, 17, 25, 26, 45, 77, 79
Portage de l'Isle, 95
Portage des Chats, 5
Portage des Paresseux, 7
Portage du Fort, 92, 94
Portage du Fort de Traite, 96
Portage la Loche (Methy Portage),
   98, 99
Portage la Prairie, 76
Potatoes, grown at forts, 49, 72,
   79, 88, 110, 111, 124, 158, 167
Primault, Andrew, 51

Also in the
CLASSICS WEST COLLECTION

The Ranch on the Cariboo
Alan Fry

"This book by Alan Fry is probably the best ever written on ranch life in the Cariboo ... While it may not make a pretty sight to the tractor jockeys, by damn it is authentic; I should know, because I was raised on a similar ranch just 18 miles north." — Eldon Lee

In this autobiographical story of small-scale ranching in the 1940s, Alan Fry shares the joys and the hardships of a time and a lifestyle few people have known. By turns humorous and poignant, *The Ranch on the Cariboo* is a vivid account of Alan's experiences growing up and discovering where he belongs.

ISBN 1-894898-02-8

Packhorses to the Pacific:
A Wilderness Honeymoon
Cliff Kopas

For four months in 1933, Ruth and Cliff Kopas slogged, scrambled and sloshed their way through some of the roughest terrain in North America, on an amazing journey across the Rockies through to British Columbia's west coast, following Alexander Mackenzie's route to the Pacific. Their story, full of excitement and suspense, is peppered with humorous observations, historical anecdotes and a deep love for the Canadian wilderness.

ISBN 1-894898-13-3

Also in the
CLASSICS WEST COLLECTION

The Rainbow Chasers
Ervin Austin MacDonald

"A vivid frontier adventure for anyone who pines for an unvarnished first-hand account of life in Cariboo in the early years of [the twentieth] century." — Paul St. Pierre

In this fascinating chronicle of fortune-hunting, close calls and pioneer life, Ervin Austin MacDonald tells the story of his father, Archie, and the hard-won wilderness home that Archie and his sons built in B.C.'s Cariboo. This is a family that survived by their wits, individual talents and, above all, through the tremendous will of their father, whose irrepressible strength made him a true western hero.

ISBN 1-894898-30-3

Klondike Cattle Drive
Norman Lee

In 1898, Norman Lee set off with a few men, a small pack train and 200 head of cattle on a 1,500-mile journey from the Chilcotin area of British Columbia to the far-off Yukon. He had heard of the gold rush in the Klondike, and he figured there was a gold mine there for himself in the form of miners who needed meat and had the money to pay for it. This story is derived from Lee's diary of that perilous expedition, and he writes with humour and zest about the strange, wonderful and often harrowing adventures they experienced.

ISBN 1-894898-14-1